I⸝⸝RACY AND DEVELOPM⸝NT

Literacy and Development is a collection of case studies of literacy projects around the world demonstrating literacy theory in practice.

The contributors present their in-depth studies of everyday uses and meanings of literacy, and of the literacy programmes that have been developed to enhance them. Arguing that ethnographic research can and should inform literacy policy in developing countries, the book extends current theory and itself contributes to policy making and programme building.

With case studies from India, Namibia, Eritrea, Peruvian Amazonia, Ghana, Bangladesh, China and Pakistan, this collection examines a wide cross-section of society and addresses in specific contexts such issues as:

- literacy, schooling and development
- multilingual literacies, ideology and teaching methodologies
- women's literacy and health
- household literacy environments as contexts for development
- literacies, gender and power.

Contributors: Sheila Aikman, Archana Choksi, Priti Chopra, Caroline Dyer, Pat Herbert, Bryan Maddox, Uta Papen, Clinton Robinson, Anna Robinson-Pant, Regie Stites, Martha Wagar Wright, Shirin Zubair; with an Afterword by Alan Rogers.

Brian V. Street is Professor of Language in Education at King's College London, and Visiting Professor at the University of Pennsylvania. His publications include *Literacy in Theory and Practice* (1991), *Cross-Cultural Approaches to Literacy* (1993) and *Social Literacies* (1995).

LITERACIES
Series Editor: David Barton
Lancaster University

Literacy practices are changing rapidly in contemporary society in response to broad social, economic and technological changes: in education, the workplace, the media and in everyday life. This series reflects the burgeoning research and scholarship in the field of literacy studies and its increasingly interdisciplinary nature. The series aims to provide a home for books on reading and writing which consider literacy as a social practice and which situate it within broader institutional contexts. The books develop and draw together work in the field; they aim to be accessible, interdisciplinary and international in scope, and to cover a wide range of social and institutional contexts.

SITUATED LITERACIES
Reading and writing in context
Edited by David Barton, Mary Hamilton and Roz Ivanič

GLOBAL LITERACIES AND THE WORLD WIDE WEB
Edited by Gail E. Hawisher and Cynthia L. Selfe

MULTILITERACIES
Literacy learning and the design of social futures
Edited by Bill Cope and Mary Kalantzis

CITY LITERACIES
Learning to read across generations and cultures
Edited by Eve Gregory and Ann Williams

LITERACY AND DEVELOPMENT
Ethnographic perspectives
Edited by Brian V. Street

LITERACY AND DEVELOPMENT

Ethnographic perspectives

Edited by Brian V. Street

London and New York

First published 2001
by Routledge
11 New Fetter Lane, London EC4P 4EE

Simultaneously published in the USA and Canada
by Routledge
29 West 35th Street, New York, NY 10001

Routledge is an imprint of the Taylor & Francis Group

The collection © 2001 Brian V. Street
Individual chapters © 2001 the contributors

Typeset in Baskerville by
The Running Head Limited, Cambridge
Printed and bound in Great Britain by
Biddles Ltd, Guildford and King's Lynn

British Library Cataloguing in Publication Data
A catalogue record for this book is available from the British Library

Library of Congress Cataloging in Publication Data
Street, Brian V.
Literacy and development: ethnographic perspectives / Brian V. Street.
p. cm. – (Literacies)
Includes bibliographical references.
1. Literacy–Developing countries–Cross-cultural studies. 2. Ethnology–
Developing countries. I. Title. II. Series.

LC161 .S83 2001
302.2'244'091724–dc21   00–059237

ISBN 0–415–23450–6 (hbk)
ISBN 0–415–23451–4 (pbk)

CONTENTS

v

CONTENTS

FIGURES

CONTRIBUTORS

Sheila Aikman is Lecturer in Education and International Development at the Institute of Education, University of London, with a special teaching and research interest in language and development, language policy, curriculum and knowledge issues, and indigenous people's education, especially intercultural and bilingual education. She holds a Postdoctoral Fellowship with the National Academy of Education/Spencer Foundation 1997–9: researching intercultural and bilingual education policy and practice in Latin America.

Priti Chopra is completing a PhD at King's College London. Her research is based on an ethnographic study of communication practices for women in three north Indian villages. She completed a postgraduate degree in Language Studies and Adult Education from Lancaster University. She has worked as an adult education facilitator in the UK and India.

Caroline Dyer (Research Fellow in the Faculty of Education, University of Manchester) and Dr **Archana Choksi** (Research Associate in the Faculty of Education, University of Manchester) have been collaborating as a North–South research team for eight years. Their research among the Rabari nomads continues through policy advocacy and regular returns to the field. They are currently leading a DfID-sponsored project which links their theoretical perspectives on literacy practices for ethnic minorities with the education of primary teacher educators in three states in western and central India.

Pat Herbert has worked in Ghana for many years and is Literacy Materials Development Consultant for GILLBT (Ghana Institute of Linguistics, Literacy and Bible Translation), an NGO working in partnership and co-operation with SIL.

Bryan Maddox studied Social Anthropology at Sussex University. He is currently a part-time teacher of Anthropology and is working on a doctorate in education based on ethnographic fieldwork in Bangladesh. He has extensive experience as both a teacher and a researcher in the adult literacy field both in the UK and Asia.

Uta Papen is currently carrying out research for her PhD at King's College London, on literacy, language and tourism in Namibia. Her background is in Social Anthropology and History with a geographical focus on sub-Saharan Africa and Asia. She carried out fieldwork on indigenous medicine in Cameroon. She worked for several years at the UNESCO Institute for Education (UIE) in Hamburg where she was involved in research and training programmes on literacy, post-literacy and adult education. She also co-ordinated an international research project on innovations in adult education.

Clinton Robinson works with SIL UK; he spent ten years in Cameroon working in linguistic research and language development. He currently heads SIL's International Programmes department in the UK. His interests and publications include sociolinguistics, African rural development, language planning and policy. He holds degrees in Modern Languages (Oxford), Linguistics (Paris), Rural Development and Sociolinguistics (Reading).

Anna Robinson-Pant is a lecturer in Education at the University of East Anglia. She has over eight years' work experience in Asia, particularly Nepal, at central and grassroots level, working in education, health and gender, using ethnographic and participatory approaches. Her particular focus is on adult literacy (training, research and planning) and NGO development administration/management. She was winner of the UNESCO/UIE International Award for Literacy Research 1998 for her study of Women's Literacy and Development in Nepal.

Alan Rogers holds the post of Special Professor of Adult Education at the University of Nottingham. Formerly Executive Director of Education for Development (1985–98) based at the University of Reading, he has worked in adult education for more than forty years, the last twenty-five mostly in developing countries, specialising for the last few of these in adult literacy programmes. He is currently engaged in research into non-formal education in the context of developing societies. He is Reviews Editor for the *International Journal for Educational Development.*

Dr Regie Stites is an evaluator and a specialist in the area of adult education and lifelong learning in SRI International's Center for Education and Human Services, California. From 1984 to 1987 he worked as foreign language teaching expert in the People's Republic of China. He has worked as a Project Director in the National Center on Adult Literacy (NCAL), at the University of Pennsylvania, where his research has focused on literacy skills retention, applications of advanced technologies to adult learning, adult literacy standards, and the evaluation of effective practices in adult basic literacy instruction.

Brian Street is Professor of Language in Education in the School of Education at King's College London, and Visiting Professor of Education in the Graduate School of Education, University of Pennsylvania. He has been active in applying theory to practice and, in addition to ten books, he has written over sixty scholarly articles and has been involved in lecture tours, workshops, training programmes and research on literacy and development in a number of countries, including Australia, USA, South Africa and Canada. He is a member of Technical Support teams on current Aid projects in Nepal and South Africa.

Martha Wagar Wright is currently a PhD candidate in educational linguistics at the University of Pennsylvania, Graduate School of Education. Her work on multilingual literacy included six months in rural Eritrea, at the Compassion of Jesus Hospital and health-education programme, conducting research as a participant observer and teachers' consultant in local schools. Presently she is completing her dissertation and preparing to return to Africa with her family, to work in another healthcare-educational outreach programme among nomadic groups in north-east Uganda.

Shirin Zubair is an Assistant Professor in the Department of English at the Baha-ud-Din Zakariya University in Pakistan. She has been a teacher and researcher in ELT in Pakistan and has been on the visiting staff of University Grants Commission, NAHE and AIOU, Islamabad. She has recently completed her PhD at Cardiff University on women's access to multiliteracies in rural Pakistan, using ethnography and extensive fieldwork. Her research centres on women's literacy and development issues in underdeveloped, multilingual communities and culturally shaped beliefs about women's education.

INTRODUCTION

Brian V. Street

Ethnographic perspectives on literacy

In recent years there has been growing awareness of the value of qualitative, ethnographic approaches to educational research and the contributions it can make to development planning. Ethnographic research
can be utilised at all stages of the project cycle, from project identification to project appraisal and can help to complement more positivist
statistical surveys by revealing the cultural and social dimensions which
may positively or adversely affect how a project is taken up.

(Yates 1994)

In many literacy projects, 'literacy experts' and planners have made prior assumptions about the needs and desires of beneficiaries. A number of literacy
projects in recent years have challenged these assumptions by stressing that
before launching into literacy programmes and interventions it is necessary to
understand the literacy practices that target groups and communities are already
engaged in (Freebody and Welch 1993; Yates 1994; Prinsloo and Breier 1996).
Researchers trained in 'ethnography' – that is, using field work methods and
sensitised to ways of discovering and observing the uses and meanings of literacy
practices to local people themselves – have conducted studies into these everyday
practices and their relationship to the programmes designed to alter them. Their
findings are now being included from the earliest stage in projects (Yates 1994;
Prinsloo and Breier 1996) and fed into the campaign design and development.

This edited volume brings together the work of a number of such ethnographers of literacy projects who have spent many years conducting in-depth qualitative studies of everyday literacies in different parts of the world and of the
literacy programmes that have been developed to enhance them. The ethnographic approach represented here is, then, more concerned with attempting to
understand what actually happens than with trying to prove the success of a
particular intervention or 'sell' a particular methodology for teaching or management. The dominant account of literacy programmes remains concerned with
'effectiveness', often measured through statistics on skill outcomes, attendance,

1

etc., and justified through correlations with important development indices such as health, agricultural production and economic take off. The findings of the ethnographic approach may lead to different measurement and claims for outcomes and to different curriculum and pedagogy than in many traditional programmes (Hill and Parry 1994; Holland and Street 1994; Black and Wiliam 1998). What counts as 'effective' cannot, then, be prejudged, hence the attempt to understand 'what's going on' before pronouncing on how to improve it.

The ethnographic approach to literacy in development programmes derives from recent theoretical approaches which argue that literacy is not just a set of uniform 'technical skills' to be imparted to those lacking them – the 'autonomous' model – but rather that there are multiple literacies in communities and that literacy practices are socially embedded (Heath 1983; Street 1993b, 1995; Barton 1994; Barton et al. 1999). The academic research emerging from this new field of interest is thus of considerable practical significance, with implications for literacy programmes in particular and development programmes more generally (Wagner 1993; King 1994; Doronilla 1996; Robinson-Pant 1997; Hornberger 1998; Kalman 1999). This volume is written in that spirit of engagement between theory and practice, academic and applied concerns. It aims to make a contribution across the divide, in clarifying conceptual issues and enhancing knowledge on the one hand and in aiding policy making and programme building on the other. The contributors are all experienced ethnographers, who have both conducted research and engaged in practice in their chosen field sites. They approach the issues in a spirit of reflective and critical enquiry, less concerned to advocate particular approaches, methodologies and theories than to extend current thinking and thereby contribute to informed practice. In order to frame their work in this context, this Introduction first establishes the wider context in which literacy and development work takes place, namely what I shall term the 'New Orders' – the New Work Order, the New Communicative Order and the New Epistemological Order. It then works through some of the theoretical and methodological responses to these changes that have been developed within what has come to be called the 'New Literacy Studies' (Gee 1990; Street 1993a; Barton et al. 1999), particularly with reference to contrasting 'models' of literacy – the 'autonomous' model and the 'ideological' model; and with reference to 'literacy events' and 'literacy practices'. I then turn to the practical implications of these theories and concepts, addressing some of the problems and objections that have been raised and anticipating some of the positive applications that could arise from a sympathetic adaptation of these approaches. This is followed by a brief résumé of the different articles, placing them in this broader context

The 'New Orders': work, communicative, epistemological

The 'New Orders' – the New Work Order, the New Communicative Order and the New Epistemological Order – require radical rethinking of what counts as literacy in the development context. This rethinking is as necessary for academics and researchers as it is for activists and practitioners: while the former have to accommodate to the needs of 'knowledge-in-use' the latter are being called upon to take account of knowledge-in-theory. This volume attempts to lay out some of the conditions for these accommodations and to bridge the divide between theory and practice in this field. In some cases (Namibia, Nepal) the New Work Order impinges directly on a particular group of people, and those working with them in terms of literacy development will need to conceptualise and accommodate these changes. In other cases, such as the transhumant Rabaris in north India, there was never a Fordist work order in the first place and the changes taking place cannot simply be conceptualised as a shift in work orders; however, the Rabaris are being continually affected by these global changes, such as the moves to settle them and the interest taken in them by outsiders. Moreover, the epistemological shifts that are suggested below also affect such people as the Rabaris in that what counts as learning and education and who has the right to define it will be salient issues for any development worker engaged with them as they are for the Rabaris themselves. I begin, then, with a brief account of the New Orders within which the experiences outlined in the chapters in this book are, to a greater or lesser extent, framed.

Gee et al. (1996; cf. Holland and Cook 1998), drawing upon the writings of economists and business theorists as well as critical sociologists, have attempted to characterise the New Work Order associated with globalisation of production and distribution, and to consider the implications of these changes for the kinds of language needed in work and in educational contexts. These changes represent the context within which contemporary literacy work is taking place and thus need addressing as much as do the theoretical underpinnings of literacy itself. Work, they suggest, is no longer defined and organised along Fordist lines, with mass production on assembly lines and its Taylorist principles of work organisation and discipline.

> There is now a shift towards forms of production which employ new ways of making goods and commodities, serving more differentiated markets, or niches, through segmented retailing strategies. There is now a great deal more attention paid to the selling environment at every level of production, from design to distribution. So while the old work order stressed issues of costs and revenue, the new work order emphasises asset building and market share.
>
> (Gee et al. 1996: vii–viii)

Associated with these defining concepts are ideas about proper organisational behaviour, including attention to flexibility and adaptation to change. Procedures are put into place to ensure both flexibility on the one hand and uniformity and guarantee of standards on the other. If consumers are perceived, through market research and company predictions, to demand the same jackets or the same tomatoes in shops across their travelling experience, then mechanisms need to be put into place to ensure that wherever these are produced they conform to those standards. This Total Quality Management has been a particular feature of the New Work Order that has impinged directly on the educational setting, in providing models for quality control there too and in imposing reductionist and unitised notions of measurement and of quality on educational outputs and 'products'.

A further organisational change that has been of especial significance for language and literacy has been the notion of team working on projects rather than hierarchical forms of organisation that simply pass orders down a chain of command. In the new project-focused work order, all members of a team combine to design, negotiate and develop 'products' for sale and distribution. In order to accomplish this, all members of a team have to be equipped with the discursive skills that such negotiation and development involve, such as ability to present and hear arguments, and to develop material for presentation on communicative devices such as overheads, slide projectors, computer displays, etc. Radical researchers confronted with these changes have particularly focused on the claims often associated with them that suggest a commitment to democracy: words like 'collaboration', 'participation', 'devolution' and 'empowerment', all cherished terms of oppositional groups, such as those working in Freirean literacy campaigns, are now used to indicate a partnership between managers and workers. Gee and his colleagues are highly suspicious of these claims and would have us examine them critically, while acknowledging that changes are indeed taking place in both the work order and the communicative demands associated with it. Literacy programmes, then, now need to take account of such shifts and such critiques if they are to handle the complex communicative needs of the New Work Order.

A number of writers working in the area of social semiotics and visual design have suggested that, in this new context, the reading and writing practices of literacy are only one part of what people are going to have to learn in order to be 'literate' in the future (Kress and van Leeuwen 1996; Heller and Pomeroy 1997; Lemke 1998). They are going to have to learn to handle both the team work literacies described above and also the iconic systems evident in many communicative practices, such as the kinds of icons and the signs evident in computer displays like the Word for Windows package with all its combinations of signs, symbols, boundaries, pictures, words, texts, images, etc. The extreme version of this position is the notion of 'the end of language' – that we are no longer talking about language in its rather traditional notion of grammar, lexicon and semantics, but rather about a wider range of semiotic systems that cut across reading, writing, speech (cf. Kress and van Leeuwen 1996). This provides a broader framework for handling questions of literacy and language in both education and the workplace that, again, new literacy programmes are going to have to take into account. Papen, for instance, describes how literacy programmes in Namibia are attempting to take account of tourism as an economic outlet for many participants: this will involve them in not simply decoding written texts but also understanding issues of layout and presentation in advertising materials as well as in developing competence in other communicative channels. These include the ability to converse with tourists in a familiar register, and to handle the body language and communicative norms expected by today's safari travellers. Likewise, Maddox comments with respect to the literacies necessary for economic activity in Bangladesh that 'this is not simply spoken language written down but involves particular types of language, form and genre'. He notes that the primers available in literacy programmes tend to look in the opposite direction, offering a 'select and relatively limited vocabulary' and narrow alphabetic skills, just at the time when the broadening of vocabulary in particular, language in general and semiotic channels more broadly are the key components of learners' requirements in the world of work and social relations.

Finally, I would like to address what Barnett and Griffin (1997) and others refer to as the crises of knowledge that are leading to a New Epistemological Order. Within the academy, they suggest, postmodernism and reflexivity have led to a valuing of the local against the universal, including a critique of Enlightenment science and the kind of modernism on which much development work has been founded. Outside the academy, meanwhile the marketisation of knowledge has likewise led to a challenge to the dominant position previously held by universities. In this new commercial world knowledge as inert commodity can be bought and sold for profit, measured as though it were inert information, and judged for 'quality' as though it were just another commercial product in which 'quality' refers to the object itself but not to the process of learning, questioning and engagement in which receivers relate to it. This new knowledge is based in numerous, non-academic settings, such as large business corporations and leisure industry outlets, for whom the critical perspective of university approaches to knowledge is less important than whether it will sell in the marketplace. Faced with this crisis of knowledge from multiple sources, Barnett asks what can be the role of the academy in the New Epistemological Order. His response is of direct relevance to the projects described in this volume: the role of the researcher is to be that of a 'practical epistemologist', involving critical engagement in real world projects and action, doing 'participatory' work. At the same time, this involves reworking the university as a forum for debate that offers a discursive space for critique of the bases of knowledge claims and frameworks in ways that for-profit knowledge industries do not. The practical epistemologist engages with knowledge in use, not simply with propositional knowledge, and he or she works *with* partners in real world contexts in the interests of equity and justice.

It could be argued that this approach to knowledge work already applied to much of the engagement of progressive literacy activists and practitioners in recent years (cf. Rogers 1994, 1999; Prinsloo and Breier 1996; Hornberger 1998) but has yet to be accepted in some policy circles, where traditional forms of knowledge and rationalist models of development predominate (Crush 1995; Grillo and Stirrat 1997). The authors in the present volume have all engaged with the reflexivity and boundary crossing required of academics working in applied areas of literacy and communication, as Chopra brings out explicitly in her chapter on how the subject of literacy programmes is constructed, which she characterises in terms of 'betrayal and solidarity'. Combining these new approaches to knowledge with attention to the New Work Order and the New Communicative Order provides the contemporary researcher on literacy with a very different agenda and framework than envisaged in the modernist era of programmes to 'eradicate illiteracy'. The argument of this book, then, is that ethnographic approaches to literacy in development can offer such an accommodation of theory and practice and address the larger issues raised in the New Orders, while maintaining a focus upon the local meanings through which we all experience such processes. The ethnographies of literacy presented here provide telling cases of the application of theoretical and conceptual tools to practical programmes. I turn, therefore, to some of the terms and concepts that have emerged within the 'New Literacy Studies' as a way of building a language of description for literacy work in this context. My aim is to operationalise these approaches as a basis both for research purposes and for practical applications.

A personal approach

In keeping with current reflexive approaches to social science research, I would like to begin by describing why I myself took on ethnographic research in this area, as a way of answering the larger question, regarding the implications of this approach for research and practice in the development field, which the authors in the volume address. As with many of the researchers whose work is featured here, the answer derives from a personal research history. I went to Iran during the 1970s to undertake anthropological field research (Street 1984). I had not gone specifically to study 'literacy' but found myself living in a mountain village where a great deal of literacy activity was going on: I was drawn to the conceptual and rhetorical issues involved in representing this variety and complexity of literacy activity at a time when my encounter with people outside of the village suggested the dominant representation was of 'illiterate', backward villagers. Looking more closely at village life in the light of these characterisations, it seemed that not only was there actually a lot of literacy going on but that there were quite different 'practices' associated with literacy – those in a traditional 'Quranic' school, in the new state schools, and among traders using literacy in their buying and selling of fruit to urban markets. If these complex variations in literacy which were happening in one small locale were characterised by outside agencies – state education, UNESCO, literacy campaigns – as 'illiterate', might this also be the case in other situations too? I have kept this image in mind as I have observed and investigated literacy in other parts of the world – urban Philadelphia, South Africa, Ghana, Nepal, the UK, etc. In all of these cases I hear dominant voices characterising local people as 'illiterate' (currently media in the UK are full of such accounts, cf. Street 1998) while on the ground ethnographic and literacy-sensitive observation indicates a rich variety of 'practices' (Heath 1983; King 1994; Doronilla 1996; Robinson-Pant 1997; Barton and Hamilton 1998; Hornberger 1998; Kalman 1999; Street 1999). When literacy campaigns are set up to bring literacy to the illiterate – 'light into darkness', as it is frequently characterised – I find myself asking first what local literacy practices are there and how do they relate to the literacy practices being introduced by the campaigners? In many cases the latter forms of literacy fail to 'take' – few people attend classes and those who do drop out, precisely because they are the literacy practices of an outside and often alien group (Abadzi 1996). Even though in the long run many local people do want to change their literacy practices and take on board some of those associated with Western or urban society, a crude imposition of the latter that marginalises and denies local experience is likely to alienate even those who were initially motivated.

Research, then, I believe, has a task to do in making visible the complexity of local, everyday, community literacy practices and challenging dominant stereotypes and myopia. This indeed has become a major drive in much recent research, of which the present volume is a key example. Following through its implications for programme design, including pre-programme research on local literacy practices and for curriculum, pedagogy and assessment/evaluation, is a major task that requires first a more developed conceptualisation of the theoretical and methodological issues involved in understanding and representing 'local literacy practices'. I now lay out some of the theoretical and methodological assumptions that underpin such work.

Autonomous and ideological models of literacy

In developing contexts the issue of literacy is often represented as simply a technical one: that people need to be taught how to decode letters and they can do what they like with their newly acquired literacy after that, an approach I have referred to as an 'autonomous' model of literacy (Street 1984). The 'autonomous' model of literacy works from the assumption that literacy in itself – autonomously – will have effects on other social and cognitive practices. The model, however, disguises the cultural and ideological assumptions that underpin it and that can then be presented as though they are neutral and universal: the research described in this volume challenges this view and suggests that in practice the approach is simply imposing Western conceptions of literacy on to other cultures. The alternative, ideological model of literacy, to which many of the chapters in this book refer, offers a more culturally sensitive view of literacy practices as they vary from one context to another. This model starts from different premises than the autonomous model – it posits instead that literacy is a social practice, not simply a technical and neutral skill; that it is always embedded in socially constructed epistemological principles. It is about knowledge: the ways in which people address reading and writing are themselves rooted in conceptions of knowledge, identity, being. Literacy, in this sense, is always contested, both its meanings and its practices, hence particular versions of it are always 'ideological', they are always rooted in a particular world-view and a desire for that view of literacy to dominate and to marginalise others (Gee 1990). The argument about social literacies (Street 1995) suggests that engaging with literacy is always a social act even from the outset. The ways in which teachers or facilitators and their students interact is already a social practice that affects the nature of the literacy being learned and the ideas about literacy held by the participants, especially the new learners and their position in relations of power. It is not valid to suggest that 'literacy' can be 'given' neutrally and then its 'social' effects only experienced afterwards.

For these reasons, as well as because of the failure of many traditional literacy programmes (Abadzi 1996; Street 1999), academics, researchers and practitioners working in literacy in different parts of the world are beginning to come to the conclusion that the autonomous model of literacy on which much of the practice and programmes have been based was not an appropriate intellectual tool, either for understanding the diversity of reading and writing around the world or for designing the practical programmes this required (Heath 1983; King 1994; Doronilla 1996; Robinson-Pant 1997; Hornberger 1998; Kalman 1999). They have instead turned to an ideological model of literacy.

One example, to bring home the significance of this argument concretely, comes from an article in *Cross-Cultural Approaches to Literacy* – a collection of articles by anthropologists who have worked in literacy around the world and have attempted to apply dynamic models of culture to dynamic models of literacy (Street 1993b). Kulick and Stroud conducted anthropological research in New Guinea villages and began with the questions that developers ask: what is the impact of literacy? However, they soon noticed that literacy was being added to the communicative repertoire in more complex ways than the concept of 'impact' conveyed. They noted that the things that people did with that literacy were rather different from what the people who had brought it had imagined. Missionaries had brought it and wanted to use it for conversion and for control and discipline; this is similar in many contexts where missionary groups have brought reading but not writing for precisely that control purpose – if people can write, they actually can write their own things down, if they can read they can only read what you provide them (Clammer 1976). They can still reinterpret a text they only read but they have rather more control over a text they write themselves. Kulick and Stroud, being social linguists as well as anthropologists, were interested in what happens to the communicative repertoire when such missionary literacy arrives: they argued that instead of talking about the 'impact' of literacy, we should ask the question, how do people 'take hold of' literacy? What they saw happening was that people were using literacy in the way that they had used oral interaction. There were precise conventions for making a speech, the dominant one being that you must not appear to put anyone else down when you make it. It is both inappropriate to put someone down and inappropriate to speak in a braggardly way about yourself, and yet at the same time you want to get your own way. So a variety of clever political discourses and conventions emerged. Kulick and Stroud discovered, when they looked at the texts being written, that people were using the same social linguistic conventions, the same discourse strategies as in this speech making. They were inserting the written into their oral. So instead of talking about impact, the researchers talk about taking hold; they talk about the way people have made use of literacy (Kulick and Stroud 1993). There are now many such examples from around the world which indicate how the communicative repertoire varies, from people simply taking literacy and doing with it what they had already done, to people discovering new functions for it which may be quite different from what the school teachers or the missionaries had in mind.

This alternative approach is termed an 'ideological' and not just a cultural model because it is important to attend not only to cultural meanings but also to the power dimension of these reading and writing processes. The example of the missionaries and of the teachers makes that clear. The concept of 'impact' then is not just a neutral developmental index, to be measured, but is already part of a power relationship. These are issues about power, assumptions about one particular set of ideas, conceptions, cultural group, being in some way taken on by another group. What is the power relation between them? What are the resources? Where are people going if they take on one literacy rather than another literacy? How do you challenge the dominant conceptions of literacy? It seems to me quite impossible to address the issue of literacy without addressing also these issues of power (Street 1996). A cultural model of literacy, particularly the reified view of culture rather than culture as process, leads one to fall back into the old reifications: a particular group of people become associated with a particular literacy; another group of people are associated with another literacy. The contestation over what counts as literacy and whose literacy is dominant gets lost. So it is called an ideological model of literacy in order to highlight the power dimension of literacy.

Instead of privileging the particular literacy practices familiar in their own culture, researchers now suspend judgement as to what constitutes literacy among the people they are working with until they are able to understand what it means to the people themselves, and which social contexts reading and writing derive their meaning from. Many of these people and others described in the accounts below might have been labelled 'illiterate' within the autonomous model of literacy and yet, from a more culturally sensitive viewpoint, can be seen to make significant use of literacy practices for specific purposes and in specific contexts. These findings, we suggest, raise important issues both for research into literacy in general and for policy in Adult Basic Education and Training in particular.

This book, then, argues that it is important for those working in the field of literacy and development equally to engage in the theoretical and conceptual debates being described here and to challenge the dominant conception of literacy work which sees it as simply applied, obvious and not in need of such theory. It is precisely the lack of such explicit attention to theory, I would argue, that has led to so many failures in development literacy programmes; behind the naturalisation of teaching and learning have lurked ideological pressures and political dogmas, often colonial but also urban/rural, or based on local ethnic conflicts and hierarchies. Making explicit our theoretical apparatus enables us to 'see' such biases and decide for ourselves whether we wish to accommodate or challenge them. On the other hand, academics have often failed to make explicit the implications of such theory for practical work. In the present conditions of world change such ivory tower distancing is no longer legitimate, if it ever was, as Barnett and his colleagues (1997) have made clear. I turn now, therefore, to some of the key concepts in the field of New Literacy Studies that I argue may enable us to overcome these barriers by applying these new conceptions of literacy to specific contexts and practical programmes: the concepts of *literacy events* and of *literacy practices*.

Literacy events and literacy practices

Barton (1994: 36) notes that the term *literacy events* derived from the sociolinguistic idea of speech events. It was first used in relation to literacy by Anderson et al. who defined it as an occasion during which a person 'attempts to comprehend graphic signs' (1980: 59–65). Shirley Brice Heath further characterised a 'literacy event' as 'any occasion in which a piece of writing is integral to the nature of the participants' interactions and their interpretative processes' (Heath 1982: 50). I have employed the phrase 'literacy practices' (Street 1984: 1) as a means of focusing upon 'the social practices and conceptions of reading and writing', although I later elaborated the term both to take account of 'events' in Heath's sense and to give greater emphasis to the social models of literacy that participants bring to bear upon those events and that give meaning to them (Street 1988). Barton (1991), in reporting on a study of everyday literacies in Lancaster, England, attempts to clarify what has been meant by literacy events and literacy practices. Baynham (1995) entitled his account of the relations between oral and written language use among Moroccans in London, *Literacy Practices*. Similarly Prinsloo and Breier's *The Social Uses of Literacy* (1996), which is a collection of case studies of literacy in South Africa, used the concept of events but then extended it to practices. My own recent book *Social Literacies* (Street 1995) tries to develop the concepts and clarify the different uses and more recently I have argued for a clarification of terminology as the field of New Literacy Studies becomes more generally known (Street 2000). So a literature is emerging that directly addresses the issue of the relation between *literacy events* and *literacy practices*. I would like to outline here my own view of these relations and their significance for the field of literacy and development.

Literacy events is a helpful concept, I think, because it enables researchers, and also practitioners, to focus on a particular situation where things are happening and you can see them – this is the classic literacy event in which we are able to observe an event that involves reading and/or writing and can begin to draw out its characteristics: here we might observe one kind of event, an academic literacy event, and there another which is quite different – catching the bus, sitting in the barber's shop, negotiating the road – and the Lancaster research projects have made good use of this concept (Barton and Ivanič 1991; Barton and Hamilton 1998). But there is also a problem, I think: if we use the concept of *literacy event* on its own, it remains descriptive and – from an anthropological point of view – it does not tell us how the meanings are constructed. If you were to observe this literacy event as a non-participant who was not trained in its conventions and rules you would have difficulty following what is going on, such as how to work with the text and to talk around it. There are clearly underlying conventions and assumptions around the literacy event that make it work.

I now come to *literacy practices*, which I would suggest is the more robust of the various concepts that researchers have been developing within a social approach to literacy. The concept of *literacy practices* attempts both to handle the events and the patterns around literacy and to *link* them to something broader of a cultural and social kind. And part of that broadening is that it attends to the fact that we bring to a literacy event concepts, social models regarding what the nature of the event is, that make it work and give it meaning. Those models we cannot get at simply by sitting on the wall with a video and watching what is happening. There is an ethnographic issue here: we have to start talking to people, listening to them and linking their immediate experience out to other things that they do as well. And that is why it is often meaningless just to ask people about literacy, as in many recent surveys (OECD 1995; Basic Skills Agency 1997) or even about reading and writing, because what might give *meaning* to this event may actually be something that is not in the first instance thought of in terms of literacy. It may be, as the chapters in this volume demonstrate, about religion (as Herbert and Robinson show with respect to the literacy programmes in Ghana), or about status (as Zubair demonstrates for women in Pakistan), or about the social relations within literacy projects themselves (as Maddox shows for Bangladesh). Heath found in discussing newspaper reading with urban adolescents in the US that much of their activity did not count in their minds as literacy, so that a superficial survey would have missed the significance of their actual literacy practices and perhaps labelled them non-readers, or more insultingly 'illiterate' as in much press coverage of this area (Heath and McLaughlin 1993). One cannot predict beforehand what will give meaning to a literacy event and what will link a set of literacy events to literacy practices. Literacy practices, then, refer to this broader cultural conception of particular ways of thinking about and doing reading and writing in cultural contexts. It is on the basis of the above theoretical debates, and in particular the development of the concept of literacy practices, that the chapters in this book could be seen as case studies that both exemplify the new ways of thinking about literacy and the ways of developing practical programmes associated with them, and also help extend, critique and reformulate those approaches.

Problems associated with these approaches

Before outlining what these chapters contribute to that development, it is necessary to address some of the problems and the objections that have arisen with
respect to these approaches. There have, for instance, been problems with the
conceptualisation of multiple literacies which the ideological model of literacy
employed to challenge the autonomous model. In characterising literacy as multiple it is very easy to slip into assuming that there is a single literacy associated
with a single culture, so that there are multiple literacies just as there are, supposedly, multiple cultures. So when we find Gujarati culture and Gujarati 'literacy' in Leicester or in Pakistan, Hindi literacy and Hindu 'culture' in India,
the two get put together in fixed lists. If we start instead from a plural conception
of culture ('Culture is a Verb'; Street 1993b) then we recognise that culture is a
process that is contested, not a given inventory of characteristics, and such easy
links of culture and literacy are not helpful. A *claim* to culture is itself a part of the
process rather than a given, as Aikman shows with respect to Peruvian Amazon
peoples (this volume). So in that sense one cannot use the concept of 'multiple
literacies' simply to line up a single literacy with a single culture.

Another problem that arises from work in New Literacy Studies and which
the authors in this volume are addressing is the extent to which rejection of what
I have termed the autonomous model of literacy can lead to a relativising of
literacy in ways that have potentially dangerous consequences. For instance, it
may be seen as celebrating local practices that are no longer appropriate in a
modern, indeed 'postmodern' condition where 'empowerment' requires high
communicative skills including formal literacy. It is also seen as leading to potentially divisive educational practice, in which the literacy of local groups is reinforced while those with access to dominant discourses and power continue to
reproduce the literacy sources of their own dominance. Papen, writing of Namibia, is acutely conscious of the ways in which a relativised view of literacy in that
context may carry echoes of the previous influence of South Africa's apartheid
system, in which local languages and cultural practices were purportedly valued
by being kept separate. Adults coming to literacy classes, whether in China,
Pakistan or India, are wary of being denied access to the language and literacy
of power. Likewise, parents of ethnic minority children in countries where
'multi-cultural' education and linguistic variation have been promoted, argue
that their children are simply getting a 'second-class' education and being denied
the genres of power (Leung and Tosi 1999).

Although the critique regarding 'relativism' may be levelled at the accounts
provided in this book, in fact the authors are extremely sensitive to this possibility and have been very careful to think through its implications and expose its
flaws. A problem with the critique, for instance, lies in its assumption that the
present condition – the current genres and forms of literacy – are fixed, universal
and given, where in fact they have been historically and culturally constructed.
The argument about 'access' to dominant genres disguises the questions about

how such genres became dominant and remain so, which will eventually determine how many others can in reality access them. For since the rules of dominant literacy genres are frequently quite arbitrary – based on surface features of language such as formal spelling rules, punctuation, pronunciation, etc. – they can easily be changed if too many people learn how to use them and thereby challenge the status quo. In that way, according to Gee (1990), those in power retain domination while appearing to provide access to the disempowered. A focus on transformation rather than on access leads to a different view. An 'ideological' model of literacy begins from the premise that variable literacy practices are always rooted in power relations and that the apparent innocence and neutrality of the 'rules' serves to disguise the ways in which such power is maintained through literacy. As Luke argues (1996), there are no 'genres of power' as such, only culturally based ways of knowing and communicating that have been privileged over others.

This argument also provides a second important retort to the 'relativism' critique: the ideological model of literacy only relativises literacy practices at an analytic level, enabling researchers and activists to recognise and describe variation where the autonomous model sees only uniformity, but it does not relativise literacy at the level of social power as the critique suggests – on the contrary, it is termed an ideological model rather than simply a cultural or pragmatic model precisely because it draws attention to the unequal and hierarchical nature of literacy in practice. Whereas many educators and policy makers see literacy as simply a neutral skill, the same everywhere and to be imparted (almost injected in some medically based discourses) to all in equal measure, the ideological model recognises that educational and policy decisions have to be based on prior judgements regarding *which* literacy to impart and why. The research described here, then, leads to the policy question of which particular literacy practices are important for, say, women in rural Mali or Nepal, school children in the new Eritrea or nomads in north India to learn. It does not suggest that they be simply left as they are on the relativist grounds that one literacy is as good as another. But nor does it suggest that they simply be 'given' the kind of formal, schooled literacy with which policy makers are familiar and which, in fact, many of them have already rejected. 'Delivering' such formalised literacy will not lead to empowerment, will not facilitate jobs and will not create social mobility.

This argument is supported not only by more than a decade of intensive research in different parts of the world, including that represented in this volume, but also by the low take up/high drop out rates on formal programmes (cf. Abadzi 1996) which indicate that people themselves see this more quickly and acutely than do planners. Formal schooled literacy practices and the autonomous model on which they are based may indeed have facilitated power for some: but they will not necessarily provide power for many, when the kinds of literacy needed in their specific contexts are often very different and, in a social sense, more complex. Developing policy and designing programmes to cater for this level of complexity and 'need' is a more challenging and difficult task than simply 'delivering' a package of 'neutral' literacy skills through centrally designed programmes.

It is in this sense, then, that the ethnographic approach relativises both literacy and the kinds of educational interventions now seen as necessary. It relativises analytically and by contextualising policy and educational planning requirements. It does not, as the critique suggests, relativise in the sense of judging each literacy as equal in social power: to the contrary, it is better placed than the autonomous model of literacy, on which much planning and policy is currently based, to elicit and analyse precisely that power dimension to literacy practices.

The approach to literacy being developed within this volume has also been critiqued for romanticising local literacies. Such research, by indicating the value of local literacies and helping readers and observers to see what they previously might have missed in the everyday uses of literacy by marginalised groups in both rural and urban settings, may appear to extol those local uses against powerful standard literacies. Developers see these local literacies as simply 'folk' practices that will need to be superseded if development is to proceed and the promise of 'progress' – in health, employment, political rights, etc. – is to be fulfilled. The authors in this volume, however, would argue that the respect their approach entails is not to be confused with romanticism or 'folk' approaches. The ethnographic approach does not involve a commitment simply to the status quo: rather the researchers are committed to social transformation – that indeed was the root of their engagement. In many cases, such as South Africa and Eritrea, the commitment is to redress with particular reference to those whose communicative resources either have gone unrecognised or have been used to maintain subordination. Changing these situations, however, involves more than simply providing formal literacy classes and abandoning 'folk' ways. Good educational practice today requires facilitators to build upon what learners bring to class, to listen not just deliver, and to respond to local articulations of 'need' as well as make their own 'outsider' judgements of it. Good political practice likewise requires developers to listen to where people are coming from and to build on local strengths, not simply wish them away. The resultant mix of local/central that a transformational programme based on an ethnographic approach would develop is quite different from the romantic vision of 'folk' paradise to be left pure and unsullied by urban or modern interference, as the 'romanticism' critique would have it.

A primary difference from the hegemonic centralism of the autonomous model is that the model of transformation which follows from an ethnographic approach to literacy research, by being sensitive to context and to local need, is able to recognise where some local literacy practices – for instance the immediate production and interpretation of documents regarding irrigation, micro-credit or health as the authors detail below – are more central to practical 'needs' (and empowerment) than the imparting of formal primer-based knowledge and 'transferable' skills. It is the dynamic relationship between local and central, between specific literacy skills focused on immediate tasks and generic skills supposedly transferable to other situations (an issue dealt with in some detail in a number of the chapters), that is the focus of policy and programme design arising from the research described here. This is neither to condone blindly the central, neutralist position nor to extol a naive romanticism but to propose a less binary and more subtle starting point.

Nor is this just a matter of researchers advocating on behalf of the people they study – what Cameron et al. (1992) term 'research for'. Rather, the people with whom the research described in this volume was conducted make their own judgements of what is really relevant and, as noted above and described at length in the literature, this frequently involves rejecting formal classes and school-based literacy where it is unconnected with local communicative practices. The research described here attempts to measure up to Cameron's call for 'research with', rather than 'research on' as in traditional methods or 'research for' as in recent advocacy approaches. This involves, as Dyer and Chokji demonstrate, listening to local critiques of apparently well-meaning programmes of adult literacy; in this case peripatetic teachers were provided for nomadic pastoralists in northern India but the Rabaris themselves associated this with state policies for sedentarisation and argued instead for programmes that would help them learn 'how to speak' the language and behaviour of power. Such grounded accounts of local responses to apparently liberal programmes remind us that people's perspectives on literacy may be very different from those of programme designers and Western educators. This volume, I hope, will help us to listen to such views and learn how to design more culturally sensitive programmes than those which currently dominate the agenda, based on grounded accounts of 'which literacies' people 'need'.

References

Abadzi, H. (1996) *Adult Literacy: A Problem-Ridden Area*, Washington, DC: World Bank.

Anderson, A.B., Teale, W.H. and Estrada, E. (1980) 'Low-income Children's Preschool Literacy Experiences: Some Naturalistic Observations', *Quarterly Newsletter of the Laboratory of Comparative Human Cognition* 2: 59–65.

Barnett, R. and Griffin, A. (eds) (1997) *The End of Knowledge in Higher Education*, esp. 'Introduction: Knowledge under Attack' by Anne Griffin; and 'Conclusion: A Knowledge Strategy for Universities' by Ron Barnett, London: Institute of Education.

Barton, D. (1991) 'The Social Nature of Writing', in D. Barton and R. Ivanič (eds), *Writing in the Community*, London: Sage.

—— (1994) *Literacy: An Introduction to the Ecology of Written Language*, Oxford: Blackwell.

Barton, D. and Hamilton, M. (eds) (1998) *Local Literacies: Reading and Writing in One Community*, London: Routledge.

Barton, D., Hamilton, M. and Ivanič, R. (eds) (1999) *Situated Literacies: Reading and Writing in Context*, London: Routledge.

Barton, D. and Ivanič, R. (eds) (1991) *Writing in the Community*, London: Sage.

Basic Skills Agency (1997) *International Numeracy Survey*, London: Basic Skills Agency (BSA).

Baynham, M. (1995) *Literacy Practices: Investigating Literacy in Social Contexts*, London: Longman.

Black, P. and Wiliam, D. (1998) *Inside the Black Box: Raising Standards through Classroom Assessment*, London: School of Education, King's College London.

Cameron, D., Harvey, C. and Rampton, B. (1992) *Researching Language: Issues of Power and Method*, London: Routledge.

Clammer, J. (1976) *Literacy and Social Change: A Case Study of Fiji*, Leiden: Brill.

Crush, J. (ed.) (1995) *Power of Development*, London: Routledge.

Doronilla, M.L. (1996) *Landscapes of Literacy: An Ethnographic Study of Functional Literacy in Marginal Philippine Communities*, Hamburg: UIE.

Freebody, P. and Welch, A. (1993) *Knowledge, Culture and Power: International Perspectives on Literacy as Policy and Practice*, London: Falmer Press.

Freire, P. (1972) *Pedagogy of the Oppressed*, London: Sheed & Ward.

—— (1985) *The Politics of Education: Culture, Power and Liberation*, Cambridge, MA: Bergin & Garvey.

Freire, P. and Macedo, D. (1987) *Literacy: Reading the Word and the World*, Cambridge, MA: Bergin & Garvey.

Gee, J. (1990) *Social Linguistics and Literacies: Ideology in Discourses*, London: Falmer Press.

Gee, J., Hull, G. and Lankshear, C. (1996) *The New Work Order: Behind the Language of the New Capitalism*, Sydney: Allen & Unwin.

Grillo, R. and Stirrat, R.L. (eds) (1997) *Discourses of Development: Anthropological Perspectives*, Oxford: Berg.

Heath, S.B. (1982) 'What No Bedtime Story Means: Narrative Skills at Home and School', *Language and Society* 11: 49–76.

—— (1983) *Ways with Words: Language, Life and Work in Communities and Classrooms*, Cambridge: Cambridge University Press.

Heath, S.B. and McLaughlin, M.W. (eds) (1993) *Identity and Inner-City Youth: Beyond Ethnicity and Gender*, New York: Teachers College, Columbia University.

Heller, S. and Pomeroy, K. (1997) *Design Literacy: Understanding Graphic Design*, New York: Allworth Press.

Hill, C. and Parry, K. (eds) (1994) *The Test at the Gate: Cross-Cultural Perspectives on English Language Assessment*, London: Longman.

Holland, C. with Cooke, T. and Frank, F. (1998) *Literacy and the New Work Order: An International Literature Review*, London: NIACE.

Holland, D. and Street, B. (1994) 'Assessing Adult Literacy in the United Kingdom: The Progress Profile', in C. Hill and K. Parry (eds), *The Test at the Gate: Cross-Cultural Perspectives on English Language Assessment*, London: Longman.

Hornberger, N. (ed.) (1998) *Language Planning from the Bottom Up: Indigenous Literacies in the Americas*, Berlin: Mouton de Gruyter.

Kalman, J. (1999) *Writing on the Plaza: Mediated Literacy Practices among Scribes and Clients in Mexico City*, Cresskill, NJ: Hampton Press.

King, L. (1994) *Roots of Identity: Language and Literacy in Mexico*, Stanford, CA: Stanford University Press.

Kress, G. and van Leeuwen, T. (1996) *Reading Images: The Grammar of Visual Design*, London: Routledge.

Kulick, D. and Stroud, C. (1993) 'Conceptions and Uses of Literacy in a Papua New Guinean Village', in B. Street (ed.), *Cross-Cultural Approaches to Literacy*, Cambridge: Cambridge University Press.

Lemke, J. (ed.) (1998) 'The Language and Semiotics of the Classroom', Special Issue of *Linguistics and Education* 10(3).

Leung, C. and Tosi, A. (1999) *Rethinking Language Education*, London: CILT.

Luke, A. (1996) 'Genres of Power? Literacy Education and the Production of Capital', in R. Hasan and G. Williams (eds), *Literacy in Society*, London: Longman.

Maybin, J. (ed.) (1994) *Language and Literacy in Social Practice*, Clevedon and Philadelphia: Multilingual Matters/Open University Press.

OECD (1995) *Literacy, Economy and Society: Results of the First International Adult Literacy Survey*, IALS Statistics Canada/OECD.

Prinsloo, M. and Breier, M. (eds) (1996) *The Social Uses of Literacy: Theory and Practice in Contemporary South Africa*, Amsterdam and Johannesburg: John Benjamins and SACHED Books.

Robinson-Pant, A. (1997) 'The Link between Women's Literacy and Development', PhD thesis, University of Sussex.

Rogers, A. (1994) *Using Literacy: A New Approach to Post Literacy Materials*, London: ODA (DfID).

—— (1999) 'Improving the Quality of Adult Literacy Programmes in Developing Countries: The "Real Literacies" Approach', *International Journal of Educational Development* 19: 219–34.

Street, B. (1984) *Literacy in Theory and Practice*, Cambridge: Cambridge University Press.

—— (1988) 'Literacy Practices and Literacy Myths', in R. Saljo (ed.), *The Written World: Studies in Literate Thought and Action*, Berlin and New York: Springer-Verlag.

—— (1993a) 'Review Article on Books on Ethnographic Research', *Journal of Research in Reading* 16(2) Special Issue, 'The New Literacy Studies'.

—— (1995) *Social Literacies: Critical Approaches to Literacy in Development, Ethnography and Education*, London: Longman.

—— (1996) 'Literacy and Power?' *Open Letter* 6(2): 7–16. Sydney: UTS.

—— (1998) 'New Literacies in Theory and Practice: What Are the Implications for Language in Education?', *Linguistics and Education* 10(1): 1–24.

—— (1999) 'Meanings of Culture in Development', in A. Little and F. Leach (eds), *Schools, Culture and Economics in the Developing World: Tensions and Conflicts*, New York: Garland Press.

—— (2000) 'Literacy Events and Literacy Practices: Theory and Practice in the "New Literacy Studies"', in K. Jones and M. Martin-Jones (eds), *Multilingual Literacies: Comparative Perspectives on Research and Practice*, Amsterdam: John Benjamins.

Street, B. (ed.) (1993b) *Cross-Cultural Approaches to Literacy*, Cambridge: Cambridge University Press.

Wagner, D. (1993) *Literacy, Culture and Development: Becoming Literate in Morocco*, Cambridge: Cambridge University Press.

Yates, R. (1994) 'Gender and Literacy in Ghana', PhD thesis, University of Sussex.

Part I

LITERACY AND DEVELOPMENT

Ethnographic perspectives on schooling
and adult education

INTRODUCTION

The chapters in this part of the book all address educational interventions, whether at the level of school or of adult programmes. Adopting an ethnographic perspective on education involves, first, suspending judgement on the educational aims and agendas of developers rather than taking them as the ground from which further analysis follows. It is not, for instance, self-evident that programmes for literacy acquisition are necessarily in the best educational or social interests of the target audience. Nor are approaches to learning and teaching considered 'state of the art' or 'progressive' by developers and Western educators necessarily the most effective or successful in different contexts. Particular approaches, such a 'learner-centred' or process writing may work in some contexts but we will not know whether they work in others until we have studied those other contexts: we cannot simply impose apparently 'effective' methods and expect to see the same results everywhere – as Wagner states, 'one shoe does not fit all'. An ethnographic perspective, then, obliges us to suspend judgement on such methods until we have understood better the context in which they are being applied. Local meanings and uses of communicative practices in general and of literacy practices in particular may indicate alternative approaches to the design of literacy programmes to those that may seem obvious from outside. The accounts in this part, based upon ethnographic research mainly in India and Africa, both on local literacy practices and on educational projects as themselves social practices, call into question such centralist sentiments. We are helped instead to 'see' local perspectives and nuances in indigenous and central conceptions of the educational process. Out of such re-viewing the authors hope that more sensitive programmes might emerge. That is, the researchers are not interested simply in the theoretical and methodological insights arising from their research but are also committed to working through their practical implications. Developers and programme designers as well as academics in the field of language and literacy should therefore find much of interest in these chapters: if these traditionally separate groups are facilitated to overlap to some extent and to learn from each other's perspectives, then the authors will feel their work has been worthwhile.

Caroline Dyer and Archana Choksi in 'Literacy, schooling and development: views of Rabari nomads, India' consider these issues with respect to nomadic people, focusing on questions of literacy and power. The Rabaris of Kachchh, Gujarat, India, are a caste of transhumant pastoralists who were traditionally camel herders, but have diversified to husband sheep, goats, cattle and occasionally buffaloes. Over the centuries, they have enjoyed an occupational niche that has enabled them to maintain their entire, holistic way of life – a careful equilibrium of God–human–animal. Since the 1980s, Rabaris have been increasingly negatively affected by the state's pattern of development, which in its focus on industrialisation and 'modernisation' is causing sources of fodder and water available to pastoralists to shrink ever more rapidly. In this era of increasing pressures which appear to be rendering their traditional way of life unviable, Rabaris have started to look for alternatives. Their way of life precludes them from making use of any of the static modes of educational provision offered by the state, yet Rabaris are unanimously in favour of 'literacy'. Under their present circumstances, peripatetic adult literacy teaching seemed the most logical form of provision for nomadic groups who cannot remain in one place for longer than three weeks at the most. In a two-year period of ethnographic research, during which Dyer and Choksi conducted several action research experiments with literacy teaching and learning, they found that Rabaris see various uses of the written word in their local environments, but that 'literacy' is seen in terms of a series of discrete functions, such as being able to read a bus destination board or sign a name. Significantly, the uses they talked of in this connection were all public literacy events – places when highly independent and self-sufficient Rabaris felt compromised by having to ask for the help of others. When it came to issues of power, Rabaris did not have much conviction of the use of adult literacy; they made very much stronger connections between power and the processes of schooling, where children would not only learn to read and write, but would also learn 'how to speak' – use the language and behaviour of power. To them, 'development' followed a path of sedentarising and sending their children to regular government schools where they would learn these skills, which their parents could not impart through their indigenous patterns of education. Schools were seen as offering the way into social and economic security in the contemporary context, where the traditional occupation of transhumant pastoralism is seen to have neither value nor social status. Conversely, Rabaris felt that peripatetic adult literacy, which attempted to validate their traditional occupation but marry it with the literacy skills required in modern times, was tantamount to condemning them to remain 'backward' and 'barbaric'. Dyer and Choksi, then, offer a careful antidote to the romanticised uses of ethnography as simply privileging local values and conditions: in New Work Order conditions, marginalised peoples like the Rabaris want to be part of economic development and are prepared to make compromises. This appears to require both traditional and progressive literacy practitioners to revise their assumptions about programme development and to work with a more nuanced understanding of their implications for literacy learning and teaching.

Uta Papen's chapter '"Literacy – your key for a better future"? Literacy, reconciliation and development in the National Literacy Programme in Namibia' likewise addresses contradictions and contestations in views of what a literacy programme should look like, in her case the National Literacy Programme in Namibia (NLPN). The NLPN was initiated by the new government after the country gained independence from South Africa in 1990. Since 1992, it has been implemented in all regions of the country. The programme begins with two years of reading and writing in mother tongues (Stages 1 and 2) followed by one or two years of English literacy (Stages 3/4). Since 1998, the 'Adult Upper Primary Education' (AUPE) programme has been added to the NLPN. It consists of a three-year (Stages 5–7) course of basic education equivalent with formal primary education.

The research on which this chapter is based combines an ethnography of literacy practices in and around the NLPN with a policy analysis of the NLPN, attentive especially to new communicative practices and to the location of literacy practices in a post-revolutionary context that is already deeply embedded in global politics. Papen's ethnography of literacy practices describes the uses and meanings of literacy in different social contexts and institutional settings of the NLPN, e.g., in the classrooms, in training sessions for literacy teachers and in the broader context that informs particular programme choices and decisions. Context, as she understands it here, encompasses institutional structures, social relationships, economic conditions, historical processes and the ideological formations or discourses in which literacy is embedded. Emphasising in particular the insights to be gained by focusing on discourses, Papen suggests that literacy in the NLPN is framed by a range of discourses about literacy and learning and about education in general. Furthermore, the NLPN is directly related to other governmental policies and their discourses. In this chapter, she is particularly interested in the broader state policies of social and economic development to which the NLPN is tied. The aim of this research is not to evaluate or to critique the programme and its policies and structures, but to understand them, that is to understand the social practices, the discourse formations and the ideological interests in which teaching and learning in the NLPN are embedded.

The chapter consists of three sections. In the first part, Papen briefly introduces the theoretical concepts which underlay her research and which link closely to those outlined above. In the second main part, she discusses the role of the NLPN as part of the government's reconciliation and development policy. The core of this section is a portrait of the National Literacy Day celebrations on 4 September 1999 which Papen attended as a participant observer. The purpose of her account of the festivities is to illustrate the meanings attached to literacy and education in the context of the development policies that she outlines. In the concluding section of the chapter, she describes some of the literacy practices used in the NLPN classrooms. She argues that the dominant conceptions of literacy and education, and the larger political aims attached to literacy, which she introduced in the second section, not only bear upon the content of the programme, but also privilege certain understandings of knowledge and influence the kind of literacy practices used in the programme. What counts as knowledge in the new epistemological order of, in this case, a post-revolutionary 'developing' society, is highly contested and fraught. Such epistemological assumptions underpin the decisions and choices made within a programme. The strength of Papen's chapter is to offer us a way of 'seeing' these processes where they are often hidden and to recognise their importance where they often appear too 'academic' to be of concern to practitioners and developers.

Martha Wright in 'Multilingual literacies, ideology and teaching methodologies in rural Eritrea' similarly offers a way of re-viewing dominant conceptions of what counts as literacy and what counts as good ways of imparting it. Like Papen and Dyer and Choksi, Wright provides a reflective and often self-critical account of the assumptions that developers (in Hobart's sense of both Northern and Southern development workers), literacy workers and researchers bring to literacy programmes. The new nation of Eritrea emerged in 1991 from thirty years of war with Ethiopia and with an ambitious programme of educational reform. The Eritreans hold out great hope that through the provision of education, especially literacy, they can bring their people into the new world order, and make restitution for the deprivations of this past generation and the previous several centuries of domination by foreign powers. As in many developing countries, much educational reform in Eritrea has been based on imported ideologies, from Christian missionaries to Marxist revolutionaries to teacher trainers armed with communicative methodology; each has left its mark on literacy instruction as practised today. Primary school teachers in modern Eritrea are the recipients of this political, cultural and educational heritage, and have been given the task of integrating their experience growing up in colonial and insurgent Eritrea with the pervasive reform which parents and educators hope will transform the lives of the new generation in one of the world's poorest countries. Wright's ethnographic study of literacy instruction in the rural town of Ghinda looks at how early literacy is accomplished, focusing on English as a foreign language and also Tigrinya and Arabic. She examines the ways in which these teachers integrate modern, Western language-teaching methodologies into their personal and cultural experience, as observed by the researcher in their classrooms and as the teachers themselves have accounted for their practices, in formal and informal interviews. The teachers' beliefs – about learning in general, about their students in Ghinda, about the practical limitations placed on them by the specific situation – are discussed in relation to the ways in which they determine their approach to the teaching of as many as three distinct literacies.

The chapter represents the kind of reflective ethnography advocated in a number of the chapters and that appears to lead to the ethnographer exposing herself to criticism and beginning to change her own cherished assumptions.

Wright had come to Eritrea espousing 'progressive' language process approaches and was rather shocked to observe teaching methods that appeared to involve traditional memorisation, choral repetition and copying: she could not at first 'see' what was going on within and behind the surface appearance of these practices. For instance, she 'found to her embarrassment that not only did I not recognise "groupwork" when it was right before my eyes, I didn't recognise "active" student participation either'. Gradually, however, close observation, interviews and conversations with the participants and self-questioning led her to recognise that what was going on did not necessarily represent the stereotypical mindless repetition that progressive Western educators have criticised. Rather, there was a complex adaptation of Islamic and Eritrean methods to modern conditions. A major contribution of her findings to literacy policy is that it might be less important to focus on what teaching methodology is being employed than to focus on what research methodology is being used to understand it. As Wagner has demonstrated with respect to Morocco and elsewhere, programmes tend to put too much weight on teaching methodologies as though these will resolve the problems of learning, drop out and motivation cited in the programme evalua-tions (cf. Abadzi above). Rather it is the conceptualisation of the whole pro-gramme and its context, including recognising the often creative meanings that teachers frequently bring to new situations, that matters more than a particular method of teaching. Wright concludes: 'The innovations and adaptations which many teachers in the developing world have already devised within the constraints of their situation need to be "mined", so to speak – scrutinised for negative and positive attributes, adjusted accordingly, tested and incorporated into more realistic teacher training . . . integrating the best from their traditions.' Indeed, state of the art methodologies from outside the context may actually lead to people being disempowered by the very thing they were led to believe would liberate them.

Priti Chopra's 'Betrayal and solidarity in ethnography on literacy: revisiting research homework within a north Indian village' addresses both educational issues of the kind raised by Wright and other authors in this part and the broader issues of literacy and development raised by authors throughout the book, but from the perspective of a more general question – how do/can re-searchers engage in research on such issues and what is their relationship with the researched? In the case of literacy, the researched are people who are fre-quently constituted as 'illiterate' by the agencies who come to 'empower' them. Chopra feels that she sits 'in a fidgety manner' in this book, because she is interested not so much in such 'illiterate' subjects, as in people 'who refuse to be "illiterate" subjects', in her case within a literacy centre in a north Indian village and within her ethnographic study. Yet her dilemma, which remains more or less explicit in the other contributions, is that these subjects still remain captured in her writing, as subjects of literacy. Is this capturing a kind of betrayal? This issue clamours for reflexivity in ethnographic research on literacy, both her own and others'.

The first purpose of her own reflexivity is to reflect upon the interplay of betrayal and solidarity as an issue for ethnographers, like herself, in re-presentations of people she knows and works *with* as subjects of literacy. Secondly, her focus on non-attendance in a village literacy centre aims to contribute to the efforts of ethnographic research, exemplified in this volume, as a way for hearing the voices of 'illiterate' subjects. She uses the chapter to review and reflect on these dilemmas, revisiting her research 'homework' in a north Indian village in order to become (under the reader's gaze) self-conscious of these acts of 'knowing' as neither innocent nor transparent. She uses the term 'home' rather than 'field' as the site of her research work since, for her, 'home is not a fixed space but rather a shifting space that encompasses acts of betrayal and solidarity. Home represents, for me, a space in which I am attached, in which I belong, but also a space which is not free from confrontation, struggle and transformation.' She presents this review in the form of three narratives based in and near a village in which she was both observer and participant in a literacy programme. The first narrative is her translation, from a literacy facilitator's writing in Hindi about a meeting, including many non-attending participants, at the village literacy centre, an account Chopra entitles 'Re-citing Saraswati's writing on meeting no.1'. In the second narrative, 'Story 1', she revisits an interview with a non-attending participant, Lakshmi, who refuses to be the 'illiterate' subject of the literacy centre and of her ethnographic study. The final narrative, 'Story 2', is based on revisiting Yamuna, a literacy facilitator, living outside the context of the village and the literacy centre. Chopra uses these narratives to reflect upon representations of the 'illiterate' subject by both herself and others and as a means to study representation as the practice of reading and writing the 'illiterate' subject as 'literate'. By studying representations of the 'illiterate' subject, as the practice of literacy theory, she hopes to extend the gaze beyond 'failure' to see limits in acts of 'knowing' the 'illiterate' subject in order to be able to critique and act upon these limits. The chapter therefore offers insights into the processes by which all of the data in the present volume were collected and indicates the similar dilemmas experienced by all of the authors. It therefore sits appropriately at the bridge of the two main parts of the book, following chapters that explicitly address the educational dimension of literacy work in development and before a series of accounts of literacy work in a number of domains of practice – land rights (Aikman), the language of literacy (Herbert and Robinson), the marketplace (Maddox), health (Robinson-Pant), state control of indigenous peoples (Stites) and the gender politics of literacy (Zubair).

1

LITERACY, SCHOOLING AND DEVELOPMENT

Views of Rabari nomads, India

Caroline Dyer and Archana Choksi

Nomads and literacy

At the World Conference on Education for All, held in Jomtien, Thailand in 1990, governments around the world pledged to intensify their efforts to provide Basic Education to all their citizens. Basic Education is conceived as 'primary . . . education for children, as well as education in literacy, general knowledge and life skills for youth and adults' (WCEFA 1990: ix). This pledge to provide literacy as part of a strategy of Education for All is underpinned by a view of literacy as neutral and universal, or 'autonomous' (Street 1984). In this chapter, we draw on two and a half years of ethnographic research among the Rabaris of Kachchh, a nomadic[1] group from Gujarat in the west of India, to illustrate some of the ways in which Rabaris' perceptions of 'literacy' contribute to an alternative view: that literacy is not neutral and singular, but that literacies are plural, social and therefore 'ideological' practices (Street 1984 and this volume).

The ideological nature of the apparently neutral, 'autonomous' model is immediately evident for nomads and other spatially mobile groups, for whom the commonplace assumption that literacy classes be regularly provided in the same place for a period of time makes attendance impossible. Sedentary classes seem at first glance to be logistical and therefore neutral; but they are not. They are a component of a developmental ideology that posits the desirability of a settled population over a population that moves, as Klute (1996: 3) observes: 'State agents consider nomads as belligerent, difficult to control, and see their continuous movement much more as a sort of offence to the requirements of any modern state and its rational administration than as a quest for water and pasture.' We suggest, therefore, that for nomads their relationship with the state is likely to be a key issue shaping their perceptions of literacy.

The desire to become literate that is growing among the world's nomadic populations is a relatively recent phenomenon (Swift et al. 1989). Ironically this

27

desire is largely fuelled by the way 'development' schemes are contributing to their social, economic and political marginalisation. Nomads have always lived 'apart' (one interpretation of the name Rabari, for instance, is *rah bahar* – lives out of the way). They have occupied a specific and unique niche resulting from their spatial mobility and their ability to exploit marginal natural resources, combined with their capacities to regulate their own law and order by recourse to their own socio-political and legal institutions. But this 'apartness' has changed in character: nomads are finding fewer and fewer places to go as development policies that favour other groups cut into the land available to them. Nomads in India, for example, do not benefit from 'development' strategies that include the intensive agriculture practices introduced through the Green Revolution (Glaeser 1987); Operation Flood (a massive dairy initiative) (George 1985); Forestry Department policies designed to protect forest cover, arrest encroaching deserts and soil erosion; industrialisation; or anti-poverty schemes to provide land for the landless (cf. for India: Bose 1975; Salzman 1986; Agrawal 1992; Vira 1993; Choksi and Dyer 1996a; Hoon 1996). The combination of these pressures is leading groups such as Rabaris to recognise that their indigenous, apprenticeship model of education is no longer sufficient to help them flourish in contemporary, modernising society. Reading and writing, for example, are acknowledged to be important, but no one among the non-literate, transhumant groups possesses the necessary knowledge to pass on to others.

Our research project 'Literacy for Migrants'[2] (Dyer and Choksi 1996) was sited at the intersection of the Indian government's pledge to provide Education for All and transhumant Rabaris' desire for something they called 'literacy'. We researched literacy events in their lives, and their literacy practices, and experimented with a model of peripatetic provision that initially appeared to offer a bridge between Rabaris' way of life and their aspirations to become literate. The ethnographic approach helped us to see how Rabaris' 'conceptions of knowledge, identity and being' (Street, this volume) influenced their understandings of 'education', providing insights into meanings of literacy in their lives that often contradicted our own initial premises and consistently revealed new facets of the complex relationship between literacy and development.[3]

The Rabaris of Kachchh: in search of 'education'

Kachchh is an arid, semi-desert area of Gujarat State that borders Pakistan to the north-west, and Rajasthan to the north-east. It lies just within reach of the south-west monsoon, which provides an erratic yearly rainfall, averaging only 300–400 mm; droughts are frequent and in summer temperatures reach 49°C. Poor agricultural conditions and formerly plentiful grasslands have encouraged widespread animal husbandry in the region: Hindu Rabaris and the non-migrating Muslim Maldharis are the prominent pastoral groups (GoI 1987).

There are five, endogamous, sub-groups of Rabaris of Kachchh: two groups, the Katchi and Gardo Rabaris, used to migrate into the Sindh in Pakistan but partition of India and Pakistan closed off this route, and they have since sedentarised in Kachchh and diversified into other occupations (Choksi and Dyer 1996a). The other three groups – Dhebar, Vagad and Kantho Rabaris – are still predominantly migratory; Dhebars have now mostly migrated out of Gujarat to other states, where they are fully nomadic, returning to Kachchh only for social or religious ceremonies. Vagad and Kantho Rabaris are transhumant within Gujarat, returning to Kachchh for the monsoon season. Rabaris were traditionally camel breeders: all five sub-groups share a myth of origin which recounts that they were put on earth by Lord Shiva to tend Parvati's camels. Nowadays they mostly keep mixed flocks of sheep and goats, and only a handful of families still rear camels, but pastoralism remains a God-given occupation and Rabaris' socio-cultural identity is deeply embedded in their occupational identity.

Highly visible as they migrate, with their large flocks of sheep, their camel trains and their distinctive, embroidered clothing, Rabaris are nevertheless more or less invisible to the state. As they are usually absent when door-to-door enumeration takes place for the decennial census, many Rabaris are not counted. As a group, they do exist officially, since they are included in the category of Other Backward Classes: but for this group, unlike those who are classified as Scheduled Caste or Scheduled Tribe (Enthoven 1922), specific demographic and socio-economic data are not solicited. As a result, basic information required for development planning for them is missing: a best guess of the population of Rabaris of Kachchh by their leaders is 90,000, but we do not have information as to the proportions of the sub-groups, or the numbers of those who migrate. Literacy among transhumant groups is reportedly virtually zero; and among sedentary Rabaris few children complete secondary schooling (Pashuara 1995) while adult literacy runs below the rural average for Kachchh of 37 per cent male and 20.7 per cent female (GoG 1990).

In common with other nomadic groups, Rabaris are confronted by shrinking pastures that are undermining the foundations of transhumant pastoralism and making it increasingly difficult to pursue animal husbandry in contemporary conditions. Rabaris migrate across wasteland and forestry land, both owned by the government, but also need to use land and water sources owned by farmers. Access to all of these resources has become increasingly problematic, and their interactions with guardians of these resources is, in various ways, leading Rabaris to consider the relevance and importance of literacy in their own lives.

In the past, transhumant animals used to consume crop residues, and agriculturalists paid pastoralists in cash or kind for the animal dung and urine that fertilised their fields. Now, as more land comes under irrigation to support intensive cultivation, fields are rarely left fallow: aggressive marketing by the chemical fertiliser industry has helped artificial fertilisers to replace animal fertilisers. Where before they were welcomed, Rabaris and their migrating animals are now perceived as a threat to standing crops, which means that farmers are reluctant to allow them to pass over their land. This problem can be solved to some extent by paying rent to farmers, agreeing a fee in advance for a finite number of days' worth of grazing.

As they migrate, Rabaris are also increasingly embroiled in disputes about land use, often because of illegal practices by lower-ranking forestry officers. These disputes have to be settled by the police, who are more likely to be sympathetic to the local farmer than to a passing nomad. Another dimension of these disputes is that, in these lower echelons of government service, the people who impact heavily on Rabaris are often people from the Scheduled Tribes or Castes, who have benefited from positive discrimination by the state to rise to positions of relative power (at least, from the Rabari point of view). Rabaris find themselves being blocked or punished by people who, to them, occupy inferior caste positions. Ascribed status, a key social ordering principle for Rabaris, no longer seems to count. Measured in secular terms, Rabaris find that others see their social status as very low, a clear contrast with times gone by: 'Before, they used to drop everything to come out and look at us as we passed by. Now they jeer at us' (personal communication, Dhebar Rabarin 1994).

Whether to pay rent, fines or bribes, if Rabaris are to be able to move – which is an imperative for the survival of their animals – they now need to generate large sums of money. In the past, they used only to sell *ghee* (clarified butter) and some wool to obtain hard cash, but such income no longer suffices. Ever-present demands for cash have forced Rabaris to sell animals for the meat market and for them, as pious Hindus, this is a moral outrage which they liken to selling the blood of their own sons (Westphal-Hellbusch and Westphal 1974). Much of what is happening as a result of unfavourable development policies is attributed by Rabaris to this disastrous development which, to them, marks their moral downfall. Apart from their own dilemma, it is evident to Rabaris that others see their way of life as socially problematic: they hear from these farmers, and from shopkeepers and other sources, that their 'wandering about' is backward and *jungli* (of the jungle, and by implication uncivilised).

There is now a very strong perception among transhumant Rabaris that literacy is implicated in their difficulties in coping effectively with the combination of pressures outlined above:

> Because we have no education we can't speak up. That's why we're beaten. Police harass us, and so do villagers. Forest officers are a problem. If someone writes a letter saying a pastoral has damaged something a pastoral can't do anything about it. He may not have any money to feed his children but he has to pay the officers. This is why the community is deteriorating, because it has no education. How can it get out of this: they don't know the law so they're stuck in a vicious circle. We get implicated in police cases and because we are uneducated we don't know what to do next. Our situation is bad but it's time to think hard how to improve it.
>
> (Personal communication, Bhudhabhai, Vagad Rabari, 1994)

Rabaris' perceptions of how these key issues of social status and power were related to what they called 'education' emerged over time in the course of conversations and observations. Because we were also working with Rabaris on the design of peripatetic provision, we also looked at literacy events in their daily lives, to identify priority areas where reading and writing would be helpful. We found that on a day-to-day basis, in less confrontational situations, Rabaris' experience of non-literacy is also constructed partly around social status and power. The link between non-literacy and dependence emerged very strongly, for example, in discussions about the use of modern transport, and in writing letters. Being able to read bus boards would not only enhance mobility:

> Without writing I do have problems, specially reading boards when I go out in the bus. Now I have to ask someone, otherwise I could read the board and get on the bus. Now I have to ask, sister, has my bus come? Sometimes people insult me, saying, can't you see? Get lost. If you were literate you would not feel dependent. This is helplessness. I have to ask the time as I can't read the clock. I would know what time the bus will go. I could read the board at the station and know this bus will start at this time. Just now, I run round and round to find out about buses.

Letters are very important, particularly for women. If they could write letters, mothers would not need to worry about their daughters' welfare:

> I won't worry if my girl goes to her in-laws' place, at least she will be able to write to me, but at the moment all we can do is sit and worry. But if she could write we could communicate. If I get a letter from here I will know what's going on, otherwise all I can do is worry about how she is, is she well, and if anything happens I am so far away.

The relationship between literacy and power is also associated in some cases with a moral dimension of the human character that is very important to Rabaris, for whom their own *mariyada* (a code of ethical conduct) is very important, and something they often find lacking in others. This, too, presents for them a disturbing component of depending on non-Rabaris for help with literacy events, as this comment shows (italics added):

> If we get a letter, we have to go to someone like you who is literate, and ask what is written. Isn't that a problem? *If someone is good they will read; otherwise they will say something is there which is not right,* or they say they don't have time, and won't read it.

Perhaps because of their sense of the distortion of the moral order, Rabaris also believe they are constantly being cheated. Cheating for men was certainly an ever-present possibility as they do not do the day-to-day domestic transactions, and so, 'We can understand the big notes but if we have to add up the little ones, we can't manage.' The situation for women was more ambiguous, since their mental arithmetic was excellent (far faster and more reliable than ours) and they knew the market rates for their purchases. Shopkeepers felt that it would be impossible to cheat Rabari women; but still the women felt that being able to read prices would be better. For both sexes, being able to read bus tickets was important as conductors could not be expected to return small change unless you could argue for how much you were owed. In unfamiliar places, if you were not comfortable with asking someone who might not co-operate, you would not know this unless you could read the ticket.

Overall, it emerged from our observations and conversations with transhumant Rabaris that they felt not being educated was one of the main reasons why they felt 'we have become backward and so we have remained backward'. They also firmly believed that 'if there was education, we would be clever, we wouldn't have to ask anyone'. As this discussion shows, Rabaris' sense of 'literacy' was very broad, covering day-to-day problems around routine literacy events, to much wider dimensions reflecting their sense of their own social position in a modernising world.

Peripatetic teaching: literacy on the move

Although non-formal educational provision in India (now known as Alternative Schooling) has expanded considerably in the decade since the Jomtien declaration, it is still very much sedentary and village-based. While many pastoralists do now see value in learning how to read and write, they feel excluded: 'We want to study but there is no scheme, no system. If we do want to fit into a system, we can't' (personal communication, Hamir Rabari, 1994).

Drawing on reports of work in other country contexts (such as Nigeria (e.g. Ezeomah 1983) and Iran (e.g. Heron 1983)), we suggested to Rabari leaders and government officials that it might be appropriate to experiment with a peripatetic teaching programme. There is no such educational provision in Gujarat, yet the exigencies of the pastoralists' occupation seem to demand that supply move with the learners as they cannot move to the supply. The notion of a moving teacher was an innovation in educational thinking, and our willingness to engage in searching for a way forward was welcomed. Rabaris had great expectations of education, and were certain that it was their key to a better future: not having education was like having impaired vision:

> If we have a cataract in our eye and go to hospital and get it removed, we'll be able to see. This [education] is like that, people will start being able to see things. They will feel relieved that the burden is gone from their heads. If there is a ditch ahead, at least they won't fall into it. It is all about seeing things. If a woman is educated, she can take care of her household better, she can teach her children how to talk, make them

understand properly, and if she teaches the child, the child won't be cheated anywhere else.

(Dyer and Choksi 1998)

The notion of peripatetic provision was also greeted with reservations from some pastoralists, who wondered whether it would be possible to overcome the potentially competing demands of caring for animals and having time to study. We were warned: 'Do you think they will study? A sheep will run off and they will run after it. How can they learn?' (personal communication, Budha Rabari, 1994).

Our initial project aims were to observe literacy events and to find out what kind of inputs, and teaching and learning strategies would be best suited to the Rabari way of life, and to establish whether peripatetic teaching within the normal migratory cycle was actually feasible. We hoped later to find literate Rabari persons to act as literacy facilitators, but would initially adopt this role ourselves. We planned to test the feasibility of the peripatetic mode by migrating with Rabaris to learn more about them and their educational needs in the first project year, and in the second year to migrate with them again, using the four-month monsoon period in between, while they were back in Kachchh, to assemble – by collecting or preparing – materials we had identified as useful.

'We' were a research team of two women, one Southern (Gujarati) and the other Northern (English). Being female allowed much freedom, as it meant we could interact freely with Rabari women, without being seen as a threat to their honour, while enjoying the 'honorary male' status conferred upon us that allowed us to work with men too. Archana, as a Southern woman, overtly seemed to have more in common with Rabaris: she is, like them, a native speaker of the Gujarati language (but was initially not fully familiar with the Rabaris' dialect or linguistic conventions governing their conversational patterns), a Hindu (but of a different sub-sect and, unlike them, not active), and is fortunately of a similar caste status, which not only engendered respect, but was an important prerequisite for being allowed to eat and drink tea with them. Caroline, as a Northern woman, was clearly none of these things, but her obvious otherness had the advantage of not creating the behavioural expectations which would govern Archana's acceptability. Neither of us was by any means an insider and the acceptability of our presence as participant observers in Rabaris' social world was something we continually had to negotiate if we were to learn about Rabaris' perceptions of education. These perceptions, like our own, were reflections of sets of historically and contextually conditioned social values, aspirations, senses of self, and so on, many of which we did not share (nor did we necessarily share these with each other).

We envisaged that the literacy work would interest Rabaris in various ways. Being able to read and write would assist for instance in reading bus destination boards, tickets and prices; and dosage instructions on modern veterinary medicine, which Rabaris are beginning to use but generally in incorrect dosages

(Ramakrishnan 1994). We hoped that this learning would be embedded in discussions about fodder and herd management, the use of veterinary medicines, and wool and meat production, to see whether it would be possible to align Rabaris' practices of animal husbandry more comfortably within the wider, modernising context. Our premise was that Rabaris should not have to leave an occupation which can have good economic returns, appears relatively safe from competition by other groups and which is for Rabaris a complete way of life. We also envisaged that through discussions about literacy events and literacy practices in Rabaris' lives, we could share our knowledge of the functioning of modern institutions, which would help Rabaris become more confident in dealing with those who attempt to mis-use their positions of power.

Our original idea of an initial 'pilot' migration simply as participant observers with a migrating group (*dhang*) proved impossible (access negotiations are discussed more fully in Choksi and Dyer 1996b). It emerged that we only had a legitimate function in a *dhang* as their teachers. Enacting this role with an interested *dhang* of forty-eight Vagad Rabaris, we arranged 'formal' teaching sessions during the day for women and children and in the evening for men: these classes were able to accommodate anyone who was interested. The *dhang* members' literacy goals were reading and writing their own letters so they would not have to depend on anyone else for help; to read bus boards so they could catch a bus without asking anyone else where it was going; to read bus tickets; and to read religious texts. There was no suggestion that literacy was in any way related to animal husbandry.

Informally, we learned a great amount about each other's worlds by living and eating together, as our very different lives intersected for a couple of months. One wonderful day came when the men came charging back from a trip in the bus to the village, waving their tickets at us for verification. They suspected they had been over-charged and although they could now read the tickets, they had not felt confident enough of their new-found skills to challenge the bus conductor. Regretfully, we confirmed their suspicions, but it turned out to be affirmative action, for then their annoyance at their own timidity redoubled their wish to read well enough to get their money back in future! We suspended the migration with the *dhang* at the onset of the monsoon, when they returned to Kachchh.

When we then began to renegotiate access with members of the same *dhang* for the next season, we found that within only three to four months, the prevalent view that 'you can't migrate and study at the same time' had reasserted itself among the *dhang* members who had actually done so, and so was never dispelled among others. We met many more Rabaris, and heard again the same enthusiasm for the idea of peripatetic teaching, but despite our protracted efforts, no arrangements actually materialised. We were also struggling with the logistics of the impact of the wettest monsoon for a century, which allowed Rabaris the luxury of staying home for an extra three months, and then migrating in groups of only two or three families. Project funding, ideology and timetabling clashed head on with the Rabaris' sensible advice to come back next season. We were also wondering why they were so insistent that we stay at home with them in their village and set up a school for their children, where there was already a village school there to use if that option was what they wanted. Trying to work out what to do, we went over our field notes and tape transcripts again, and recalled the conversations we had had with each other. We needed to understand better the Rabaris' reservations about peripatetic teaching, before pursuing this idea: it did not seem to be presenting a way forward in the way that we, and community leaders, had imagined.

Rabaris' notions of 'literacy': the ethnographic findings

Our research had already shown that transhumant Rabaris thought learning to read and write while migrating would help them with events such as reading bus destination boards, bus tickets and ration cards, and writing letters – a series of discrete tasks. This was welcome as it would reduce the dependence on others to perform literacy tasks for them. Rabaris clearly did not regard literacy as a means by which to gain information – an 'alternative form of language behaviour' (Downing 1987) that overarches the individual tasks – although this understanding might have developed over time; and nor did they link literacy and their occupation. They liked the way we taught, but to them a programme within pastoralism held out the promise only of providing technical skills to solve a finite and identified range of literacy problems. This was not enough.

Reviewing the ethnographic evidence more carefully, we appreciated better how the cumulative outcomes of changes in the wider socio-political and economic contexts are actually serving to de-legitimise pastoralism. After our migrations, we could now comprehend better the holistic nature of pastoralism as a religious way of life, and we suddenly realised that what we were witnessing was the shattering impact of these changes. It was no longer possible for pastoralists to adapt and change in the ways they have been doing before: external changes have now begun to exert pressures on pastoral production that draws into question this whole, delicately balanced and holistic mode of existence. The moral economy on which Rabari pastoralism is based has been irrevocably undermined, and transhumant pastoralism as practised by Rabaris cannot readily be reconstructed as part of a modern market economy. No literacy classes we could offer could change this. Things that people had told us before took on new meanings: now we could appreciate the depth to which Rabaris feel their occupation is incompatible with the modern world when they made comments like this man had done:

> In the past, we had everything. But now the animal husbandry we do today does not give us enough to survive on. God gives us and we are carrying on with it, but truly there is no hope from these animals now.

> We are still doing animal husbandry because we are illiterate and so we can't find anything else. If we found something else we could change, we are very hard-working, but now pastoralists can't survive. With God's grace, and if education increases, we will be able to find a way, and that will be very good.

Non-formal, peripatetic teaching was not the answer to what, for them, is a new twist in the historical quest to adapt and survive. Although peripatetic classes were facing problems which were articulated in terms of logistics, we were gradually reaching more fundamental reasons why they were not what transhumant Rabaris aspired to. A programme of literacy within pastoralism, centred on their knowledge and experience, conflicted with Rabaris' sense of the future in several ways which we pieced together from the ethnographic data.

Parents had frequently reiterated that they, but particularly their children, should 'improve' (*sudhare*) and become 'clever' (*hoshiar*). These are qualities that Rabaris associate with people who have learned the ways of the 'developed' (which they express as 'improved') world. This world is quite other than the jungle[4] where Rabaris spend their lives, and which makes them *jungli* (of the jungle, used to mean uncivilised, and by implication needing to be improved) and backward. Valabhai, a father of three in our *dhang*, made this link explicit. He wanted to sedentarise because: 'I don't like the jungle because I can never hear anything new there, or meet any new people. I don't get any news, I won't be able to learn what is happening in the world if I stay there.'

To Rabaris, the jungle is not a place where one can improve and become clever. While conceptually the idea of a teacher moving with them was acceptable, in practice, there is no precedent of an educational programme on migration. Being 'literate' is, for Rabaris, intrinsically linked with being sedentary; and while our ideology of development embraced the possibility of non-sedentary literate persons, this was at odds with the ideology prevailing in this context. The formal school (village schools, or the one boarding school for Rabaris with only 200 places) is seen as the only option.

In the face of failing transhumant pastoralism, Rabaris sought to assure their children's futures, and this was a greater priority than adult education. If pastoralism is no longer going to provide the means of subsistence, occupational diversification is a necessity. Manual labour is an option for those with no educational qualifications, but a better job in the non-pastoral economy requires a school certificate. Apart from having an appropriate certificate, however, Rabaris recognise that it is important to be able to interact easily with other people. Such socialisation does not occur in the jungle, which has led to difficulties for sedentarising adults that a sedentary community leader has observed:

> They have grazed animals for forty years, they don't know the characteristics of [other caste groups]. They don't know how to behave with them, they don't come into contact with them because they don't have

the opportunity. So when they come back, and when they try to change their business, they don't fit in with anyone else.

(Personal communication,
sedentarised Dhebar community leader, 1994)

'Literacy', then, involves becoming appropriately socialised, and schools are seen as the places where such socialisation will take place.

Another thing that Rabaris thought was an important part of being 'literate' was being able to 'talk'. Knowing 'how to talk' seemed to represent liberation from feeling disempowered and intimidated by modern institutions where they do not know how to talk to those who work there (and are licensed to do so by their educational qualifications): 'even if we do get to the door of the hospital we won't know what to say next'. Difficult relationships with police and forestry officers provide for Rabaris similar evidence of this link between literacy and speaking the language, and using the behaviour, of power. This language and behaviour can be learned at school.

The currency of literacy programmes: do they measure up?

While we established that literacy teaching and learning can physically take place within a transhumant pastoral way of life, Rabaris had reservations about this approach. Their assessment was that transhumant pastoralism itself is not likely to continue to be a viable way of life and that therefore 'literacy' should offer an alternative future option. Through their contacts with sedentary people and their own assessments of the current trends in their situation, Rabaris' perceptions of 'literacy' encompass far more than technical literacy skills, which were useful only for solving discrete and immediate tasks. Literacy emerged as a whole ideology, shaped by the social, economic and political circumstances of their lives, and their sense of self in relation to other groups.

Rabaris, therefore, seek under the banner of literacy a means of meeting a variety of needs for capital, in Bourdieu and Passeron's (1977) terms: economic capital (via certification for a job); cultural capital in the form of language, or social manners; and symbolic capital – the power to convert economic and cultural capital into material resources and social authority. A literacy programme that fulfils Rabaris' developmental aspirations will be judged by the extent to which it offers the promise of providing them with access to such forms of capital. For this nomadic group, in this part of India, a literacy programme would have to compete with the hegemony of formal schooling as the only provider of this capital. It would have to make a claim to be an alternative place which is capable of furnishing access to the types of capital and knowledge which have been legitimised as those which 'count', even by those, like Rabaris, who until recently have had no interest in possessing such capital. Although the type of schools which are available for Rabari children to use may be highly unlikely to provide all three forms of capital, given the role of such schools in reproducing, rather than challenging social inequalities (Carnoy and Levin 1976), they offer that promise. A literacy programme, even if it is based on Freirean notions of 'conscientisation' (Freire 1972, 1985), to encourage critical reflection on the relationship between literacy practices and the (mis)exercise of power, will have to be able to offer currency at least equal to that which schools, whatever their quality, can offer.

As this research study has demonstrated, there were substantial differences between our own and Rabaris' perceptions of 'literacy'. We have tried to show here that by empirically testing a promising approach in the context of an ethnographic study, we were able to develop a much more substantial set of understandings about the complexity of what Rabaris understood by literacy, and therefore what a total programme of 'literacy' for Rabaris would need to provide.

Returning, in conclusion, to our concern at the outset with adult literacy as a component of Education for All, we believe that the existence of many different ideologies of literacy – one of which we have illustrated here – needs urgently to be acknowledged, and subsequently acted upon. Only then can this pledge to act become a real call to action, by linking the advances made in conceptual understandings of literacies with practical action through well-designed and appropriate literacy programmes.

Notes

1 Rabaris are transhumant pastoralists, rather than nomads, since they migrate with their animals in search of pastures in a fixed annual cycle, generally returning home once a year: nomads are permanently migratory.
2 The research project 'Literacy for migrants: an ethnography of literacy acquisition among the nomads of Kachchh' was funded by the UK's Economic and Social Research Council, whom we thank for their support.
3 The search was made all the more complicated by the colloquial use of a single generic term in Gujarati, derived from the verb 'bhanvun' which covers to study, to go to school, to be educated and to be literate/illiterate. 'Aabhan' which Rabaris used to describe themselves actually means one who has not studied, but is the usual term for illiterate. We tried to be specific about reading and writing, going to school, gaining knowledge, etc. to differentiate between these various meanings of 'literacy'.
4 Jungle (the Gujarati and English word is the same) is used here in the sense of a wild place, and does not necessarily connote trees.

References

Agrawal, A. (1992) *The Grass Is Greener on the Other Side: A Study of Raikas, Migrant Pastoralists of Rajasthan*, Drylands Programme Issues Paper no. 36, London: International Institute of Environment and Development.
Bose, A.B. (1975) 'Pastoral Nomadism in India: Problems and Prospects', in L. Leshnik and G.-D. Sontheimer (eds), *Pastoralists and Nomads in South Asia*, South Asian Institute of the University of Heidelberg Wiesbaden: Otto Harrassowitz.
Bourdieu, P. and Passeron, J.-C. (1977) *Reproduction in Society, Education and Culture*, London: Sage.

Carnoy, M. and Levin, H. (1976) *The Limits of Educational Reform*, New York: David McKay.

Choksi, A. and Dyer, C. (1996a) *Pastoralism in a Changing World: Patterns of Adaptation among the Rabaris of Kutch, Gujarat*, Drylands Programme Issues Paper no. 69, London: International Institute of Environment and Development.

—— (1996b) 'North–South Collaboration in Educational Research: Reflections on Indian Experience', in M. Crossley and G. Vulliamy (eds), *Qualitative Educational Research in Developing Countries*, New York: Garland.

Downing, J. (1987) 'Comparative Perspectives on World Literacy', in D. Wagner (ed.), *The Future of Literacy in a Changing World*, New York: Pergamon Press.

Dyer, C. and Choksi, A. (1996) *Literacy for Migrants: An Ethnography of Literacy Acquisition among Gujarati Nomads*, Final Report to the Economic and Social Research Council, UK.

—— (1998) 'Education Is Like Wearing Glasses: Nomads' Views of Literacy and Empowerment', *International Journal of Educational Development* 18(5): 405–13.

Enthoven, R.-E. (1922) *The Tribes and Castes of Bombay*, Bombay: Government of Bombay.

Ezeomah, C. (1983) *The Education of Nomadic People: The Fulani of Northern Nigeria*, Driffield: Nafferton Books.

Freire, P. (1972) *Pedagogy of the Oppressed*, London: Sheed & Ward.

—— (1985) *The Politics of Education: Culture, Power and Liberation* (trans. D. Macedo), London: Macmillan.

George, S. (1985) *Operation Flood: An Appraisal of Current Indian Dairy Policy*, Delhi: Oxford University Press.

Glaeser, B. (1987) *The Green Revolution Revisited: Critique and Alternatives*, London: Allen and Unwin.

GoG (1990) *Primary Education Statistics, Gujarat State*, Gandhinagar: Government of Gujarat.

GoI (1987) *Report of the Sub-committee for Studying the Problems and Suggesting the Remedial Measures for the Salinity Ingress in the Banni Area of Kutch District*, Central Design Organisation, Gandhinagar: Government of Gujarat Water Resource Dept.

Heron, P. (1983) 'Education for Nomads', *Nomadic Peoples* 13: 61–7.

Hoon, V. (1996) *The Bhotiya of the Himalaya*, New Delhi: Sage.

Klute, G. (1996) 'Introduction', *Nomadic Peoples* 38: 3–10.

Pashuara, H. (1995) Personal communication, Katchi community leader and secondary school teacher, Kachchh.

Ramakrishnan, K. (1994) Personal communication, Director, Sheep and Wool Development Board, Kachchh, Gujarat.

Salzman, P. (1986) 'Shrinking Pasture for Rajasthani Pastoralists', *Nomadic Peoples* 20: 49–61.

Street, B. (1984) *Literacy in Theory and Practice*, Cambridge: Cambridge University Press.

Swift, J., Toulmin, C. and Chatting, S. (1989) 'Education', in *Providing Services for Nomadic People: A Review of the Literature and Annotated Bibliography*, New York: UNICEF.

Vira, S. (1993) *The Gujjars of Uttar Pradesh: Neglected 'Victims of Progress'*, Drylands Programme Issues Paper no. 41, London: International Institute of Environment and Development.

WCEFA (1990) *The World Conference on Education for All: Meeting Basic Learning Needs – a Vision for the 1990s*, Background document, New York: Inter-Agency Commission for the World Conference on Education for All.

Westphal-Hellbusch, S. and Westphal, H. (1974) *Hinduistische Viehzuechter im nord-westlichen Indien. Vol. I, Die Rabar*, Berlin: Duncker & Humblot.

2

'LITERACY – YOUR KEY TO A BETTER FUTURE'?

Literacy, reconciliation and development in the National Literacy Programme in Namibia

Uta Papen

Introduction

This chapter deals with meanings and uses of literacy in the National Literacy Programme in Namibia (NLPN). The new government initiated the NLPN after the country gained independence from South Africa in 1990. Since 1992, it has been implemented in all regions of the country. The programme begins with two years of reading and writing in local languages (Stages 1 and 2) followed by one or two years of English literacy (Stages 3/4). Since 1998, the 'Adult Upper Primary Education' (AUPE) programme has been added to the NLPN. It consists of a three-year (Stages 5–7) course of basic education (in English) equivalent with formal primary education.

The research on which this chapter is based combines an ethnography of literacy practices in and around the NLPN with a policy analysis of the NLPN. My ethnography of literacy practices describes the uses and meanings of literacy in different social contexts and institutional settings of the NLPN, e.g., in the classrooms and in training sessions for literacy teachers. Context, as I understand it here, encompasses institutional structures, social relationships, economic conditions, historical processes and the ideological formations or discourses in which literacy is embedded (see Gee 1999). Literacy in the NLPN is framed by a range of discourses about literacy and learning and about education in general. Furthermore, the NLPN is directly related to other governmental policies and their discourses. In this chapter, I am particularly interested in the broader state policies of social and economic development to which the NLPN is tied. The aim of this research is not to evaluate or to critique the programme and its policies and structures, but to understand these, i.e., to understand the social practices and the discourse formations in which teaching and learning in the NLPN are embedded.

The chapter consists of three sections. In the first part, I briefly introduce the theoretical concepts which underlay my research. In the second and main part, I discuss the role of the NLPN as part of the government's reconciliation and development policy. The core of this section will be a portrait of National Literacy Day celebrated on 4 September 1999. The purpose of my account of the festivities is to illustrate the meanings attached to literacy and education in the context of the above mentioned development policies. In the concluding section of the chapter, I describe some of the literacy practices used in the NLPN classrooms. I will argue that the dominant conceptions of literacy and education, and the larger political aims attached to literacy, which I introduce in the second section, not only bear upon the content of the programme, but also privilege certain understandings of knowledge and influence the kind of literacy practices used in the programme.

Theoretical background: literacy and literacy teaching as social practices

My understanding of literacy is of reading and writing as social practice (see Street, this volume). Literacy, in this perspective, is not conceived as a single set of competencies, but as different practices 'embedded in political relations, ideological practices and symbolic meaning structures' (Rockhill 1993: 162), and, I would add, discourses. Therefore, literacy can be defined not in terms of technical skills alone, but in terms of a variety of conventions or modes of using written language. What counts as literacy varies depending on the people using it and the social and political context within which reading and writing take place.

If, as the social theory of literacy suggests, reading and writing is always located in a social context from which it derives its meaning, the same must be the case for literacy education (see Luke 1997). Kell (1996) has suggested that what is taught in a literacy programme is always a specific type of reading and writing. In my research, I start from the assumption that what is actually happening in the classrooms, what is taught and how learners 'take hold' (Kulick and Stroud 1993) of new literacy practices, depends *inter alia* on the conceptions of literacy held by planners and policy makers, and the degree to which these are being accepted, refuted or transformed by regional and local literacy workers, by the teachers and by the learners in the classrooms.

In the NLPN, literacy teaching is embedded in a set of social and institutional relationships, which have a direct influence on teaching and learning. These include the relationship between the teacher and the learners, between the government as provider of the programme and the participants as its recipients, between textbook knowledge and personal knowledge, between expert and lay knowledge, between official language and community languages, etc.

41

Literacy, development and reconciliation: the role of the NLPN as part of the government's economic and social policies

Introduction

A literacy programme such as the NLPN has its own goals, and, as I show in this chapter, these go far beyond imparting reading and writing skills. But literacy programmes are also part of broader political aims and are embedded in related policies. In the case of the NLPN, the 'ideological package' (Rassool 1999), which the programme carries with it, relates to economic development, societal modernisation, nation building and racial/ethnic reconciliation. Teaching to read and write in the NLPN is framed by these policy goals as well as by the fact that it is a government service provided to its citizens.

In order to understand the meanings and functions of literacy in the NLPN and the role of the NLPN for the government's development and reconciliation policy, I studied policy documents, evaluation reports and political speeches. I attended staff meetings and training sessions and participated in the National Literacy Day celebrations on 4 September 1999.[1] I use Foucault's concept of discourse (1980, 1988, 1997) to analyse how, in the above texts and practices, the symbolic and ideological meanings of literacy are framed in discursive statements. Discourse in this perspective refers to themes, attitudes and values, expressed through written or oral statements, symbols, images and behaviour, which at a given time and place, within a certain institutional or non-institutional context, are deemed appropriate and meaningful and make a claim to truth (adapted from Gee 1999: 37).

It is in the above sense that, in this chapter, I conceptualise literacy as discourse, i.e., as a historically and politically constructed field of knowledge and practice that consists of a range of discourses and practices embedded in social and institutional relationships. The starting point of my analysis is that discourses are interrelated with practice, thus 'affecting the actual design and implementation of projects' (Gardner and Lewis 1996: 73). Studying literacy as discourse, or as 'a regime of representation' (Escobar 1995: 6), allows me to uncover and explicate the concepts and assumptions that underpin literacy teaching in Namibia. By doing so, I pay particular attention to how different conceptions of literacy shape institutional and pedagogical practices in the NLPN. Furthermore, I unravel the connections between literacy discourses and other discourses that are at the core of current policy debates in Namibia, namely discourses of development, reconciliation, redress and equity. Using National Literacy Day as an example, I discuss literacy as itself being a discursive practice, i.e., I examine the role of written language in disseminating and promoting certain ideas about education and development as well as about reading and writing itself.

National Literacy Day: a national literacy event

National Literacy Day (NLD) is a crucial event in the NLPN's annual calendar.[2] It is celebrated towards the end of the NLPN's yearly programme, after the final examinations, which are normally held in the last weeks of August. During the festivities, which are held all over the country, learners who passed the exams receive their certificates.

The account of the day that I present in this chapter, although far from being exhaustive, nevertheless is understood as a 'thick description' (Geertz 1972) of this important social and political event. My description pays particular attention to the role of language and discourse during the festivities. I portray National Literacy Day as a literacy event, i.e., a social event in which written texts are essential for interaction and meaning making (Heath 1983; Barton and Hamilton 1998; Hamilton 2000). Although communication during the day was mainly oral, most of it was based on written texts. The speeches, which dominated the entire ceremony, were either read from a pre-written document or composed by the speakers on the basis of their pre-prepared notes. Other literacy events included the posters and banners carried during the festivities and the handing over of the certificates to the learners at the end of the ceremony.

Conceptualising National Literacy Day as a literacy event – which included different literacy practices (see Street, this volume) – provides an analytical framework which helped me to understand the social meanings of the celebrations by focusing on the role of different texts and communicative practices during the day. As Maybin (2000) points out, the concept of literacy practices offers a methodological tool for looking at the interrelationship between the immediate situational context and the wider bureaucratic and institutional context. I am particularly concerned with the role of the speeches during the day. What image of the NLPN was presented in the speeches? What messages did they convey regarding the relationship between the state and its citizens? On what texts and practices did the contributions rely to carry over their message? Furthermore, I will ask how literacy practices and discourses positioned the different actors involved.

Celebrating literacy and celebrating the achievements of the NLPN: National Literacy Day

The celebrations for National Literacy Day were held in Lüderitz, the main coastal city of the south. Learners, promoters and district literacy officers from the southern educational region travelled to Lüderitz to participate in the festivities. A delegation from the central office in Windhoek, headed by the Director of the NLPN, attended as well.[3] The guests of honour included the Minister of Labour of Namibia, the Minister of Basic Education and Culture and the Minister of Works, Transport and Communications. Also present were several high-ranking officials from the municipality and the regional education office.

The official purpose of National Literacy Day was to celebrate literacy and the achievements of those who had succeeded in becoming literate through the programme. Underlying this aim, however, was another important purpose: to mobilise support for the programme and to invite new learners to enrol. As much as the event was meant to be a celebration of literacy, it also needs to be seen as a celebration of the achievements of the new nation and its government. Three months before the general elections, with the government, although firmly in place, increasingly under attack for its ineffectual development policies, National Literacy Day was a big propaganda event for SWAPO, the ruling party. Its aim was to celebrate the success of the government's education policy.

The proceedings: speeches, songs and slogans

The festivities were held near the municipal football stadium of Lüderitz, located between the city with its mostly white middle-class neighbourhoods and the former townships for black and coloured Namibians. A podium had been erected for the guests of honour and several rows of chairs put up for the public.

The day was officially opened by the arrival of the guests of honour. Next on the agenda was the raising of the flag and the singing of the national anthem. Immediately before the opening of the festivities, a group of learners, promoters and DLOs had organised a promotional march through the nearby townships.[4] The marchers carried with them banners and posters telling people about the merits of literacy. Their songs invited people to join the programme. The march ended at the podium in front of which a crowd of spectators had started to fill the rows of seats. When the marchers arrived at the podium, they sang one of the NLPN's popular literacy songs. Easy to sing and to memorise 'Come along, sister, come along brother, we all go to literacy class' is the ideal promotional song.[5]

The front group of the marchers carried a huge banner of painted cloth on which appeared one of the most prominent slogans of the NLPN: 'Literacy – your key to a better future' (see book cover). It was used *inter alia* on the cover of the first policy guidelines of the NLPN (DABE 1993). 'Literacy – your key for a better future' symbolises the programme's belief in the capacity of literacy to help people improve their lives. This is an example of a 'mobilising metaphor' (Shore and Wright 1997:3) which is used to promote the government's literacy programme. That literacy does lead to a better future is an unquestioned assumption. The sentence refers to a goal most people can easily identify with: a wish to change and a belief in the future. The banner directly addresses its readers, and appeals to their responsibility in making the dream happen: literacy is *your* key. At the same time, the slogan offers the means to achieve the dream: *literacy*. The use of the second person signals the difference between the addresser, presumably the government, and the addressee, the people, since it is assumed that only the latter need the remedies advocated for.

On the two sides of the banner, the logo of the NLPN is printed. It shows two people helping each other with reading and writing. The figures, drawn to have no specific age, race or sex, are supposed to reflect equality (DABE 1992), although they look more male than female. They are encircled by the sun, the national symbol of Namibia, emphasising the significance of the NLPN as a national programme. Throughout the day, the banner remained in prominent view.

The speeches: literacy, individual advancement and National Development

The main events of the day were the 'addresses' by the invited regional and national politicians and government officials. Although interrupted by the 'cultural performances', i.e., literacy songs, dances and short plays, the biggest share of the five hours had been reserved for the speeches.

The keynote speaker of the day was the Minister of Labour, Andimba Toivo ya Toivo. He began his address congratulating the learners and the promoters 'for the job well done' (Toivo ya Toivo, 4/9/99: 2).[6] In his speech, he sketched out the government's policy towards literacy. The government regards it as its responsibility to provide education for all its citizens. It is committed to a policy of redress and affirmative action. The NLPN is presented as 'a truly national plan' (Toivo ya Toivo 4/9/99: 5) and literacy is seen as a priority for national development.

The Minister summarised the main goals of literacy. These are social and economic development, building democracy and citizenship, reconciliation and nation building. The expected contribution of the NLPN to development in Namibia is expressed in the following statement: 'It [literacy] makes possible better communication, which is often at the core of *progress* and *development*' (Sam Nujoma, quoted in Toivo ya Toivo, 4/9/99: 7).

This statement is part of a speech by the President of Namibia, which was quoted in full by the Minister. The assumed link between education and development is further illustrated in the following quote, again from the President's speech: 'Of course, literacy is also a basic skill, without which it is difficult to add the modern skills of agriculture and industry which we now promote as a nation' (Sam Nujoma, quoted in Toivo ya Toivo, 4/9/99: 7/8).

A modernisation theory underlies these statements. This is illustrated in the next quote, once again from the President's speech: 'The progress of a nation depends to a very large extent on the abilities and attitudes of its people' (Sam Nujoma, quoted in Toivo ya Toivo, 4/9/99: 8).

In her welcoming address, the Mayor of Lüderitz addressed the same issue. Namibia had already achieved political independence; now, she said, it needed to 'reach economic freedom' (Fieldnotes, 4/9/99). In order to do so, she explained, the country needs skilled people.

The above excerpts from several speeches held during National Literacy Day depict a view of literacy as a key instrument in the promotion of social and economic development. From this perspective, literacy is primarily conceived in terms of the development of human resources for the economy (see Oxenham 1980). Literacy is regarded as a basic skill, a necessary requirement for the acquisition of vocational and professional skills and knowledge. How, in practical terms, education is supposed to lead to economic development was not explained in Toivo's speech. But in a later intervention, the Minister of Basic Education and Culture, under whose responsibility the NLPN is being implemented, explained that education could of course not directly create jobs. The government, he said, had to stimulate economic growth (Fieldnotes 4/9/99).

Underlying the above views is a conception of literacy that bears resemblance with the model of functional literacy introduced by UNESCO in the sixties (Verhoeven 1994). Initially, functional literacy was used to refer to the needs of employment and economic development. The concept was then broadened to include 'the print demands of occupational, civic, community and personal functioning' (Verhoeven 1994: 6). Throughout the eighties, in international definitions of literacy, the functional model lost its influence as it was largely replaced by the empowerment-oriented concepts inspired by the work of Paulo Freire (1972). In the nineties, despite growing interest in the new social and ideological models, alongside the growing impact of neo-liberal policies worldwide, the economic dimension of literacy reappeared strongly in the debates. Belanger (1994: 92) calls this the 'over "economisation" of literacy issues' which according to him is related to the 'economisation' and the 'de-politicisation of citizenship'. I want to argue that economic aspects are given a central place in the NLPN, in policy documents and speeches as well as in the teaching materials. By contrast, references to democracy as a political goal of the NLPN are limited to people's participation in the elections and their role in community development.[7]

In all the speeches, the purpose of literacy was framed mainly in terms of the 'typical' development indicators, ranging from child health and nutrition to poverty alleviation. The following quote about the benefits of literacy for women illustrates this point: 'The benefits of women becoming literate are well documented, not only in terms of their own emancipation, but also in terms of education, health and economic progress of the whole family and nation' (Toivo ya Toivo, 4/9/99: 9/10). Again, the Minister's words build on a range of unquestioned assumptions regarding the positive impact of literacy. These are backed by the reference to some documented 'proof'. Such assumptions are part of a conception of literacy which Street (this volume) has termed the 'autonomous' model. It builds on two important suppositions: first, that literacy is a technical skill and therefore independent of its context of use, and second, that the acquisition of literacy promotes social progress, cognitive development, democracy and economic development (see also Street 1995). It is assumed that literacy by itself can bring about these benefits. Accordingly, illiteracy is often seen as impeding the development of high-level analytical skills, a 'modern' inventive and adventurous attitude, etc. (Goody and Watt 1968; Oxenham 1980).

Undoubtedly, poverty, poor housing, ill health, lack of economic opportunity and lack of access to information are 'real' issues for the majority of the Namibian population.[8] Ten years after Independence and the end of Apartheid, many Namibians still have not found their 'key' and are still waiting for their better future to come. Not surprisingly, development, in particular economic development, is perhaps the strongest theme in all government politics in Namibia. Having promised to redress the inequalities of Apartheid, the government has put strong emphasis on providing education, health and housing for all Namibians. Political and financial commitment for literacy and adult education is exceptionally high. However, while significant improvements have been achieved in the social services and education, economic growth has lagged behind and did not have a substantial effect on minimising inequalities and poverty (Hansohm 2000). Progress in addressing the main structural differences has been slow, and the very unequal distribution of land remains a highly controversial issue (see Werner 2000).

What is the nature of an academic literacy practice at a popular festival?

Was the day a school lecture, a government propaganda day, an information session for the population, a lesson on the merits of literacy or a popular festival? Mostly advocated as the last, to an outsider it appeared to be mainly a mixture of the first three elements.

As the main purpose of the day was to win support for the NLPN and to invite learners to join the programme, the primary goal of the speeches was not to inform but to attract, to persuade (Apthorpe 1997) and even to command. In order to achieve these aims, a range of literacy practices and linguistic devices were used. The speeches were a mixture of lecture and propaganda event. Toivo's speech, read from a pre-written manuscript, resembled at times a school lecture, at other times a fatherly advice to his children. Its language was relatively formal and bureaucratic, reflecting its origin in a written text. As in all of the day's speeches, the choice of words emphasised the distance between the Minister, as the representative of the government, and his audience. The Minister's words signalled authority and symbolised governmental power and technical expertise. Potential learners were 'instructed' about the problems of illiteracy, both for the nation as a whole and for each of them individually. The attending public was assigned the place of recipients of knowledge and the frequent use of the second person positioned the addressees at a distance from the speakers.

During the speeches, the distance between speaker and listener was accentuated by the height of the podium from which the Ministers addressed the seated audience. Distance was further increased by the fact that all speeches were given in English, the official language, which is not spoken by all Namibians. The need for translation had only been realised minutes before the beginning of the day. Consecutive translation into Oshivambo and Afrikaans was then arranged.

Reconciliation, nation building and the new Namibian citizen

Namibia is a highly divided country. Recent events in the Caprivi, the north-eastern region, are an indicator of the mixed feelings of some regions and ethnic groups towards the nation and the central government in Windhoek. Existing tensions are linked to ethnic, racial and socio-economic differences. They are related to a variety of factors, among others the perceived unequal support of the government for the country's different regions and populations.[9]

In this political climate, the NLPN stands for the government's commitment to a policy of redress and development for all Namibians. The programme attempts to disseminate and promote national unity and a better understanding between the different population groups (DABE 1996). Closely related to this aim, other goals figure prominently in the NLPN's policy discourse, i.e., to foster democracy, participation and citizenship. The mayor of Lüderitz, in her contribution to NLD, referred to the potential of literacy to help learners 'better exercise their rights and responsibilities as Namibian citizens' (Fieldnotes 4/9/99).

Partnership, joint commitment, unity and reconciliation were highlighted in several speeches of the day. The NLPN's expected contribution to nation building was particularly addressed in Toivo's speech:

> As we work together to help all our people learn to read and write, whether in our local languages or in English, I am sure that we are going to develop a better sense of what it means to be a reconciled, united nation, and what we can accomplish when we set out with a will to deal with the inherited inequalities and backlogs which are an obstacle to our development.
>
> (Sam Nujoma, quoted in Toivo ya Toivo, 4/9/99: 6/7)

The above quote exemplifies how in the speeches the issue of reconciliation was merged with the development goals of the NLPN. In fact, reconciliation is expected to come along with development. In this discourse, education is presented as a common purpose of all Namibians. Literacy is perceived as apolitical, as a neutral means to attain the supposedly shared goals of reconciliation and nation building. Kell (1994) draws similar conclusions regarding the meaning of literacy within the new discourses of human resource development in South Africa. In these discourses, she argues, literacy is not being problematised; it is 'precon-structed' as 'a common and social need' (Kell 1994: 7).

The government's commitment to 'education for all' was emphasised several times during the day. But the speakers also made it clear that the citizens have a responsibility to make use of the opportunities provided by the state and to contribute to the nation's development. The following quotes reveal the type of partly inviting, partly prescriptive language the Minister used: 'The constitution of Namibia guarantees your right to basic education and the Government is expecting you to make use of this opportunity.' 'You are entitled to basic education and literacy. Do not let this good chance slip away' (Toivo ya Toivo, 4/9/99: 12).

As the above quotes show, in Toivo's speech a discourse of democracy and state obligation is linked to a discourse of duties and obligations. He invites his audience to conform to and identify with the image of the new Namibian citizen outlined in his speech. Literacy has an important symbolic quality in this discourse; it is associated with the 'modern' citizen who identifies with the new nation and the shared goals of development and reconciliation.

The discourses of development and reconciliation prominently referred to during National Literacy Day originate in a narrow vision of development. In her study of the NLPN, Tegborg (1996) argues that the NLPN's view of development is limited to investment in human capital and 'political socialisation' rather than promoting 'liberation' and 'transformation'. National Literacy Day certainly reveals the NLPN's function as an instrument of 'political socialisation' into the values of the old and new elite, i.e., acceptance of the current distribution of resources between different population groups, commitment to reform rather than revolution, the priority of economic growth over redistribution, an acceptance of individual responsibility and duty towards community and nation, and an agreement with capitalism.

The NLPN is part of the government's reformist orientation to change (Tegborg 1996). Education has a crucial function within this strategy, as it is highly valued by the population and provides the opportunity to disseminate and promote new social identities. In this discourse, literacy no longer figures as part of a revolutionary ideology, as it did in the earlier phase of adult education in Namibia. The narratives of liberation and socialist transformation, inside which much of Namibia's literacy provision before independence had found its ideological ground, have been replaced by new rather apolitical development discourses. These discourses are manifested in the government's commitment to providing access to education for all Namibians. In this discourse, education, including mother tongue literacy, is seen as a right (see also Aikman, this volume). Empowerment is understood to be achieved by enhancing the individual's capacity to operate more successfully in the current system.

Posters and banners: 'Educate the woman, educate the nation'

Throughout the festivities, posters and banners carrying important messages about the goals of the literacy programme were held up (some of these are pictured on the cover of this book). These slogans displayed similar assumptions regarding the need for and the benefits of literacy as those expressed by the speakers. 'Eradicate poverty through skills' resonates with the government's trust in education as a means for economic development. 'Educate the woman, educate the nation' alludes to the assumed impact of women's education for the community and the nation, while at the same time appealing to women's roles and responsibilities towards society.

The striking element of these slogans for me is the 'persuasive power' of this kind of promotional language. Perhaps even more strongly than the speeches, slogans such as the ones above make huge promises regarding the benefits of literacy for the individual and for the nation. The above statements not only appear to be totally deduced from the actual social situation, they also seem deliberately plain (Apthorpe 1997). The addressed correlation is presented as a 'simple truth', which does not need explanation or proof. Apthorpe (1997: 44) argues that such a language can achieve 'symbolic force', its goals being to persuade and to win support.

Images of literate and illiterate people: deficit discourses

A deficit discourse (see also Robinson-Pant, this volume) underlies many of the views put forward during National Literacy Day. Despite some remarks, which were meant to convey a positive image of illiterate people, negative stereotyping was hidden behind many of the assumptions made regarding the positive impact of literacy. Referring to the forthcoming elections, one of the posters said: 'Elections – Literacy will help you to make the best choice.' This seemingly simple statement disguises two assumptions: first, that literate people are more likely and better able to vote than people who cannot read and write; second, that those who cannot read and write will find it difficult to choose the best candidate. Prinsloo and Robins (1996) noted similar misreading regarding illiteracy as a problem for the first democratic elections in South Africa.

Another striking example came from the mayor's speech. She addressed the problem of HIV/AIDS in Namibia. Referring to HIV/AIDS and tuberculosis, the mayor made the following remark: 'Only if they [the people] are able to read and write can they be aware of the danger of these diseases and precautions' (Fieldnotes 4/9/99). Again, the statements testify the huge assumptions made regarding the power of literacy to bring about behavioural changes in people. Second, they assume that people labelled as 'illiterate', and thereby expected to be 'in deficit', cannot identify diseases such as HIV/AIDS and tuberculosis.

Deficit discourses are often related to a discourse of societal modernisation. In this view, literacy is regarded as a motor for the emergence of the 'modern man' and 'the development of attitudes and dispositions of flexibility, adaptability, empathy, willingness to accept change, proneness to adopt innovations' (Lanksheer 1987: 47). By contrast, illiteracy is believed to be related to ignorance and backwardness. People are categorised as either literate or illiterate, depending on how the political and educational establishment in each society sets the criteria for the minimum requirement of 'basic skills'. Foucault (1997) calls such a process 'normalisation' achieved through 'dividing practices'.

Literacy policy in Namibia starts from the assumption that Namibians lack basic reading and writing skills. Little attention is paid to existing literacy and language skills, non-dominant literacy practices and prior knowledge. According to the official guidelines, four years of schooling are regarded as the threshold for literacy (DABE 1996). But many people in Namibia, in particular those who grew up under the South African regime, left school after one or two years. However, as a recent study has shown, among those who are officially categorised as illiterate, many have acquired reading and writing skills through other means, e.g., in church or at their workplace (Melaku-Tjirongo and Devereux 1993). The non-recognition of skills acquired outside the formal system has important consequences for placement of learners in the three stages of the NLPN, an issue which, as I discovered, is much debated by learners and teachers.

Cultural performances and the handing over of the certificates

In many ways, how the festivities were organised reflected the relatively hierarchical nature of the NLPN itself. As I tried to show above, this was partly achieved through the language and communication practices of the day. The event was dominated by the officials from the government and the NLPN. This changed only during the cultural performances, when learners and promoters took on a more active role.

The so-called cultural performances consisted of songs and short plays by groups of learners, a dance performance by a group of local school children and a popular theatre group. The popular theatre is a relatively new component of the NLPN. Its main purpose is to help the regions campaign for the literacy programme.

The short plays depict the hardships of being illiterate. One of the stories performed during NLD was about a young man who was cheated over his salary. Because he could not count, he found out too late and his complaint to the management of his factory was rejected. In the second play, two young men applied to the Ministry of Home Affairs for a passport. Because they could not read, write or speak English, the officer in charge had to fill out the forms for them. An interpreter was needed, because the officer did not speak the two boys' language. The climax of the story, and certainly the most comical moment, was when the two had to be photographed. Illiterate as they were, they had never seen a camera and where terribly afraid when they were asked to stand still and smile for the picture.

Both stories are examples of the 'classic' narratives of the problems of illiteracy. These assumptions are part of the 'literacy myth' (Gee 1990) that ascribes cognitive and social developments to literacy while at the same time relating illiteracy to underdevelopment and 'traditional' non-Western cultures who do not know cameras and cannot count money.

The cultural performances shifted the focus of the celebrations away from the big policy discourses towards the learners and their immediate problems. There was much less distance between the players and the audience. Although even the plays were performed in English, the language no longer signalled distance and authority, but emphasised commonality. The bureaucratic and abstract terminology of the speeches had been replaced by a popular discourse, using colloquial language and the kind of English many Namibians are familiar with. Nevertheless the plays served to illustrate similar points to the speeches. In the stories, illiterate men were stereotyped as backward and ignorant, albeit this time in a comical way, which made the audience laugh and identify with the victims. Their antagonists were the women who because they were learning in the NLPN could no longer be cheated. In the plays, they took on the speakers' roles and invited their husbands and colleagues to join the programme.

The last item on the day's agenda was the handing over of the certificates to a group of learners. This was done by the Minister of Labour, Toivo ya Toivo, together with the Director of the NLPN.

The certificate is an important document, both for the learners and for the NLPN. It is an institutional literacy practice, which conveys official recognition of a personal achievement. It certifies that the learners have passed the exam and therefore successfully accomplished a stage of the NLPN. It allows them to continue their learning in the next higher stage. For the Ministry, its role is to certify and symbolise the success of government policy.

The gesture of handing over a certificate confirms the authority of the document. Toivo ya Toivo, as a cabinet member, represents government authority and, in this context, the central examination authority that decides over who passes and who fails. The importance of the certificates was often referred to in my discussions with staff, teachers and learners of the NLPN. For the learners it is a sign of their accomplishment and conveys status and a sense of self-fulfilment. The importance attributed to the formal certificate is not unusual in a context where many people have not been to school. For many, school education is a desired goal and formal certificates have a great symbolic significance (see also HAI 1998).

Conclusions: what does all this have to do with what is going on in the classrooms? Literacy practices and learner–teacher–textbook interaction in the classrooms of the NLPN

The main purpose of my description of National Literacy Day was to examine the meanings and goals attached to literacy in the context of the government's development policy. In my conclusions, I will try to point out the possible implications these meanings may have for the models of teaching and learning promoted in the NLPN. I will briefly introduce some of the issues, which emerge from my classroom observations and analysis of learning materials.[10]

A look at the curriculum and the materials used in the NLPN reveals the influence of the dominant development paradigm and the national education goals for the choice of the content. The NLPN privileges 'practical', 'life skills' and development issues; it has textbooks on primary health care, agriculture and small-scale business. The primers for Stages 1 and 2 and the English textbook for Stage 3 include lessons on health and nutrition, housing, community development and employment. Democracy and citizenship are addressed in several of the textbooks, although, as I mentioned earlier, in a rather limited perspective compared with economic themes.

Overall, the programme is strongly oriented on a school model of education. The curriculum of the post-literacy stages for example relies heavily on the formal primary school curriculum. As Street (this volume) argues, the focus on formal schooled literacy practices is based on the autonomous model. Since the government presupposes that a certain level of basic education is a necessary requirement for the development of a skilled labour force, the curriculum emphasises skills and formal knowledge and equivalency with formal qualifications. But I believe that this decision is also the result of other factors, e.g., the positive image of school education among many adult Namibians and the government's focus on equality and redress. The NLPN promotes school-based literacy practices although in many domains of adult life these may not necessarily be powerful or even functional literacy practices (see for example Aikman's example of legal literacies, this volume). However, for political and historical reasons, in the present context affective congruence supports formal education. Literacy is strongly associated with being 'educated' and knowledgeable (Stites, this volume). In this sense, it also denotes the ability to read, write and access information in English, the official language of the country. As Aikman (this volume) notes, 'knowing' the official language is associated with being developed and modern. In the Namibian context, this statement also has a racial connotation.

My classroom observations confirm the strong presence of school-based practices in the NLPN. Teaching materials play a central role in the NLPN classrooms. Teaching and learning is heavily 'textbook-based' (see Brown et al. 1999) and teacher-focused. Typically, a lesson is developed around a chapter in the textbook and it is very rare that teachers deal with any topics not related to the lesson.

The learning materials contain mainly descriptive and factual information (Tegborg 1996). Figure 2.1 shows an excerpt from the Primary Health Care book, which is used for Stage 3 of the NLPN. The chapters concentrate on imparting information and giving instructions.[11] The example is taken from a lesson in which a health worker, the expert, tells a village chief, the listener, about water-borne diseases. A similar kind of relationship between expert and lay person is perpetuated in the classrooms. Teachers rarely invite learners to share their own knowledge. Working from the textbook, they initiate questions and assign tasks. In general, classroom discussions tend to remain closely focused on the content of the textbook. Teachers hold a position of authority, although it stream. Animals are in the water too. He sees that there is only one latrine. This is used by chief Kapana. The rest of the village pass their stools and urine in the bush.]

Health worker: The stream, and pond are dirty, that is why your people are sick because of the dirt. Dirty water causes stomach ache, diarrhoea and vomiting. It spreads many diseases, such as worms, diarrhoea, cholera, typhoid. Do you boil the water before drinking it?

Chief Kapana: No, we put it in containers to keep it cool.

Health worker: Drinking dirty water makes you sick. You must boil the water and then leave it to cool off. This will make it clean. Even bathing in dirty water can make you ill.

Chief Kapana: Why is the water dirty?

Health worker: Some of your people are passing stools in the bush. The rains wash the stools and leaves and soil into streams. People bath and wash clothes in the stream. Children play in the stream. You let animals drink in the stream. Your people make the stream dirty.

Figure 2.1 National Literacy Programme in Namibia, Primary Health Care, Learner's Work Book, p. 22

seems that the 'real' authority is grounded in the textbook with its anonymous experts, the teacher's role being to pass on knowledge from textbook to learner.

The primers and textbooks contain discussion exercises and group work, but in the classroom situation these are often being left out, or turned into a conventional teacher-guided question–answer session. Figures 2.2 and 2.3 show examples of exercises commonly used in the NLPN materials, e.g., multiple choice questions, sentence completion, gap filling or matching drawings with sentences or individual words.[12] These types of literacy practices focus on transfer of knowledge, correct repetition and full retention rather than discussion or critical engagement with the content of the lesson.[13]

The influence of the school model and the related deficit discourse may also be a cause of what has been criticised as the 'meagre content' (Bhola, in Lind

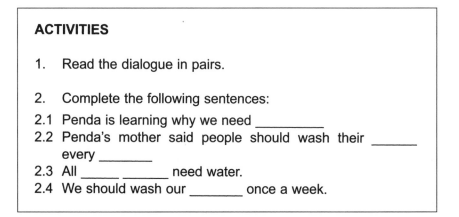

EXERCISE 7:   What should we do to help these children be happy like Petrus?
Read the list and tick with an **X** if you think Yes or No.

		YES	NO
1.	Give them food three times a day.	☐	☐
2.	Beat them and shout at them all the time.	☐	☐
3.	Let them rest especially after school.	☐	☐
4.	Let them do all the house work.	☐	☐
5.	Give them something to take to school.	☐	☐
6.	Give them time to study and do homework.	☐	☐
7.	Keep them at home and play by themselves.	☐	☐
8.	Let them play with friends.	☐	☐
9.	Shout at them while eating.	☐	☐
10.	Praise them when they have done good.	☐	☐

Figure 2.2 National Literacy Programme in Namibia, Basic English, Learner's Work Book, 1st edition, 1992, p. 39

ACTIVITIES

1. Read the dialogue in pairs.

2. Complete the following sentences:

2.1 Penda is learning why we need _____

2.2 Penda's mother said people should wash their _____ every _____

2.3 All _____ _____ need water.

2.4 We should wash our _____ once a week.

Figure 2.3 National Literacy Programme in Namibia, Primary Health Care, Learner's Work Book, p. 19

1996: 44) of the materials. My own assessment is that the materials undervalue the experience and the level of knowledge learners bring with them to the classes, a tendency which has been observed by other practitioners and researchers. The assumed ignorance of people who have no or little formal education results in unchallenging learning materials unappealing to the adult learner (see DSE/ZED 1995, Rogers et al. 1999). In one of my discussions with a group of learners in Windhoek, I asked them about the Primary Health Care book, which they had been studying over the previous weeks. They told me that the book did not contain any new information for them. However, they said, they 'had not known these things in English' (Fieldnotes 6/7/99), so they wanted to learn the English words and expressions (see also Robinson-Pant 1997).

I would like to end by signalling that the current school orientation of the programme is not unchallenged within the NLPN. Many people inside the programme have expressed their scepticism regarding the viability of the school-based approach. They argue that the adult learners who join the programme arrive with concrete practical needs and want to gain skills which are immediately applicable. These critical voices question the assumption of the 'autonomous' model regarding the transferability and applicability of skills presumed to be universal and technical in nature. Their claim is supported by the learners who drop out or never enrol because they feel alienated by the formal nature of the programme and wonder how on earth all this textbook knowledge will help them in their daily struggle for a decent life.

In my conversations with learners, the school model was commented on both positively and critically. But many participants spoke about concrete and practical literacy-related needs. When I asked learners about the differences they had experienced since they enrolled, they mentioned things such as to be able to read the 'closed' sign in a shop, to sign a paper, or to understand the English-speaking doctor in the clinic. Such achievements reflect the diverse life situations of adult Namibians and their varying learning goals (Rogers 1996). Furthermore, what learners had to say confirmed that their learning demands are grounded in literacy practices they already engage in and want assistance with (Rogers et al. 1999).

Many of these demands are related to individual learners' desires to explore new economic opportunities and to participate more fully in new social practices that arise with the changing life styles of post-Independent Namibia. As Aikman's example (this volume) shows, venturing into new economic and social practices entails the necessity to participate in new literacy and discourse practices. With regard to the NLPN, the important question further ethnographic research needs to address is whether the type of literacy privileged in the programme helps learners to acquire the language and communication practices they need in order to participate fully in the new Namibian society and economy.[14]

A related issue is the question of individual and local conceptions of development that may differ from the government's views on literacy and development (see also Aikman, this volume). Changes reported by learners (see the examples above) may look small compared to the big promises the Ministers made during National Literacy Day. But these changes appear to be real achievements, which have their own potential to bring about transformation. Participants' stories, although remaining silent about any grand changes, testify to the many successes of the NLPN. Literacy may not be the only key to a better future, but it certainly is an essential ingredient of what Namibians aspire to for their future.

Acknowledgement

I would like to thank the Director of the Namibian Directorate of Adult Basic Education for permission to reprint three pages of teaching material from the National Literacy Programme.

Notes

1 During my fieldwork in Namibia from May to November 1999, I was based in the head office of the NLPN, the Directorate for Adult Basic Education (DABE), in Windhoek. My research was supported by a King's College London Association (KCLA) research studentship.
2 The idea of a national literacy day to celebrate and promote literacy was originally born by UNESCO when it declared 8 September as 'International Literacy Day' to be celebrated by all its member states.
3 I travelled to Lüderitz with the group from the NLPN head office.
4 In the official terminology of the NLPN, teachers are called promoters. District Literacy Officers (DLOs) have a supervisory role and are responsible for the implementation of the programme in a district. The 'classes' (often called as such by the learners themselves) are called literacy groups.
5 It is a popular practice in the classes to teach learners songs. Promoters learn these songs as part of their own training. Some of the songs are written in local languages, others – like the one above – in English.
6 The quotes are extracts from the manuscript from which the Minister read his speech.
7 *Know Your Land and People*, the social studies textbook developed for the AUPE course, for example, discusses democracy in terms of people's rights and duties as citizens. Its second module includes a longer section on how democracy developed historically and how the current system in Namibia works. Also included is a short section on 'How democracy works', which contains a paragraph on how citizens can express their opinion, for example through the media. *Know Your Government*, a reader for Stage 2, deals with similar topics. The English primer for Stage 3 has a lesson about a water self-help project set up in a community. These materials provide a lot of information about the principles of the government and the democratic system. However, there are no examples that take up concrete problems learners may face when dealing with the government at local or central level (e.g., communication with local ministerial offices).
8 These issues were strong themes in my discussions with learners, promoters and staff of the Ministry of Basic Education and Culture in Windhoek, Rundu and Otjiwarongo. They were repeatedly addressed by learners during interviews and group discussions. Furthermore, my understanding of the current economic and political situation in Namibia is based on my readings of the relevant literature and of national and international newspapers, and on my many informal discussions with Namibians. The

collection of papers published in Melber (2000) provides an overview of the achievements made since Independence and the difficulties experienced in the government's attempts to address the inherited inequalities and the persistent regional disparities.

9 Separatist tendencies in the Caprivi, a long-standing political factor, escalated in August, when a group of rebels from the 'Caprivi Liberation Army' attacked the military base and several buildings in the region's capital Katima Mulilo. In the aftermath of the event, the government's strong reaction to the attack provoked a nation-wide public debate about the state of the Namibian democracy, the government's development policy and its attitude towards human rights.

10 This section is based on my classroom observations in Windhoek and Rundu. A much more detailed analysis of classroom interactions, literacy practices and textbooks, will follow in my forthcoming dissertation.

11 A similar point is made by Robinson-Pant (this volume).

12 The chosen examples do not cover the full range of exercises contained in the teaching materials of the NLPN. However, they indicate types of exercises and tasks which can be found in all learning materials and which I have seen being used regularly and extensively in all the classes I have visited.

13 Writing this chapter, I am aware of the possibly negative judgements I may make about teaching practice in the NLPN. Reading Martha Wright's chapter (this volume) once again made me aware of the necessity to analyse critically my own perceptions and interpretations of classroom practice and textbooks.

14 In my current research, I examine tourism as a domain of social and economic activity that has its own literacy and communicative practices. Tourism is a growing sector of the Namibian economy. Learners of the NLPN mentioned the spread of tourism as a reason why they want to learn English. They also discussed it in relation to employment and income.

References

Apthorpe, R. (1997) 'Writing Development Policy and Policy Analysis Plain or Clear: On Language, Genre and Power', in C. Shore and S. Wright (eds), *The Anthropology of Policy: Critical Perspectives on Governance and Power*, London and New York: Routledge.

Barton, D. and Hamilton, M. (1998) *Local Literacies: Reading and Writing in One Community*, London: Routledge.

Belanger, P. (1994) 'Literacy and Literacies: Continuity and Discontinuity', *Language and Education* 8(1&2): 87–100.

Brown, S., Katjavivi, J. and Walters, S. (1999) *External Review and Advisory Mission*, Draft Report, Windhoek: Ministry of Basic Education and Culture (MBEC).

DABE (1992) *NLPN Progress Report June 1992*, Report to the National Literacy Committee, Windhoek: MBEC.

—— (1993) *Guide to the National Literacy Programme in Namibia*, Windhoek: MBEC.

—— (1996) *Policy Guidelines for the Second Phase 1996–2000 of the National Literacy Programme in Namibia*, Windhoek: MBEC with the assistance of UNICEF.

DSE/ZED (1995) *Annual Report*, Deutsche Stiftung für Internationale Entwicklung (German Foundation for International Development, Education, Science and Documentation Centre), Bonn: DSE/ZED.

Escobar, A. (1995) *Encountering Development: The Making and Unmaking of the Third World*, Princeton, NJ: Princeton University Press.

Foucault, M. (1980) *Power/Knowledge: Selected Interviews and Other Writings 1972–1977*, Hassocks, Sussex: Harvester Press.

—— (1988) 'On Power', in L.D. Kritzman (ed.), *Michel Foucault: Politics, Philosophy and Culture. Interviews and Other Writings 1977–1984*, London and New York: Routledge.

—— (1997) *The Archeology of Knowledge*, trans. A.M. Smith, 6th edition, London and New York: Routledge.

Freire, P. (1972) *Pedagogy of the Oppressed*, London: Sheed & Ward.

Gardner, K. and Lewis, D. (1996) *Anthropology, Development and the Post-Modern Challenge*, London and Chicago: Pluto Press.

Gee, J.P. (1990) *Social Linguistics and Literacies: Ideologies in Discourse*, London: Falmer Press.

—— (1999) *An Introduction to Discourse Analysis*, London and New York: Routledge.

Geertz, C. (1972) *The Interpretation of Cultures*, New York: Basic Books, HarperCollins.

Goody, J. and Watt, I. (1968) 'The Consequences of Literacy', in J. Goody (ed.), *Literacy in Traditional Societies*, Cambridge: Cambridge University Press.

HAI-HelpAge International (1998) 'Annual Progress Report on Older People's Literacy in Clermont, South Africa'. HAI Ref. RSA 37 141, London: HAI (internal document).

Hamilton, M. (2000) 'Expanding the New Literacy Studies: Using Photographs to Explore Literacy as Social Practice', in D. Barton, M. Hamilton and R. Ivanič (eds), *Situated Literacies: Reading and Writing in Context*, London: Routledge.

Hansohm, D. (2000) 'Macro-Economic Framework', in H. Melber (ed.), *Namibia: A Decade of Independence, 1990–2000*, Windhoek: NEPRU.

Heath, S.B. (1983) *Ways with Words: Language, Life and Work in Communities and Classrooms*, Cambridge: Cambridge University Press.

Kell, C. (1994) 'An Analysis of Literacy Practices in an Informal Settlement in the Cape Peninsula', unpublished Masters thesis, University of Cape Town.

—— (1996) 'Literacy Practices in an Informal Settlement in the Cape Pensinsula', in M. Prinsloo and M. Breier (eds), *The Social Uses of Literacy: Theory and Practice in Contemporary South Africa*, Amsterdam and Johannesburg: John Benjamins and SACHED Books.

Kulick, D. and Stroud, C. (1993) 'Conceptions and Uses of Literacy in a Papua New Guinean Village', in B. Street (ed.), *Cross-Cultural Approaches to Literacy*, Cambridge: Cambridge University Press.

Lanksheer, C. (1987) *Literacy, Schooling and Revolution*, London: Falmer Press.

Lind, A. (1996) *Free to Speak Up: Overall Evaluation of the National Literacy Programme in Namibia*, Windhoek: DABE/MBEC, Gamsberg/Macmillan Publishers.

Luke, A. (1997) 'Critical Approaches to Literacy', in V. Edwards and D. Corson (eds), *Encyclopedia of Language and Education*, Vol. II, *Literacy*, Dordrecht: Kluwer.

Maybin, J. (2000) 'The New Literacy Studies: Context, Intertextuality and Discourse', in D. Barton, M. Hamilton and R. Ivanič (eds), *Situated Literacies: Reading and Writing in Context*, London: Routledge.

Melaku-Tjirongo, E. and Devereux, S. (1993) *Adult Literacy in Uukwaludhi, Northern Namibia*, Windhoek: University of Namibia, SSD.

Melber, H. (ed.) (2000) *Namibia: A Decade of Independence, 1990–2000*, Windhoek: NEPRU (The Namibian Economic Policy Research Unit).

Oxenham, J. (1980) *Literacy: Writing, Reading and Social Organisation*, London: Routledge & Kegan Paul.

Prinsloo, M. and Robins, S. (1996) 'Literacy, Voter Education and Constructions of Citizenship in the Western Cape during the First Democratic National Elections in South Africa', in M. Prinsloo and M. Breier (eds), *The Social Uses of Literacy: Theory and Practice in Contemporary South Africa*, Amsterdam and Johannesburg: John Benjamins and SACHED Books.

Rassool, N. (1999) *Literacy for Sustainable Development in the Age of Information*, Clevedon, Philadelphia: Multilingual Matters.

Robinson-Pant, A. (1997) 'The Link between Women's Literacy and Development', unpublished PhD thesis, University of Sussex.

Rockhill, K. (1993) 'Gender, Language and the Politics of Literacy', in B. Street (ed.), *Cross-Cultural Approaches to Literacy*, Cambridge: Cambridge University Press.

Rogers, A. (1996) *Teaching Adults*, 2nd edition, Buckingham and Philadelphia: Open University Press.

Rogers, A., Maddox, B., Millican, J., Newell Jones, K., Papen, U. and Robinson-Pant, A. (1999) *Re-defining Post-literacy in a Changing World*, Education Research, Serial no. 29: London, Department for International Development,.

Shore, C. and Wright, S. (eds) (1997) *The Anthropology of Policy: Critical Perspectives on Governance and Power*, London and New York: Routledge.

Street, B. (1995) *Social Literacies: Critical Approaches to Literacy in Development, Ethnography and Education*, London: Longman.

—— (forthcoming) 'Literacy "Events" and Literacy "Practices": Theory and Practice in the "New Literacy Studies"', in K. Jones and M. Martin-Jones (eds), *Multilingual Literacies: Comparative Perspectives on Research and Practice*, Amsterdam: John Benjamins.

Tegborg, M. (1996) *Adult Literacy and Empowerment: A Study of a National Literacy Programme in the Caprivi Region*, Institute of International Education, University of Stockholm.

Verhoeven, L. (1994) 'Modelling and Promoting Functional Literacy', in L. Verhoeven (ed.), *Functional Literacy: Theoretical Issues and Educational Implications*, Amsterdam: John Benjamins.

Werner, W. (2000) 'Agriculture and Land', in H. Melber (ed.), *Namibia: A Decade of Independence, 1990–2000*, Windhoek: NEPRU.

3

MORE THAN JUST CHANTING

Multilingual literacies, ideology, and teaching methodologies in rural Eritrea

Martha Wagar Wright

Researchers going into the developing world may, in good faith and with all heartfelt compassion for the desperate plight of the people there, fall rather short of the mark in interpreting what is happening between the very teachers and students they are trying to help.[1] It is understandable that the sight of such dreary classrooms, often dark and cold, even in North Africa, lacking all the niceties of modern Western elementary schoolrooms – or even the *necessities*, to Western eyes – could be overwhelming: the small, thin children dressed in little more than rags, crowds of them packed on to broken desks, with only broken pencils, a blackboard they can barely see, no textbooks and only a few thin copybooks donated by some aid organisation. The din of these sixty children shouting their replies to the teacher's questions, seemingly at the top of their lungs, only to be told to say it louder, can be stupefying to the researcher trained to look for communicative methods, who sees no literacy being practised and only 'chanting' taking place in these classrooms. Perhaps those of us going into the field need to consider if we have failed to recognise what the people we are studying already do have; perhaps we need to see if we have allowed ourselves to be blinded to the gifts and abilities of the people themselves because we have, perhaps unwittingly, assumed them to suffer an intellectual impoverishment commensurate with the material. Some have already begun to do so, as the 'number of literacy projects in recent years have challenged [Western] assumptions by stressing that before launching into literacy programs and interventions it is necessary to understand the literacy practices that target groups and communities are already engaged in' (BVS, p. 1).[2]

In working with the teachers of Grades 1 and 2 in one town in Eritrea, I endeavoured not to tell them what to do, no matter how often they asked, but to see how early literacy was accomplished in these classrooms, to discern what *they* did so I might be able in turn to tell them what they were already doing; some of my teacher contacts there seemed to assume I wanted to promote a 'particular intervention or "sell" a particular methodology for teaching or management' (BVS, p. 1), although I did not consciously set out to do so. In the process of trying to see what was 'going on' in early literacy instruction, I uncovered a good deal of institutional prejudice – of which I was a perpetrator myself – towards methods that did not appear to be in keeping with the 'modern' ideology. However, at the same time I gained a genuine appreciation for kinds of adaptation I had not theretofore even recognised. But it took many, many visits and conversations, being bored and confused, frustrated by what I did *not* see, for me to begin to question the gospel of 'student-centred', 'communicative' methodology.

More than just chanting

In the new nation of Eritrea there is a great deal more than chanting going on, even in the earliest grades. The town of Ghinda is a bustling hub of multilingual commerce midway between the capital and one of the busiest ports in Africa, and the teachers there draw on a pedagogical heritage including many hundreds of years of indigenous education, both Christian and Islamic, in addition to several recent generations of hideous colonial oppression exercised in part through the educational system. Close examination of classroom methods in second-language (L2) instruction in English, compared with those used for the national languages of Eritrea (Tigrinya, in particular, and Arabic), reveals some of the ingenuity of this new generation of teachers in coping with the variety of pedagogical demands placed on them in the face of ongoing material deprivation.

In much the same way that non-standard forms of a language are viewed by many as deficient, as failure to achieve (Labov 1972), interpretations of classroom methodology which differ from what is expected may then be taken as teachers' failure to comprehend and implement the curriculum. I would contend, however, that in fact, rather than *failing to understand*, the teachers may instead be *choosing to interpret* the L2 curriculum in their own ways, and that these choices are based on their own concerns about what is best for the students, what is possible given the constraints of their material circumstances, their beliefs about the students and their families, and in some cases awareness of their own capabilities and limitations as teachers. I would suggest that it is important for those investigating language policy and instruction, especially when outside familiar environments, to consider whether they need to incorporate the above perspective, to allow for a fuller understanding of the interaction under analysis; that they cannot begin to suggest improvements to an educational system which they have analysed only in terms of how it fails to resemble their own.

Much of the literature available on classroom interaction has been done in the US (Cazden, Mehan, Sinclair and Coulthard, and others) and looks at more advanced levels than the ones I observed, often more spontaneous and less controlled speech or more intricate interactions involving a larger number of individual interlocutors. Perhaps the relative paucity of studies on classroom discourse in the developing world is because it may have seemed almost pointless to examine student–teacher interactions around text, in classrooms where it appears there is almost no text and only one type of interaction taking place – 'mindless' repetition. A few researchers, however, such as Street and Wagner, have brought to scholarly attention the variety of literacy practices which can be found in the developing world, emphasising the value of indigenous practices as *resources*, rather than seeing them only as *problems* to be fixed, impediments to modernisation which need to be eradicated.

The 'rich and diverse' (Wagner 1993: 271) history of 'rote' literacy instruction in the developing world includes accounts of traditional educational systems which are in many ways similar to that of Eritrea. Common to all of these are the practices of choral repetition and extensive memorisation which were 'supposed to have been eliminated from so-called modern schools in most countries many decades ago' (Wagner 1993: 271). Like many Westerners, I found myself in the camp of those who would be very slow to attribute much if any value to these old-fashioned methods. However, serious inquiry into the current literature shows that in addition to the varieties of literacy outside schooling which Street discovered in Iran, Wagner's study in Morocco revealed unexpected degrees of effectiveness of indigenous methods: 'evidence suggests that recitation and memorisation facilitate reading acquisition in Arabic, particularly for children whose native language is not Arabic' (1983: 187). Eisemon likewise found in his study of children in Kenya whose earliest education had consisted mostly of memorising portions of the Quran that these children 'develop an *understanding of the meaning* of religious texts which they have learned in Arabic by recitation; second, that such children may acquire from a disciplined study of the Quran skills in *comprehending other kinds of written texts* in another language and, third, that *comprehension declines* when children are presented with texts and questions *in a language used only for school instruction and examination*' (1988: 95, italics mine).

Eritrea is about one-half Muslim, and Quranic schools not unlike those in Iran or Morocco have operated throughout much of the area, especially in the areas like Ghinda, below the Highland ridge, for many hundreds of years. In addition, 'Ethiopia [of which Eritrea was formerly a province] . . . maintained a highly structured, organised system of church education from at least the sixth century of the Christian era' (Wagaw 1979: viii). In both these types of schools, memorisation of sacred text in an archaic language otherwise unfamiliar to the students (Classical Arabic or *Ge'ez*, the 'Latin of Ethiopia'), has been the primary goal, and classroom activities have been oriented to that end, emphasising memorisation through individual and choral repetition as well as copying down text. Literacy of any kind was limited to a very small group of people, in the Coptic church to the class of prospective clerics; even among the nobility, only a very small number – and virtually no women at all, of any class – well into the nineteenth century had been schooled in reading or writing any language (Pankhurst 1992: 131).

The Eritrean People's Liberation Front describes its people's educational history in a 1984 document from a rather different angle:

Precolonial education in Eritrea was essentially religious and totally dominated by the Orthodox Christian Churches and the Islamic Mosques . . . divid[ing] the people on religious and tribal lines . . . even the rudiments of scientific outlook were lacking. This greatly hampered the people's ability to be equipped with even the elementary know-how that could be useful in an improvement of their living conditions . . . Furthermore, a fatalistic attitude . . . was a great obstacle to any organised struggle that they could have waged against the bonds of ignorance and oppression.

(EPLF, cited in Gottesman 1998: 68)

While the Ethiopian system employed memorisation as the primary mode of learning in the early grades, higher levels were available to successful students, where instruction focused more on analysis of text and application of doctrine.

Changes in this educational system have, over the centuries, involved interaction with other cultures to varying degrees. Although Protestant and Catholic missionaries at times established primary schools in Eritrea and Ethiopia, they have also been expelled regularly, beginning in the 1500s and continuing into the 1990s; as a result, the impact of missionary educators on the primary school system which currently obtains in Eritrea is difficult to trace with any certainty. Indeed, in the early part of this century it was claimed that the missions' schools did 'not a great deal . . . their contribution to the education of the masses is not as yet of much value' (Rey 1927: 208, cited in Wagaw 1979: 27); by another account, 'Christian missionaries were not as important in founding secular education in Ethiopia as in other African countries' (Jasperdean 1966: 62). Wagaw recounts that 'at the turn of this century a timid effort was made to initiate a secular system of education independent of church influence, an effort which required the importation of new ideas, philosophies, personnel, and methodology from abroad' (1979: viii–ix). This included Ethiopians going abroad themselves to experience firsthand foreigners' educational systems and teaching methods.

At about this same time, however, Eritrea had come under the official control of the Italian government, and educational policy reflected the oppressive, exploitative agenda of the colonial power: 'it was contrary to the policy of the Italian government to encourage industries in Eritrea . . . The standard of teaching had been low; its scope designedly narrow . . . To keep the Eritreans as ill-trained and ill-informed as possible, the Italians systematically developed and strengthened the color bar . . . they [the Eritreans] could at best hope to be low-paid clerks or orderlies . . . There were to be, in perpetuity, rulers and the passive ruled' (Wagaw 1979: 95). The memory of this repression is very much alive in modern Eritrea, for during the period of federation with and subsequent annexation by Ethiopia, the educational system was employed in a similar fashion: again the oppressors' language – in this instance, Amharic – was made the mandatory medium of instruction in the primary schools, and standards were kept artificially low so as to contain a potentially insurgent populace.

Many people, including many teachers, attribute present-day problems with students' and parents' lack of confidence in education to the repression which the Italians and then the Ethiopian Dergue regime exerted on Eritrea through the schools, what might be termed a sort of 'diseducation' – belligerent or clearly apathetic teachers, passing students to keep them in the system whether they failed or not, etc. As one of the older teachers in Ghinda explained to me, 'that is I think the problem for now this generation, and it killed their what-you-call their feeling of education . . . because if he knows he has to pass [anyway] if he fails in five subjects, why should I start?' (BS, 4/28/97). Throughout its history as a colony, 'The only schools that had aspired to teach the inherent equality of man or to provide normal standards of instruction were those run by the Swedish Evangelical Mission and a few similar organizations' (Wagaw 1979: 96), which reached only a minute portion of the population.

A remarkable burgeoning of educational development has taken place since independence in 1991, reflecting I think a widespread adherence to national (EPLF) policy regarding the fundamental necessity of literacy for personal and national liberation and continued political autonomy, as well as for internal harmony through interethnic understanding and tolerance, and for provision for cultural and linguistic expression for all nine indigenous groups. The work of the fighter teachers during the struggle for liberation played no small part in impressing this philosophy upon the masses. Postcolonial educational policy now prominently features support for mother-tongue education, although like the Harakmbut in Peru, 'not all [Eritreans] consider their indigenous language a resource' (SA, p. 6); there remains some controversy over what 'vision of development, their self-development' (SA, p. 6) is truly their own and not imported from the outside. As in Peru, 'each different literacy brings a different range of social practices, meanings, and power relations' (SA, p. 13), and in the past, 'in Eritrea, educational *policy* has been an instrument of colonial control and an instrument of liberation. Educational *experience*, however, has tended to be seen (with the exception of Asmara's youth educated under the Dergue 1980 to 1991), as liberating and possibility-opening' (Gottesman 1998: 67). With their intense fervour for 'the struggle' and the liberation they hoped for their country, the fighters can also be credited with laying the groundwork for new and innovative approaches to literacy instruction in several of the national languages of Eritrea, especially the mother tongue of the majority political party, Tigrinya, which is usually written, interestingly enough, in a form of the Ethiopic script adapted slightly from that of the Eritreans' former oppressors. As in Namibia, 'having promised to redress the inequalities of Apartheid, the government has put strong emphasis on providing education, health, and housing for all' (UP, p. 7), the citizens of a free Eritrea hope to redress the deprivations of at least three generations of oppression through similar provisions for their people.

Early literacy instruction in Ghinda

In the few years since liberation in 1991, the Eritrean government has opened dozens of primary schools throughout the country and developed an impressive array of materials to try to provide for the nine major ethnic groups. In Ghinda, two of the three public primary schools utilise Tigrinya as medium of instruction, introducing Arabic and English as subjects in Grade 2, while the other primary school, serving mostly former refugees recently returned from Sudan, has Arabic as medium of instruction, with Tigrinya introduced as a subject in Grade 2, along with English. These language choices were apparently those of the community, as that is government policy regarding selection of medium of instruction; while there are some Tigre-medium schools in the Lowlands, Tigre was not favoured as medium of instruction in Ghinda, probably because of the perceived material advantage of competence in the two national languages, Tigrinya and Arabic. It is estimated that the population of the Ghinda region is approximately 80 per cent Muslim, roughly equally divided between Saho and Tigre (a language distinct from Tigrinya) speakers, the remainder being mostly Coptic Christians and native speakers of Tigrinya. Nearly all the teachers are from the Highland region and ethnically Tigrinya, although a few are native speakers of Tigre or other national languages, and most – but not all – in the Arabic-medium school have themselves been educated in Arabic.

For first-year Tigrinya – Grade 1 or 2, depending on the school – the teachers had the beginning texts developed 'in the struggle' as the Eritreans would put it, written and used by Eritrean People's Liberation Front fighter-teachers throughout the country, mostly for adult and youth literacy classes beginning back in the 1980s. The manner and sequence of emergent literacy instruction, that is to say, the basics of the syllabary, had been reconfigured by the EPLF text writers, following on some other innovations developed over the course of the 1960s and 1970s by experienced educators. The new sequence in which the characters are taught is, in my opinion, quite well thought out and capitalises on the visual salience of characters, introducing them in gradually increasing complexity; in addition, the new method takes into account the relative frequency of certain characters which happen to fall towards the end of the traditional sequence, but which if included earlier in the year will facilitate students' reading and writing a much greater number of common words.

While the Ethiopic syllabary appears at first glance to be overwhelming in its array of symbols (roughly 240), in fact even a non-speaker can catch on to the mostly regular pattern of vowel diacritics or alterations and memorise all but a few characters in as short a span as a few weeks. However, because many if not most of these symbols require more strokes each than, for instance, most roman letters, careful and consistent orthography is essential if a person hopes to be able to write with even moderate speed. This first year of Tigrinya instruction therefore is devoted almost entirely to acquiring just the basics of this syllabary, along the way practising some two- and three-character words, and eventually two- and three-word sentences made from them. The Eritrean students I observed usually sounded out characters and words aloud as they followed the teacher writing them on the board, and often murmured them as they wrote; it was common to hear a rising swell of humming as more and more students recognised words appearing before them on the board. In the lower grades of course the children decoded slowly (I estimated one second per character or even longer), and often displayed that same burst of word-recognition young children in the English-speaking world do when the item they've just sounded out 'clicks'. In spelling out words to each other or to me, using their fingers, the students would say each syllable, slowly and distinctly, starting with an open hand and closing in one finger at a time, then repeat the whole word at full speed, much the way we might in English for 'kuh-ae-tuh – cat!' Even people we met who had had little or no schooling demonstrated this consciousness of syllabification and would break down words in the same way for us.

Teachers likewise read from the board, first one syllable at a time and then the whole word; in quizzes or classwork they sometimes helped students with a fill-in-the-blank exercise by tapping off the syllables at the board, drawing dots where the missing syllables should fit, and helping students count out and sound out the words. My impression of this continual breaking down and recombining words was that it served very well to make the phoneme–grapheme correspondence salient and memorable, particularly for those children – the majority of the school – who were not only acquiring a first or second literacy but were also learning Tigrinya as a second or third language. By the end of that first year, students were expected to have acquired the skills to write 'any word they want to, they can spell it' (HY, 4/23/97) because the phoneme–grapheme correspondence was so consistent and they had been taught to sound out by syllables. (Still, some teachers in the early grades did complain that the non-Tigrinya speakers had difficulty reading and writing beyond the word stage, once they had got more into sentences; they attributed this to the children's limited Tigrinya, but the only accommodation to these children I observed was the occasional translation of single lexemes.) Many second-language instruction programmes in the West include this very same kind of technique, sometimes called 'scaffolding'.

In response to my inquiries about where these and other techniques originated, most of my informants would say 'from my experience' rather than the Teacher Training Institute. Most of these teachers had been educated under the oppressive Ethiopian Dergue, and the language of public instruction was Amharic, so they had had little or no instruction in Tigrinya as young children, except the few who had attended mission schools. However, they explained that they were able to transfer their Amharic literacy easily to Tigrinya, both as learners and as teachers. Some of my informants had had a little primer *Arki Temeharay* ('friend of student') at home, but had been discouraged from practising Tigrinya songs or stories because of the very real risk of persecution by agents of the Dergue for what might be termed 'linguistic insurrection' – that is, cultivating any language other than the official one. Some teachers had enjoyed other kinds of home instruction: for example, one of my informants described the way his mother would practise his letters with him, drawing them in the air as he sat watching her cooking; he also recalled his delight when she would point out the letters on shop signs on their way to the market together (YT, 2/2/97).

Indigenous adaptations to circumstances

Since even in the best private schools in Asmara texts have never been plentiful – at best one book per two students, a generation ago – Eritrean teachers are accustomed to exploiting teaching methods which do not require that the children have a book of their own. These include lively blackboard demonstrations of letter formation – drawing with a flourish, erasing, redrawing, counting strokes aloud, all the while asking the class if what has been written is acceptable – 'tsebuq ala?' ('is it good/correct?') – letting the children critique the teacher's demonstration or that of another student. The configuration of the vowel alterations lend themselves well to physical demonstration also, so there is a good deal of quite humorous posturing on the part of the teachers and students, as they distinguish, for example, 'ka' from 'ko' by putting first one leg up and then the other. They mime other characters by leaning to one side, putting a hand up, pointing an arm to the left or right, drawing loops in the air, and so on. This kind of physical involvement in teaching and practising letters is a regular part of emergent literacy instruction in the US as well, of course, and could be considered rather like the Total Physical Response method. The teachers in Ghinda also clearly take into consideration which characters are most likely to be mistaken one for the other, inverted, or otherwise confused, and explicitly contrast them, when they are first introducing them and then during later practice and review: they may reinforce the instructional sequence and test the students' understanding by, for example, offering a jumble of cards or characters out of their usual order on the board, for students to resequence, set aright or otherwise correct, and thereby demonstrate that they recognise the distinctions in question. The children can point out which character has the 'hat' on it, for a palatalised consonant, or a 'crippled leg' to distinguish one consonant–vowel combination from another.

Because much of the basic Tigrinya lexicon is made of words containing a core of three consonants, it is relatively easy to build students' basic literacy skills, even long before they have learned the entire syllabary; over the course of the year high-frequency lexical items are introduced, regardless of the position of their core characters in the syllabary, so as to facilitate students' ability to read and write simple sentences. The teachers expand this three-character system to include sentences of two and then three words by mid-year. However, because of the absence of schoolbooks, the only texts the students have to study are the few sentences they have copied into their exercise books during classtime. The teachers admit that some students are 'careless' in their writing and so have very flawed texts to be learning from at all. Nevertheless the improvement in fluency from Grade 1 to 2 is considerable and unmistakable.

In the early stages of Tigrinya instruction, the teachers model reading at the board using a stick to point out each character; a sizeable amount of classtime is spent having the students walk up one by one to the board and repeat what the teacher has demonstrated. While this may at first appear inordinately repetitive, it provides teacher modelling of basic decoding techniques, as well as opportunities for feedback and correction which some students clearly need. There are always a few, usually younger students who do not appear to understand how to point and read at all – but rather flail the stick around haphazardly and 'read' without looking at the board; the teachers use this time to stop and correct them (and usually hush the rest of the class for laughing at their classmate) and to show them the way to decode, pointing at and saying one syllable at a time. This explicit instruction may be to try to ensure that students do not simply learn all the sentences off by ear and not know how to read from print; because of the large number of students, for each to have a chance to read at the board results in a large amount of repetition, but the teachers say they must do this because their students have no other opportunity outside to learn to read or write. Teachers reported that most of their students' parents were illiterate and/or completely unschooled, the children bore heavy workloads in the household, and had no print media in their home environments anyway, so they had to learn everything at school.

Implementing the new curriculum

The new English curriculum, covering Grades 2 to 11 (English is medium of instruction from Grade 6 on), had been put together just after liberation with remarkable efficiency by an experienced team working with the British Council. My impression of the textbooks and overall curricular design was that the team had taken great pains to make the content relevant and accessible to young children in Eritrea. They had adapted terms, personal names, types of houses, clothing, household items, and daily routines and activities in the texts to represent the everyday lives of most people in Eritrea, including both urban and rural settings as well as different ethnic groups.

At the English Panel office it was explained to me that the writers felt that the 'look and say' system, rather than a phonics-based approach, was better suited to the English as a Foreign Language (EFL) situation, based on their past experience in other developing countries, and so Grade 2 (first-year) English curriculum emphasises core vocabulary as sightwords, and spelling or phonics rules are not introduced until Grade 3. The Grade 2 student's textbook was designed to be a workbook for students to keep, much like the kinds of supplementary workbooks American parents buy their young children to use at home. However, after the first year these workbooks were not reprinted, and as of the time of my data collection in Ghinda were only to be found in bits and pieces, a page here or there, or ripped apart and used as exercise-book covers. The teachers in Ghinda each had a copy and shared the Teachers' Guide, passing it around as necessary. The Guides contain quite specific instructions about the way each lesson is to be presented, so as to save teachers a lot of work preparing lesson plans or devising ways of presenting the material. However, the absence of student texts in Ghinda (and throughout the country, I would imagine) drastically altered the situation for the students and teachers in ways that they may not have been prepared to handle; for example, the Teachers' Guide explicitly tells teachers not to have students copy from the blackboard, since that activity, as is known throughout the developing world, can consume much valuable classtime. But since the students did not have their workbooks, the teachers were left with the more difficult job of revising the lesson plan prescribed in the Teachers' Guide in some way that would be in keeping with their training.

Most of the English teachers I worked with had attended at least a year of training in the Teacher Training Institute in Asmara, and some had attended during the Ethiopian Dergue and then again after liberation. (One outstanding teacher was of Eritrean descent but had been educated and trained in Ethiopia.) Among my informants were several former fighters, and nearly all the teachers I observed had themselves been educated under the Dergue, through the medium of Amharic. During their year at TTI they were trained in how to teach all the primary subjects, and the English training included a considerable amount of theoretical material as well, on communicative methodology and other 'modern' perspectives on language instruction. An important feature of the training my informants had received at TTI was the emphasis on 'motivation' (mentioned to me frequently by teachers and administrators) and making the children 'active learners' (*Grade 2 Teachers' Guide*, p. 2).

Without exception the English teachers I observed and interviewed told me they believed that the new method was a great improvement over the way they had been taught English themselves. All had been taught the alphabet, 'ABCD' as they call it, in the first year, 'simply memorising the alphabet' (BS, 4/28/97), but none could recall phonics instruction; in some of our informal meetings, we discussed spelling and sound–symbol relationships, and it did not appear to me that any of these primary teachers had a conscious knowledge of core English spelling rules. My informants' recollection of the English instruction in their primary years was of a lot of memorising, from letters to words, eventually to whole sentences, recited in class, then copied from the board to be memorised. But 'the sightword system is good, because students learn how to spell now' (JO, 4/18/97). Teachers had never had textbooks of their own nor any English books in their homes; most had parents whose own education had been only up to 5th Grade, and in almost all cases their mothers were unschooled. While some had had years of experience teaching adults during the war for independence, most had their initial introduction to the profession of teaching in the Teacher Training Institute and expressed great confidence in the education system and the enthusiasm of the Eritrean people for education, now that Eritrea was a free country: 'but from the freedom, up to this place [point], the people are interested . . . is very hard work' (JO, 4/18/97).

Interpretations of 'groupwork'

One of the 'learner-centred' activities which caught my interest was 'groupwork' which I had seen mentioned in the Teachers' Guide and heard the teachers and administrators refer to as a distinctive feature of the curriculum, one of its modern innovations. I had observed several weeks of classes without recognising this 'groupwork' at all, because I had been looking for the small-group, face-to-face peer interaction commonly practised in language classes in the United States. What the Eritrean teachers called 'groupwork', however, was having segments of the class, perhaps one-sixth as recommended in the Guide, stand and repeat, or echo, or answer questions, in chorus; this activity was usually a duplicate of whatever the teacher had done with the entire class immediately prior to the groupwork. It seemed to me at first that this was a perfect example of how these poor souls could not understand what they were supposed to do and had failed to implement the curriculum; instead I had the opportunity for 'making visible the complexity of local, everyday, community literacy practices and challenging dominant stereotypes and myopia' (BVS, p. 1), those of my very own. And when I attempted to I discovered that this was in fact a good example of a decision on the teachers' part to do what they felt was best for their students.

It took no small amount of discussion with my informants, even arguing, for me to appreciate what value this 'mistake' might have in the situation: for one, nominating several groups to repeat the day's material served as a rather more interesting way to practise the new words and expressions than saying them over and over again as a large group; this offered the children some variety which my informants often mentioned as important to 'motivation'. I must admit that standing up row by row would not probably impress a Westerner like myself as being very motivating at all, since even young children in America are accustomed to much more elaborate and entertaining schemes than that on a regular basis (and still may not be motivated to learn). However, changing the pace of the class was a technique first-year teachers regularly employed, including prompting the class to burst into song as a group, or inviting a couple of talented children to lead the class in singing popular Tigre songs. From my informants' explanations I gathered this was expected to help students maintain their attention; in fact it did appear that they returned to the lesson material with renewed enthusiasm and less 'disturbing'.

Breaking up such large numbers of students into smaller units was also an efficient way for the teachers to be able to watch and listen more closely to each pupil, which they would not be able to do one by one because of the amount of time that would take (the oral exams consumed enough of that time). It also put students on the spot without their having to perform in front of the class alone, which might bring on a debilitating degree of anxiety and actually *impede*

71

learning (Bailey 1983). The proclivity of the students and teachers for choral repetition may have been not merely habitual, but evidence of the kind of 'safetalk' observed in other developing countries (Chick 1996). Some teachers felt the group recitations also fostered camaraderie which helped the children engage in class group competitions, which I was told they 'loved' (MT, 2/97).

The Eritrean teachers and administrators I worked with expressed the belief that a good teacher must *control* the class and that interactive groupwork, of the kind I described to them, would lead to children 'disturbing'. Some teachers' reluctance to invite 'disturbance' was, in my opinion, well founded, given the degree of mayhem which regularly broke out in their classes. (It appeared that certain teachers had consistently disruptive behaviour from students who behaved perfectly fine in adjacent classes with other teachers; I must assume there were factors beyond the scope of my knowledge which influenced these behaviours.) From observing their classes, I found that the teachers who *insisted* that peer interaction was absolutely impossible had certain practices in common: they controlled all *initiation* of interaction, and students only communicated or responded either directly with the teachers (i.e., answering a question), or upon their direct instruction (teachers told them to ask a question and answer it).

The teachers did, I think, try to make the very best of the time they had, usually forty minutes per lesson, six days a week. Based on prior information, when I came to Ghinda I probably had low expectations of time use in developing countries – for example, in highland Peru (Hornberger 1987: 220). In fact, in Eritrea the teachers I observed were extremely punctual, even for 6.30 a.m. classes, got right into the lesson without spending more than a minute or two setting up and getting their materials ready, and usually had the students work right up till the end of the class, when the 'bell' – a shell-casing or wheel-rim – would be struck. With only a few individual exceptions, the teachers of first-year Tigrinya, English and Arabic frequently varied the activities in their classes, from echoing to pointing to chanting to copying to singing, and so on, in blocks of only about two to five minutes per activity. Contrary to what I had expected, the children did not simply chant and chant by the hour.

By mid-year, when I conducted most of my observations, students were clearly accustomed to the most common types of activities and would follow the patterns with little if any prompting or explanation, or any overt 'framing' of the lesson activity, unlike more typical American lessons. The Tigrinya teachers marked openings and closings with '*Herrai!*' ('OK') or a hearty '*tseBUQ!*' ('good'); so also did the one outstanding first-year English teacher, but otherwise the English classes appeared not to be overtly framed for the students. I suspected, however, that because of the different variety of activities called for by the English curriculum, the students would actually have benefited from more overt explanation of what was expected of them, as at times they appeared confused or slow to join in, in contrast to the rapid, uniform response in their Tigrinya classes. I have heard Western educators complain that such 'conditioned' behaviour is evidence that the students have been brainwashed so to speak, able only to respond in fixed ways to a small range of stimuli; from my experience, I would argue that maintaining a certain level of predictability in classroom activities is preferable with younger learners. In dealing with such large classes, employing a small repertoire of activities may be an efficient way of keeping the level of order in the class requisite to the students' receiving L2 input and having opportunity to compose linguistic output in the target language themselves.

Communicative methods revealed

I found to my embarrassment that not only did I not recognise 'groupwork' when it was right before my eyes, I did not recognise 'active' student participation either. Only one teacher told me he had ever actually tried interactive groupwork but explained that because the children quickly got noisy and off-task he would only have any kind of peer interaction for a few minutes now and again. It took me quite some time to recognise that in fact this teacher had devised a kind of classroom interaction that resulted in student participation and even initiation of talk, which was actually much closer to the aims of groupwork than I had perceived. This teacher appeared to maintain unusually good attention and participation in his class (without beating any students, either); in many of his lessons he had a way of gradually leading the class into taking over his role – but as a group: he would nominate a student to be the 'questionee', who would come to the front of the room; the teacher would at first ask the questions of the student directly, then ask the class to repeat each of his questions, and then as the series progressed – for example, naming parts of the body from head to foot – the teacher would drop out and let the class ask the questions themselves. By the time the second or third individual student would come to the front, the class could initiate the questions without even prompting. The result was nearly complete student participation, some individual initiation and even student feedback if the 'questionee' made a mistake. By so doing the teacher in actuality ceded some control over the lesson but did not *appear* to and therefore did not *lose* control.

As a regular part of most lessons this teacher would, in a similar fashion, give his role as teacher over, by stages, usually to the class as a whole, or else would nominate individual students to the front to act as 'teacher' so that they might correct an answer, written on the board for example, or orally. In discussion afterwards, however, the teacher did not at first understand that he had done anything noteworthy and was not really able to answer my questions about how he had come up with these activities. His only explanation was that 'you must not give the chance to disturb'.

When I compared this to what teachers did in first-year Tigrinya, however, I saw a striking similarity, in the teacher's inviting the class to comment on their fellow student's writing or reciting, while still retaining ultimate authority over what was happening in the classroom. It seemed to me that neither the teachers nor the trainers recognised that Eritrean teachers *already* employed effective and I assume culturally acceptable methods for involving students in appraisal, feedback and correction, and other kinds of peer evaluation which Americans would expect to use in small groupwork; that because the behaviour does not *look exactly like* what we outsiders, including development experts, think ought to be there, we see nothing at all, and tell the teachers they have to do everything completely differently. I was reminded frequently by the teachers' request for my correction and instruction that they too discounted their own abilities in much the same way outsiders did and instead believed we had the solution to their problems and that they had to do things the way we told them.

First Literacy (Lit1) – Second Literacy (Lit2) Pedagogical transfer

Apparently, however, Eritrean teachers are not unique in the developing world in trying to exclude traditional methods from the 'modern' curriculum. There is no evidence that teachers in other developing countries such as Tunisia transfer methods of literacy instruction from a national language to the language of wider communication any more than my informants in Ghinda did with Tigrinya and English (M. Maamouri, pers. comm., 1999).

However, I felt strongly that in certain areas the English curriculum could have incorporated indigenous practices. One of my concerns about the 'sightword' system was the risk of excessive repetition of chunks of language too small to develop the kinds of retention and retrieval necessary for L2 and Lit2 acquisition. Keeping in mind that none of the national languages was the mother tongue of any majority of the students in Ghinda, then learning English was only somewhat more foreign. While the literature does support the value of memorising sentence- or verse-length stretches of discourse in the target language, there is no research to support the effectiveness of memorising decontextualised single lexemes, which occupied no small part of the sightword instruction. I suspect that the reason may be that the children are repeating such small pieces – words, syllables – that it does not encourage real cognitive engagement and, in the long run, they do indeed just 'forget everything' as the teachers complained. Decontextualised, even semi-comprehensible stretches of discourse at the sentence level may engage the cognitive faculties in ways that high numbers of repetitions of very small elements do not.

In another very important aspect of emergent literacy instruction, that of orthography, I felt the Eritrean teachers had really thrown out the proverbial baby with the bathwater by not transferring some of their indigenous techniques to the L2 setting. Despite some explicit instructions in the English Teachers' Guides about how to teach handwriting, in most instances the letters to be copied and practised in Grade 2 were written on the board without any comment from the teacher other than 'take out your exercise books'. However, since many of the children were then occupied with the usually very busy scene getting their pencils and copybooks ready, lobbing erasers across the room, walking around looking for a sharpener, etc., they did not even observe the teacher as s/he formed the letters. This 'silent way' seemed to me to be very inadequate as orthographic instruction and I felt it was probably a large part of the reason that the children 'drew' the letters, in inconsistent ways and also quite slowly, both of which inhibited their fluency and made all writing activities in the L2 very, very slow. Even 'clever' students' exercise books showed ample evidence of these inconsistent patterns of letter-formation, and their 'bad handwriting' was cited by a number of the primary English teachers as a serious problem. Some of that bad handwriting had to do with not separating words clearly, orienting similar letters in the wrong direction, resulting in, for example, confusion of d and b, or even of capital D and small a, since the relative heights were also not clearly demonstrated by the teacher or practised by the students. I noticed words with similar 'footprints' such as 'day', 'dog', 'boy', and 'bag' might all end up being confused with each other; I suspected the children were often guessing which word was which based only on its shape.

The teachers were not unwilling to expand the range of activities in their English classes beyond repeating and copying, to make instruction more explicit and the children more 'active'. A particularly memorable example of this occurred during one of the informal workshop-type meetings I held at the request of some of the primary English teachers: a Grade 2 teacher took an interest in an alphabet chart I had for our children, which had numbered arrows along the edges of the letters, indicating the manner in which the strokes were to be applied. He explained that he hadn't known there was a standard sequence of strokes for forming English letters and said he thought that might help his students. Not long after, I visited this first-year English teacher's class, and he had incorporated overt, numbered-strokes orthographic instruction into the handwriting lesson, something like what was written on my alphabet chart, but also like a Tigrinya lesson; he had taken the basic handwriting lesson a couple of steps further, by capitalising on the children's custom of echoing and repeating the teacher's instructions, and drawing in the air along with him, much as they did when pointing and singing 'My eyes, my ears . . .'. From this they received a quite 'motivating' lesson in writing, which by our standards made salient those features which it was the teacher's responsibility to make clear, and also engaged the children as 'active' learners, drawing on a variety of channels, including visual, auditory, and physical or corporal. I was impressed that this teacher had found a way to adapt his technique in a way that capitalised on the kinds of classroom interactions that were already there, integrating methods which outsiders like myself would consider inherently good – techniques which, I would contend, are already operating in more instances than outsiders take the time to discern.

I hear from this teacher, now nearly three years later, that he still uses the methods he 'learned' from me. I have not been able to follow up to see exactly what he means by that or if these methods have made any difference in his students' acquisition of English. Nevertheless I think it likely that when a point of method can be incorporated into already existing methods, 'indigenised' so to speak, it is more likely to be retained as part of the teacher's repertoire and perhaps also will be more effective in the long run.

Conclusion

Street suggests (Introduction, this volume, p. 9) that 'Instead of privileging the particular literacy practices familiar in their own culture, researchers now suspend judgement as to what constitutes literacy among the people they are working with until they are able to understand what it means to the people themselves.' The experience outlined above would suggest that such an approach is necessary in the design and implementation of literacy instruction as well. And what teachers and students in Eritrea and other impoverished parts of the world need is not a radical restructuring of their entire school system from the outside, based on what *ought* to exist according to Western standards; instead of seeing traditional methods as a *problem* to be eradicated, these need to be reconsidered by those within and without the system as *resources*.

Looked at through a different set of glasses, so to speak, traditional L2 methodology in Eritrea, with all its memorisation, might be considered by American 'neo-Classicists' to be a prime example of the 'grammar' stage, just before dialectic and rhetoric, and altogether on target in terms of addressing the intellectual demands of the young child and his/her cognitive limitations. In North America not inconsiderable numbers of parents are devoting large amounts of time and money to Classical Education which espouses a style of teaching for younger children much closer to what has been practised traditionally in Eritrea and other parts of the developing world for generations, which when called 'classical' is no longer 'mindless' but is believed to be uniquely suited to the cognitive limitations of younger learners (Wilson 1999).

The innovations and adaptations which many teachers in the developing world have already devised to cope with the constraints of their situation need to be 'mined', so to speak – scrutinised for negative and positive attributes, adjusted accordingly, tested, and incorporated into more realistic and relevant teacher training. The teachers and students need to be encouraged to integrate what is best from their traditions into the modern system, and the teachers enabled to adapt, given the uncertainties of material supply and the ongoing increase in demand on their skills. State-of-someone-else's-art methodology does not serve any purpose, if it is so inapt and inadequately supplied that the practitioners are, ultimately, disempowered by the very thing that they were led to believe would liberate them.

Notes

1 This chapter is based on a six-month study of classroom interaction in the Ghinda primary schools conducted during the academic year 1996–7. Many details of the

school conditions no longer obtain in Eritrea as the country has made great progress even in this short time in reprinting textbooks and improving the infrastructure.

2 Initials followed by dates in the text refer to informants and dates of interviews, drawn from field notes and tape-recordings.

References

Bailey, K. (1983) 'Competitiveness and Anxiety in Adult Second Language Learning: Looking at and through the Diary Studies', in H. Seliger and M. Long (eds), *Classroom Oriented Research in Second Language Acquisition*, Rowley, MA: Newbury House.

Cazden, C. (1988) *Classroom Discourse: The Language of Teaching and Learning*, Portsmouth, NH: Heinemann.

Chick, K. (1996) 'Safetalk: Collusion in Apartheid Education', in H. Coleman (ed.), *Society and the Language Classroom*, Cambridge: Cambridge University Press.

Eisemon, T. (1988) *Benefiting from Basic Education: School Quality and Functional Literacy in Kenya*, New York: Pergamon.

Gottesman, L. (1998) *To Fight and Learn: The Praxis and Promise of Literacy in Eritrea's Independence War*, Lawrenceville, NJ: Red Sea Press.

Hornberger, N. (1987) 'Schooltime, Classtime, and Academic Learning Time in Rural Highland Puno, Peru', *Anthropology and Education Quarterly* 18(3): 207–21.

—— (1989) 'Continua of Biliteracy', *Review of Educational Research* 59(3): 271–96.

Labov, W. (1972) *Language in the Inner City*, Philadelphia: University of Pennsylvania Press.

Mason, J. (1994) *Tigrinya Grammar*, Ghinda: American Evangelical Mission.

Mehan, H. (1979) *Learning Lessons: Social Organization in the Classroom*, Cambridge, MA: Harvard University Press.

Pankhurst, R. (1992) *A Social History of Ethiopia*, Addis Ababa: Institute of Ethiopian Studies.

Sinclair, J. and Coulthard, M. (1975) *Towards an Analysis of Discourse: The English Used by Teachers and Pupils*, Oxford: Oxford University Press.

State of Eritrea, Ministry of Education (1994) *English for Eritrea: Grade 2 Teachers' Guide*.

Street, B. (ed.) (1993) *Cross-Cultural Approaches to Literacy*, Cambridge: Cambridge University Press.

Wagaw, T. (1979) *Education in Ethiopia: Prospect and Retrospect*, Ann Arbor: University of Michigan Press.

Wagner, D. (1983) 'Rediscovering "Rote": Some Cognitive and Pedagogical Preliminaries', in S.H. Irvine and J.W. Berry (eds), *Human Assessment and Cultural Factors*, New York: Plenum.

—— (1993) *Literacy, Culture, and Development: Becoming Literate in Morocco*, Cambridge: Cambridge University Press.

Wilson, D. (1999) *Recovering the Lost Tools of Learning*, Moscow, ID: Canon Press.

4

BETRAYAL AND SOLIDARITY IN ETHNOGRAPHY ON LITERACY

Revisiting research homework in a north Indian village

Priti Chopra

> The starting point is the self: how we perceive ourselves and our relations with others. People are not some form of textbooks to be read or written by others. They should all be authors.
>
> (Archer 1999: 8)

Para-cites re-citation ex-citation: writing readings of others' self-expression

In this book, a variety of ethnographers, including myself, are concerned with representations of the 'illiterate' subject. This concern is primarily motivated by a desire to understand and explore 'ways of discovering and observing the uses and meanings of literacy practices to local people themselves . . . and their relationship to the programmes designed to alter [express] them' (Street, this volume, p. 1). Sitting (in a fidgety manner) within the frame of this book, I write about 'illiterate' subjects, who refuse to be 'illiterate' subjects (within a literacy centre and within my ethnographic study) yet remain captured, in my writing, as subjects of literacy. Capturing a person-as-identity relates to two purposes clamouring for reflexivity in my ethnographic research on literacy. The first purpose is to reflect upon the interplay of betrayal and solidarity as an issue for ethnographers, like myself, in re-presentations of people as subjects of literacy. Secondly, my focus on non-attendance in a literacy centre aims to contribute to the efforts of ethnographic research, in this volume, as a way for hearing the voices of 'illiterate' subjects.

My emphasis is on attempting to displace claims of 'knowing'-as-authority, in readings of the 'illiterate' subject, constructed by literacy programmes and by ethnographers, such as myself. By being more reflexive about the nature of authorship, contained in one literacy programme and one ethnographic research we can reread reasons for non-attendance, in a literacy centre and in my re-presentation, as the active refusal of people to be defined as the 'illiterate' subject of others. I write limits in 'knowing' the 'illiterate' subject as an act of transfor-mation both in the literacy centre and in my research. Transformation, in (not all) perspective, that exposes the boundaries of clarity as recognition of mis-understanding the opaque.

Prior to revealing a con-text[1] I will paint a pre-text for this knowledge making (see Barnet and Griffin 1997) gymnastics by unpacking what I mean by literacy, solidarity, betrayal and 'home' as ethnographic research features explored in this chapter.

In my study of literacy practices I draw upon Street's definition (this volume) of literacies as fluid and dynamic practices situated in different domains. I approach literacies as hybrid practices which are produced by a variety of people for different purposes. I see these hybrid practices as communicative practices expressing relations of power that are historically situated within political, social, economic and cultural processes (see Street 1984 and 1993; Archer and Costello 1990; Gee et al. 1996; Archer 1998: 100–8; Barton et al. 1999).

It is within this understanding of literacy that I place the constructed 'illiter-ate' subject and her refusal to be 'illiterate'. Through her refusal, I hope to displace homogeneous re-presentations of the 'illiterate' subject, which situate her in the role of 'dependant' or 'victim', as failed attempts to rob her of her historical and political agency (Mohanty 1996). By narrating 'refusal' I hope to recognise different individuals' sense of agency as embedded in and evolving through forms of collective action that activate differences in order to transform practices. This, for me, defines my position of solidarity in the relationships I express and re-presentations I construct for subjects of literacy.

I define betrayal as the utterance of individual desire and personal interest, embedded in relations of power. By expressing individual desire and personal interest, in acts that represent other people, I re-produce my identity as author-ity-in-knowing. I demonstrate my position, as a subject of ethnography, occupy-ing spaces where boundaries between betrayal and solidarity become blurred in my interpretation and production of other subjects of ethnography. I understand my occupied 'in between' spaces as critically negotiated slippage that not only reveals how 'I think I know what I know' but also engages me in a process of realising, critiquing and acting upon limits in my acts of 'knowing' (Clifford 1988) the 'illiterate-as-literate' subject.

I revisit my research homework in a north Indian village in order (under your gaze) to become self-conscious of these acts of 'knowing' as neither innocent nor transparent (Visweswaran 1994). I make use of the term 'home' rather than 'field' as the site of my research work. For me, home is not a fixed space but rather a shifting space that encompasses acts of betrayal and solidarity. Home represents, for me, a space in which I am attached, in which I belong, but also a space which is not free from confrontation, struggle and transformation. I occupy home, in many sites, as a flexibly situated and produced subject of communicative practices implicated in relations with other versatile, situated and produced subjects of communicative practices.

I re-present refusal to be the 'illiterate' subject and the interplay between acts of solidarity and betrayal in the form of three narratives based in and near NIV village.[2] The first narrative, named 'Re-citing Saraswati's[3] writing on meeting no. 1', is my translation, from Saraswati's Hindi writing about a meeting, attended by many non-attending participants, at NIV literacy centre. In the second narrative, 'Story 1', I revisit an interview with non-attending participant, Lakshmi, who refuses to be the 'illiterate' subject of the literacy centre and my ethnographic study. The final narrative, 'Story 2' is based on revisiting Yamuna, NIV literacy facilitator, as living (in my experience) outside the context of NIV village and the literacy centre.

I reflect upon re-presentations of the 'illiterate' subject by my and other selves as (un)blemished surfaces in-actions-re-actions. I study re-presentation as the practice of reading and writing the 'illiterate' subject as 'literate'. I explore the action of practices, in reading and writing subjects of literacy, as impinging on three issues: the issue of social space; the issue of responsibility and blame; and the issue of dialogue.

By studying re-presentations of the 'illiterate' subject, as the practice of literacy theory, I gaze beyond 'failure' to see limits in acts of 'knowing' the 'illiterate' subject in order to be able to critique and act upon these limits.

Betrayal and solidarity in moments of interstitial intimacy

> One night . . . a [researcher] appeared . . . and said, I have been sent
> by – and here he [she] named the dear name – to comfort you. Then
> drawing a worn volume from the pocket of . . . [a] long black coat he
> [she] sat and read till dawn. Then disappeared without a word.
>
> (Beckett 1986: 447)

Over the period of one year, I travelled and resided in many organisations implementing a variety of literacy programmes in north Indian villages. YDFMP is one such local organisation working in thirty-five north Indian villages. The organisation has a long history of work in mobilising marginalised groups for the implementation of development interventions. All programmes were implemented through the formation of *mahila sangathans*[4] within the village. In new villages, the literacy centres provided the basis for developing *mahila sangathans*. NIV is one such village with a population of forty-five scheduled caste[5] families. The literacy centre is based on a programme for women that has been operating for several years.

Naming a few names present in the narratives

- Saraswati?[6] female, brahmin[7] caste, from a north Indian village, early twenties, YDFMP literacy centre facilitator . . .[8]
- Mdevi? female, scheduled caste, from NIV . . .
- Adevi? female, scheduled caste, from NIV . . .
- Bdevi? female, scheduled caste, from NIV . . .
- Rdevi? female, schedule caste, from NIV . . .
- Yamuna? female, thakur caste,[9] from a north Indian village near NIV, late twenties, NIV literacy centre facilitator for YDFMP . . .
- Lakshmi? female, scheduled caste, from NIV, early thirties . . .
- Sita? female, scheduled caste, from NIV, early twenties, student . . .
- I? female, kshatriya caste,[10] from Delhi, late twenties, student-researcher . . .

Re-citing Saraswati's writing on meeting No. 1

On the 18th at 3.15 pm, at the literacy centre of NIV village, a meeting was organised by the *mahila sangathan*. Thirty-five different women participated in this meeting which included members of the *mahila sangathan* and seven organisation members (the field programme officer, five different literacy centre facilitators and one research-student).

The aim of the meeting was to discuss the following issues raised by *sangathan* members enrolled in the literacy centre:

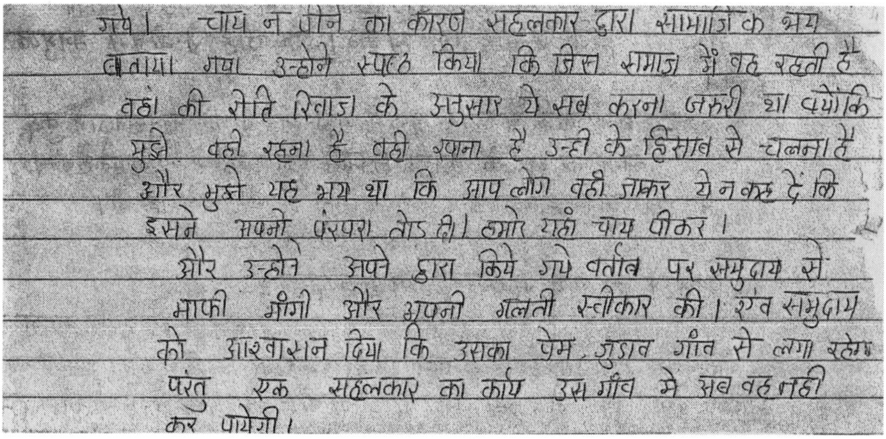

गए। चाय न पीने का कारण सहलकार द्वारा समाज का भय बताया गया उन्होंने स्पष्ट किया कि जिस समाज में वह रहती है वहां की रीति रिवाज के अनुसार ये सब करना जरूरी था क्योंकि मुझे वही रहना है वही रचना है उन्ही के हिसाब से चलना है और मुझे यह भय था कि आप लोग वही जिक्र ये न कर दे कि इसने अपनी परंपरा तोड़ दी। और यहां चाय पीकर। और उन्होंने अपने द्वारा किये गये वर्ताव पर समुदाय से माफी माँगी और अपनी गलती स्वीकार की। एवं समुदाय को आश्वासन दिया कि उसका प्रेम, जुड़ाव गाँव से लगा रहेगा परंतु एक सहलकार का कार्य उस गाँव में सब वह नहीं कर पायेगी।

Figure 4.1 An extract from Saraswati's writing on meeting No. 1

- to discuss reasons for non-attendance of *mahila sangathan* members in the literacy centre and ways to improve the situation;
- to discuss the ways in which stronger trust can be built between YDFMP and the *mahila sangathan*;
- the preparation of a second line facilitator for the literacy centre;
- the possibility of opening a children's crèche in the village.

During a participatory discussion the following two reasons for non-attendance emerged.

Reason one: the unfair distribution of sweets and saris during diwali[11]

From the participants' discussion it was felt that problems of non-attendance were caused by the manner in which sweets and saris were distributed by YDFMP during diwali. There is a total of thirty-one members in the literacy centre but only twenty-two of them received these diwali gifts. During distribution gifts were given to those women who either did not or rarely participated in the literacy centre's activities. Not all regular participants in the literacy centre received gifts.

One of the *mahila sangathan* members expressed the following opinion (in pahari – her local language): '*Dina saben barabar din, ne dina ke na din . . .*' (If you are going to give then give equally to all or give to none at all . . .) (Mdevi).

They said that this was not the issue of receiving something; this was more an issue of being insulted by neglect. They especially felt this insult when they were asked by other people in the village why they had failed to receive anything when others had received gifts. The organisation apologised for this incident and said that they would take care not to repeat such a mistake. The participants also felt that the *sangathan* should develop some rules to ensure that members were not treated like this again, i.e., to take responsibility for the distribution themselves and to ensure that no one received any gifts if there were not enough for everyone.

Reason two: NIV facilitator's[12] inappropriate behaviour

The second reason for non-attendance raised by the participants was the inappropriate behaviour of the facilitator towards NIV centre participants. Some of the following experiences were shared by enrolled members of the literacy centre during discussion.

Adevi said that once she had not been able to learn her lesson properly, and the facilitator lost her temper, took off her shoe and hit her with it. She said that this left her feeling hurt and humiliated. Following this incident she got up from the class and returned to her home. She said (in Hindi): '*Aaj tak mere pati na mere gharwalon ne mujhe mara aur purey samaj ke samne inhone mujhe mara*' (Till today neither my husband nor any other member of my family has ever hit me and in front of everyone she hit me). She said that this was the reason why she stopped attending classes at the literacy centre. Bdevi said to the NIV facilitator (in Hindi): '*Jab hamne apko bola ke ap yahan aise vyvhar karenge to hum nahin ayenge apko achcha vyvhar rakna chaiye tha*' (When we told you that if you behaved like this we would stop attending you should have behaved in a good manner with us).

Instead she said that the facilitator would lose her temper and use abusive language. She would also threaten them that the organisation was working in several villages so if they did not attend she would leave and the organisation and herself would end their work in the village. Bdevi said that the fear of losing contact with YDFMP and its other programmes caused them to be silent. She said that they had never worked with an organisation in their village before and that they did not know the organisation very well. She said (in Hindi), '*ye soche kar chup rahe ki hamari kaun sonega*' (We kept quiet thinking who would listen to us).

The literacy centre members also complained that the facilitator was casteist in her behaviour towards them within their village. Rdevi said (in Hindi): '*Sabke liye chai banie thi samudai mai sabne pii. Sahilkar ne nahin piya aur pochney par bataya ki 'mujhe ulti ho jayegi mai bimar ho jaoungi*' (Tea was made for everyone and everyone drank it. The facilitator did not drink it and on being asked said 'It will make me vomit, I will get sick').

All the centre members had felt humiliated by this incident. The facilitator told everyone that she had not wanted to humiliate anyone. She explained that her reason for not drinking tea with them was due to social pressure. She said that she has to live according to the traditions and customs of the society within which she resides. She has to live there and eat there so she also has to walk in life according to their norms. She said that she was scared in case anyone of them would say in her village that she broke her traditional values by drinking tea with them in their village. The facilitator then asked for forgiveness for her behaviour towards the literacy centre participants. She told the participants that her attachment and love for the village would remain but she would no longer be able to continue working as a facilitator in their village.[13]

The field programme officer then initiated a discussion on possible steps to be taken by NIV centre members and YDFMP in order to overcome the difficulties they had been experiencing.

Revisiting Lakshmi's refusal to be the 'illiterate' subject: Story 1

I went through attendance registers and made a list of all non-attending literacy centre participants. I then went to Sita in order to find out some background information about the participants. Where did they live in the village? Were they neighbours? Or relatives? Sita and I discovered that all the women resided in the upper part of the village. She then explained the differences, to do with sub-castes and social status, between people who resided in the upper part and the lower part of the village. She said that we should go and visit some of the non-attending participants in the afternoon (after they returned from work in the fields and had eaten lunch). Lakshmi was the first person we visited. Sita had provided me with some background information about Lakshmi and her own speculations on reasons for Lakshmi's 'drop out'.

On meeting Lakshmi, Sita introduced me and explained the purpose of our visit. She then asked Lakshmi if she could speak with me. Lakshmi invited us into her home and we sat down together. I then tried to initiate a general conversation, based on her family, but Lakshmi refused to be drawn into a conversation beyond polite formality. Sita, all the while, kept on insisting that Lakshmi speak openly about herself. Feeling under pressure myself, that Lakshmi, thus, must speak, I then asked about the literacy centre and how long she had attended, why she had joined, when and why she had left. Lakshmi, under our pressure, responded that she had attended the NIV centre for one month and had joined in order to learn to read and write. She said that she left because there were too many things to attend to at home. Sita then interrupted her and told her to speak openly. She said, 'she will not put you in trouble, she wants to know what the difficulties are and she'll write it for us'. Sita then, herself, started to explain reasons for why Lakshmi had left NIV centre.

I was now feeling more and more uncomfortable as Lakshmi felt awkward. Either staying or leaving was becoming difficult. So, I asked for a glass of water. This surprised Lakshmi. By the time I was slowly sipping my water Lakshmi's children and mother-in-law had joined us. Sita then, in response to the mother-in-law's questions, began to reintroduce me. I took this opportunity to tell Lakshmi that I really did not want to disturb her and that I could now leave. But everybody insisted, 'no, no stay . . .'. We then started talking about the children. This led to a very long conversation about the operation Lakshmi had, to stop having children, in return for some government money. Lakshmi spoke about the difficulties experienced with her treatment during and after the operation. This eventually led to more discussion, which they meant for me to write down, with Lakshmi actively speaking about her unsatisfactory experiences in a variety of government income-generation schemes.

After some time I tried to reintroduce her non-attendance at the literacy centre back into the conversation. However, Lakshmi dismissively responded, 'I should have been taught all the alphabet in the amount of time I spent there. Then at least I could have written a letter.'

Revisiting Yamuna: Story 2

While we[14] were washing our feet, in a small stream outside NIV village, a snake went past Yamuna and she screamed. I saw half the snake and screamed. Saraswati screamed because she knew there'd be a reason. On the way home, Saraswati and I argued about whether it was lucky or unlucky to see a snake.

Yamuna really laughed and said that it was pretty lucky to see the snake without it seeing us.

Yamuna and I spent loads of time together. I lived with her and her family during my second week in the area. Working in NIV village literacy centre is only a part of the million and one things she has to do. She has to get up at five in the morning and start with household chores, see to the animals and deal with the crops. She also has to attend to her younger brother and sisters. After having lunch she sets off on her one-hour trek to the NIV literacy centre from her nearby north Indian village. On her way back she may stop in town to do some shopping. Once she's back home, in the evening, she has loads more chores to sort out.

I asked Yamuna why she is so 'strict' with the children at home. She told me you have to beat the nonsense out of them while they are young so they learn to do as they are told and don't get spoilt. I asked, 'what about your nonsense?' She laughed and said it wasn't as much as my nonsense.

(Un)blemished surfaces in-actions–re-actions

a single leaf turns not yellow but with the silent knowledge of the whole tree

(Gibran 1988: 34)

The narratives are my partial truths (Clifford 1986). They are written constructions based on reading and rereading self-expressions of the 'illiterate' subject as different people who decide actively to 'opt out' not passively to 'drop out'. Moments of 'interstitial' intimacy shared between betrayal and solidarity are re-produced, for your reading, through a variety of gazes: 'knowing' gazes exchanged between constructed 'illiterate–literate' subjects situated inside and out of NIV literacy centre, NIV village, YDFMP, my ethnographic study and this chapter.[15]

Here, I continue to reflect upon re-presentations of the 'illiterate' subject by my and other selves. I engage in reflection on the practice of reading and writing the 'illiterate as literate' with two desires. One desire, as an ethnographer researching literacy, is to displace re-presentations of people as the homogeneous 'illiterate' being who becomes passively 'literate' as an occupant of margins in other people's Centres. This desire constructs my position in acts of solidarity. Another desire is to critique my endeavour to 'know' perfectly the 'illiterate-as-literate' subject through an ethnographic study on literacy practices. Where I claim to 'know' perfectly is where I reveal my betrayal. Critiquing my endeavour to 'know' makes me self-conscious of how I slip between the fluid spaces of betrayal and solidarity. With these two desires in mind I explore the action of reading and writing subjects of literacy.

I consider actions of reading and writing the 'illiterate' subject as 'literate', in the narratives, to impinge on three interlinked issues: the issue of social space; the issue of responsibility and blame; and the issue of dialogue.

The issue of social space

Drawing upon Street's definition of literacies (this volume) as a lens for viewing the 'illiterate' subject, it becomes clear that the 'illiterate' subject is not a free-floating object a 'literate' vision fixes in a space outside its own. The 'literate' and 'illiterate', as subjects of literacy, have relations. They share the same moving social spaces. Within social space they are constructed as each other by themselves and vice versa. In order to understand these historical acts of construction we, ethnographers of literacy, focus on the economic, cultural, social and political processes, expressed through our understanding of everyday practices, as grounded in shared social space. I think within social space we also occupy moral and critical spaces that influence the lens through which we not only gaze but also act upon each other when we construct our and other selves as subjects of literacy. Reflecting on how and why we occupy positions, as selves within these spaces, determines our purpose for engaging in actions of reading and writing subjects of literacy as critically negotiated slippage between betrayal and solidarity.

The issue of responsibility and blame

Homogeneous re-presentations of the 'illiterate' as 'victim' or 'dependant' create roles of responsibility and blame that sustain inequality in relations of power. Blame is placed on the 'victim of illiteracy' as 'failing' to take responsibility for becoming 'literate'. Responsibility is located in the 'literate' as authority in making the 'illiterate' 'literate'. Through ethnographic research on literacy such constructions for blame and responsibility can become displaced. However, for me, the issue of blame and responsibility becomes equally problematic if ethnographic practice constructs an inverse relationship where blame is simply removed from the 'illiterate as literate' body and placed on the head of a programme instead. I see blame and responsibility as the expression of relationships shared between different individuals and between individuals and the structures that function, at a variety of levels, to sustain subjects of literacy. Researchers, such as myself, are implicated in these relationships through our ethnographic practice – the purpose of which defines the ways in which we express solidarity and betrayal. Re-presenting refusal to be the 'illiterate' subject, through ethnographic research, for me is the recognition of different individuals' sense of agency asserted through collective acts for transforming practices. In this recognition, blame and responsibility become evolving and shared processes established through the relationships built between different individuals and between individuals and structures which operate, at many levels, for reading and writing subjects of literacy. These relationships are constructed through historically situated everyday communicative practices, that reveal and conceal relations of power, involved in social, economic, political and cultural processes.

The issue of dialogue

To think the closure of representation is . . . to think the cruel powers of death and play which permit presence to be born to itself, and pleasurably to consume itself through the representation in which it eludes itself in its deferral . . . And it is to think why it is fatal that, in its closure, representation continues.

(Derrida 1997: 250)

Reading and writing re-presentations of the 'illiterate' subject also involve ways of listening and speaking which all contribute, together, to form the production of dialogue (see Shor and Freire 1987). Dialogue involves the experience of speaking to be heard and hearing in order to be able to reply.[16] Thus, the experience of dialogue reveals the impossibility of dialogue (Spivak 1988). In my re-presentations, (un)conscious interruptions in listening, speaking, reading and writing, refusals of the 'illiterate' subject, made explicit ways in which our dialogue communicated desire captured in self-interest and relations of power. Absence and presence produced by the engagement of my desire with the desire of other people make me confront the 'failure' of dialogue and closure of re-presentation as limits in acts of 'knowing' through my ethnographic practice. However, it is also my ethnographic practice that enables me to critique and act upon these limits of 'knowing' as a way for continuing the action of dialogue and practice of re-presentation.

Practising the action of reading in re-presentation

. . . whenever we set about reading 'our' texts and find them leading us obsessively back to ourselves, it is a good idea not to stop there, with ourselves as centres of meaning, but rather to go on and to think through the possibility that the personal might necessarily lead us outside 'ourselves' to the political.

(Landry and Maclean 1996: 12)

The action of reading people, as subjects of literacy, in order to re-present their practices, as the creation of our gaze construction, for me, involves a continuous process of rereading. Rereading in order to become conscious of the gaps and absences hidden in my reading as an act of 'knowing' other people's practices. For me, this is the action of responsibly engaging in re-presentation through the practice of reading (and being read) actively with a critical embrace. Reading with myself becoming conscious of how and why I critically embrace is what makes possible my experience of the impossible: dialogue. The moment I read other people, to construct re-presentations of the 'illiterate as literate', with a hostile gaze is for me the moment of betrayal: the site at which I realise the 'failure' of dialogue and the closure of re-presentation to be critiqued and acted upon as my limits of 'knowing'.

Practising the action of writing in re-presentation

The action of writing readings of others' self-expressions, as an ethnographer narrating refusals to be the 'illiterate' subject, involves the practice of translating and articulating (see Spivak 1988 and 1993) the self-expressions of other people. My practice of translating and articulating readings of other people, as actions of writing in re-presentation, involves a continuous process of questioning how and why I am unable to transcend the construction of my identity-as-authority in 'knowing' through the practice of these actions in writing. By becoming self-conscious, I am able to negotiate critically the slippage of my position between acts of solidarity, displacing my identity-as-authority, and acts of betrayal, re-claiming my identity-as-authority, in 'knowing' refusals to be the 'illiterate' subject.

Closure? Gazing beyond 'failure' to see limits of knowing

> ... there is nothing but action ... action of theory and action of practice which relate to each other as relays and form networks.
>
> Deleuze[17]

The inter-action between theory of literacy and practice of literacy, within this con-text, determines how I revisit research homework, as re-presentations of people's refusals to be the 'illiterate' subject, in NIV literacy centre and my ethnographic study. I explore 'failure' to know refusals, of non-attending participants, as acts revealing the 'interstitial' intimacy shared between betrayal and solidarity. It is by becoming conscious of the positions that my and other selves occupy in this intimacy that I am able to gaze beyond the 'failure' of dialogue and closure of re-presentation to realise and act upon my limits of 'knowing'.

My experience of ethnographic practice engages with two desires. One desire is to reread, through ethnography, 'failure' of the passive 'illiterate' as 'drop out'. By rereading the 'illiterate' subject I re-present some reasons for non-attendance as historically situated communicative practices, involving power relations, acted out in social, economic, political and cultural spaces. Through this rereading, I hope to recognise the 'failure' of 'drop out' as limits of 'knowing' the practices of the 'illiterate' subject – who actively 'opts out'. My second desire is to reread ethnographic practice as re-presentations of 'knowing' the 'illiterate-as-literate' subject: a 'knowing' that engages myself, as an ethnographer, in experiencing the impossibility of transcending 'failure' of dialogue and closure of re-presentation. However, by gazing beyond 'failure' I can recognise and act upon limits in my acts of 'knowing'. 'Knowing', as an ethnographer researching literacy, engaged in critically negotiated slippage 'in between' the spaces of solidarity and betrayal. As continuation with-'n-closure,[18] while Spivak spoke:

> If the project of Imperialism is violently to put together the episteme that will 'mean' (for others) and 'know' (for the self) the colonial subject as history's nearly selved other, the example of these deletions indicate explicitly what is always implicit: that meaning/knowledge intersects power
>
> (Spivak 1999: 215)

I heard:

> Is the project of ethnographic researchers (like myself) to make knowledge that will 'mean' for 'illiterates' and 'know' for 'literates' the 'illiterate' subject as my stories nearly made 'literate illiterate'? How am I going about making explicit in different ways what remains implicit in many ways – 'that meaning/knowledge intersects power'?

And within this chapter lives (in hope) my imperfect-as-incomplete reply.

Notes

1 I thank Bryan Maddox for questioning my use of the word con-text. I have used context to frame context as a construction of reality contained by fabrication shaped in the interest of a (not always) 'known' agenda. I use it in an effort to make explicit that 'context' is not a neutral pre-existing entity. As a written representation of others' reality, my con-text conceals and reveals an (un)known context as con-text.
2 The names of people, place and time period, from North Indian Village (NIV) homework, have been disguised for identity protection in the case of (un)wholly sensitive exposure.
3 Saraswati is one of the many literacy facilitators with whom I lived and worked at YDFMP. She once said, 'I know how to work but not how to speak so that others recognise me. Others who know how to speak but not how to work never seem to have this problem.' For me, she has no problem speaking (honestly, I heard her) and she 'knows' how to write as well. We were a team, for some time, learning and sharing experiences together. I learnt a lot from Saraswati. This chapter is a product of such a process of shared learning. I wanted to displace my authority in writing by sharing authorship, as I did learning, with Saraswati. But in conventional reading this gesture is seen to displace my accountability and not seen as sharing my claimed authority. By translating all conversations and Saraswati's writing from Hindi I knowingly and unknowingly re-write the absences and presences of other unaccountable authors within this text.
4 Grassroots-level women's organisations.
5 With 'out-caste' residing as 'untouchables' at the base of the caste hierarchy through the 'impure' and 'pure' acts of others, involving, for instance, the social practice of food consumption as a marker of status.
6 ? attempts to displace the closure in naming. ? opens the question of who the person-as-name is being and becoming.

7 Within priest caste.
8 . . . fills the space of absences in this re-presentation of a person's multiple identities.
9 Within landlord and warrior caste.
10 Landlord and warrior caste.
11 Diwali is an Indian festival.
12 Yamuna – NIV literacy centre facilitator.
13 One literacy facilitator, Yamuna, re-cited, in Hindi, through the writing of a different literacy facilitator – Saraswati. Re-presented, in English, through my translation. Saraswati's re-citation of Yamuna is also placed, as a photocopied extract of Saraswati's own writing, within this text.
14 In case you are wondering, 'who is we?', we are Yamuna, Saraswati and myself.
15 I would like to thank Brian Street for drawing my attention to the role of intertextuality, and many other aspects involved in the drafting process of this chapter, as influences on your gaze construction.
16 I'd like to learn (to reply) from your reply at choprapriti@hotmail.com.
17 Deleuze cited in Foucault 1997: 206–7, and in Spivak 1999: 256.
18 The symbol ' in its situated presence represents the located absence of both i and e, thus, paradoxically, enabling the simultaneous presentation of 'with-in-closure–with-en-closure'.

References

Archer, D. (1998) 'The Evolving Conception of Literacy in REFLECT', *PLA Notes* 32: 100–8, London: IIED.
—— (1999) 'REFLECT in Nicaragua', Draft Report, July 1999, London: ActionAid.
Archer, D. and Costello, P. (1990) *Literacy and Power*, Earthscan: London.
Barton, D., Hamilton, M. and Ivanič, R. (eds) (1999) *Situated Literacies: Reading and Writing in Context*, London: Routledge.
Barnet, R. and Griffin, A. (eds) (1997) *The End of Knowledge in Higher Education*, London: Institute of Education.
Beckett, S. (1986) 'Ohio Impromptu', in *The Complete Dramatic Works*, London: Faber & Faber.
Clifford, J. (1986) 'Introduction: Partial Truths', in G. Marcus and J. Clifford (eds), *Writing Culture*, Berkeley: University of California Press.
—— (1988) *The Predicament of Culture: Twentieth-Century Ethnography, Literature, and Art*, Cambridge, MA: Harvard University Press.
Derrida, J. (1997) *Writing and Difference*, London: Routledge.
Foucault, M. (1997) *Language, Counter-Memory, Practice: Selected Essays and Interviews*, trans. D. Bouchard and S. Simon, Ithaca, NY: Cornell University Press.
Gee, J., Hull, G. and Lankshear, C. (eds) (1996) *The New Work Order: Behind the Language of the New Capitalism*, London: Allen & Unwin.
Gibran, K. (1988) *The Prophet*, London: Heinemann.
Landry, D. and Maclean, G. (eds) (1996) *The Spivak Reader*, London: Routledge.
Mohanty, C. (1996) 'Under Western Eyes: Feminist Scholarship and Colonial Discourses', in P. Mongia (ed.), *Contemporary Postcolonial Theory: A Reader*, London: Arnold.
Shor, I. and Freire, P. (1987) *A Pedagogy for Liberation: Dialogues on Transforming Education*, New York: Bergin & Garvey.
Spivak, G. (1988) 'Can the Subaltern Speak?', in C. Nelson and L. Grossberg (eds), *Marxism and the Interpretation of Culture*, Urbana: University of Illinois Press.

—— (1993) 'The Politics of Translation', in M. Barrett and A. Phillips (eds), *Destabilizing Theory: Contemporary Feminist Debates*, Cambridge: Polity Press.

—— (1999) *A Critique of Postcolonial Reason*, Cambridge, MA: Harvard University Press.

Street, B. (1984) *Literacy in Theory and Practice*, Cambridge: Cambridge University Press.

—— (1995) *Social Literacies: Critical Perspectives on Literacy in Development, Ethnography and Education*, London: Longman.

—— (ed.) (1993) *Cross-Cultural Approaches to Literacy*, Cambridge: Cambridge University Press.

Visweswaran, K. (1994) *Fictions of Feminist Ethnography*, Minneapolis: University of Minnesota Press.

Part II

LITERACY AND DEVELOPMENT
Local literacies and development agendas

INTRODUCTION

While the chapters in Part I explicitly addressed the educational dimension of development interventions, the chapters in Part II of the book address the broader contexts within which such debates take place and focus on specific aspects of development agendas – land rights (Aikman), the language of literacy (Herbert and Robinson), the marketplace (Maddox), health (Robinson-Pant), state control of indigenous peoples (Stites) and the gender politics of literacy (Zubair). In each case the ethnographic perspective adopted by the authors suggests a more sensitive approach to local meanings and understandings of the development process in general and of literacy in particular than is usually the case when large state or international agencies address such issues. Whether such large institutions have an interest in or are able to recognise such local and nuanced meanings is an issue addressed from various directions by the authors – their collective agreement appears to be that we cannot afford *not* to take such a view and indeed this perspective does appear to offer some explanation for the general disaffection shown by many of the target audience for literacy campaigns. If we do address what literacy and development mean to those for whom the programmes have been designed, then those programmes – or rather revised versions of them, including redesign from the ground up – might stand a better chance of success. That at least is the message of the research documented here.

Sheila Aikman's chapter, 'Literacies, languages and developments in Peruvian Amazonia' deals with the Arakmbut who are involved at community level and through their representative indigenous organisation in the implementation of three projects: an intercultural bilingual schooling project, an integrated land and economic strengthening project and a project for the development of eco-tourism. The chapter examines the theories of development and approaches to literacy which the Harakmbut have experienced over the twentieth century and relates these to the approaches to language and literacy in the three projects. The Harakmbut have had a subdued response to the project for a biliterate intercultural model of schooling in their villages but are much more motivated and responsive to the two more economically focused projects. An examination of the literacy practices and literacy contexts which the Harakmbut encounter in their daily activities and protection of their territories, as well as in the course of the implementation and management of the development projects themselves, reveals their need to utilise a diverse and challenging range of literacy skills. The findings of Aikman's ethnographic studies may not always be in keeping with dominant assumptions among developers, including those who see themselves as 'progressive': the attention to local meanings that an ethnographic perspective generates may, for instance, lead to different emphases than even the researcher's own preferred approach to literacy teaching (as Wright also found). Aikman comes to the conclusion that, in order to understand and facilitate literacy development, we need to analyse political and economic contexts that might not at first sight appear to prioritise literacy. These include, for instance, a local emphasis on rights and on economic development that resists centralised planning, taking account of global economic changes through local interpretations. The chapter argues, then, that the training processes involved in the projects that have an economic focus, though not prioritising literacy learning, establish the conditions for the Harakmbut to acquire a facility with literacy skills through using writing in a meaningful context. This not only applies to becoming competent users of a wide range of Spanish-language literacy practices but also, through support for Harakmbut self-development, can lead to a more informed and committed support for mother-tongue literacy as a strategy for cultural strengthening and the achievement of their self-development. This process is, however, contingent on the Harakmbut developing their own integrated development plan, which brings together the aims of these projects within one Harakmbut agenda with clearly articulated goals. The role of the committed ethnographer in such a context is to help document the context in which this agenda is meaningful and perhaps to help outsiders understand and recognise it in more sensitive ways.

Pat Herbert and Clinton Robinson provide a nuanced account of different literacies in their chapter 'Another language, another literacy? Practices in northern Ghana'. They examine the place of language in differentiating literacies and in shaping the nature of literacy acquisition and practices, in the multilingual context of northern Ghana. They describe the characteristics of this multilingualism and report on observed literacy practices in the religious, economic, personal and 'meetings' domains, in an attempt to understand how multilingual usage by individuals and communities affects such practices. Their work demonstrates the value of close ethnographic descriptions of literacy in context but they point out that such work does not always make reference to the language in which people have acquired their literacy competence. This is particularly significant in cases where one language has a script or a long written tradition and others do not.

In Ghana most of the local languages were formerly unwritten and have been written down only within the last fifty years – chiefly by missionaries but also by NGOs. Literacy programmes have been initiated in these languages, particularly in association with Bible translation or with development concerns. More recently, however, it has become clear, as noted above for other contexts, that literacy activities are relevant only in so far as they are linked with a broad range of communication needs, including the language of literacy. In the case of Ghana and the activities of mission groups such as SIL, this contemporary understanding of the broader communicative dimension of literacy activities has led to a revised view of the role both of schooling and of adult literacy programmes. A range of 'real life' programmes has developed, such as the Danish inspired 'School for Life' which focuses on shepherd boys and on girl and boy traders who have dropped out of school. The chapter documents a number of such programmes in terms of the languages in which participants have become literate and asks not how literacy affects them but how the users have affected this literacy.

Herbert and Robinson describe a complex mix of languages and religions – from recitation of Quranic verses by heart in the north (see Wright's chapter on Eritrea for a further analysis of the meanings of such recitation) to Catholic practices among the Deg where a Paramount Chief used the Bible to make judgements about people suspected of sheep stealing. The authors suggest that a range of meanings may be attached to such practices, from the surface appearance of mysticism to which most Westerners are likely to respond to the deeper epistemological frameworks regarding problem-solving and explanation, akin to anthropologists' accounts of witchcraft. At the same time local literacies may be used for funeral records and for economic purposes, such as the traditional letter writer composing and typing letters for customers in a number of languages and frequently translating a message delivered in one language to one written in another. 'Meetings literacies' are already familiar to literacy students from the work of Barton, Hamilton and Ivanič (1999) among others and Herbert and Robinson document further examples among Deg and Dagomba peoples in Ghana, where again languages are mixed between what is said at meetings and what is recorded.

What are we to make of this complex mix of practices around oral, symbolic and literate practices and why should they be of interest to either theorists or developers? Herbert and Robinson suggest first that their empirical data are of theoretical concern since they force us to ask not only what association there may be between different literacies and different domains – religious, economic, personal – but also what link there may be between these and different languages. Their answer to the title question 'does another language therefore mean another literacy?' appears to be yes but not on language grounds alone. Different languages may be not simply communicative channels, but rather carriers of symbolic and cultural difference: 'Along with language differences go cultural patterns, made up of ancestral customs, historical antecedents, external influences and political forces. The resulting differences are carried and symbolised by particular languages, not caused by them.' In the sense of multiple literacies outlined throughout this book, then, each time a literacy is embedded in another language its meanings alter – new literacy practices are involved not just translations from one language to another. Why this is important for developers designing literacy programmes as well as for theorists interested in the nature of diversity is that such diversity cannot simply be read off from a language or a script – if the social and symbolic practices associated with different languages and scripts are what give them salience for their users, then developers cannot simply prescribe beforehand which languages a literacy programme should be conducted in or simply translate primers written in one language into another for different users: at each point the users if not the planners will recognise a different social practice and will make their choices whether to come to the programme or to drop out once started, accordingly, as Papen describes for the Namibian case. Such nuanced accounts, then, can provide explanations for the massive failures of literacy programmes documented by the World Bank and UNESCO which failed to take account of the symbolic significance of the language of literacy, but may perhaps also offer some beginning of an alternative route for designing literacy activities in which local people will engage, that take account of local literacies and languages.

A similar practical outcome from detailed empirical study follows from Bryan Maddox's chapter, 'Literacy and the market: the economic uses of literacy among the peasantry in north-west Bangladesh', which is based on recent ethnographic and action research with poor farming communities in the north-west of Bangladesh. As part of collaboration between researchers and literacy programme planners and administrators, Maddox explores the practical and theoretical tensions between a practice-based notion of literacy and numeracy learning and the idea of imparting universal 'skills' to adult learners.

The chapter begins by describing the uses of literacy and numeracy in the religious practices of the communities involved, for example highlighting the contrast between the widespread use of Arabic for Islamic religious purposes and the use of Bengali literacy and numeracy in economic activity. It then looks in detail at the connections between genre, form and practice in small-scale economic activity (the local bazaar and fish market) and the ways in which literacy and numeracy become fused in practice rather than existing as separate objects or 'skill' areas. This includes in-depth micro-ethnographic examples based on the presentation and analysis of actual texts, as well as a broader account of local numeracy concepts and practices. Finally, Maddox examines the theoretical and practical implications of the research, contrasting the politics of 'universalistic' (or autonomous) notions of literacy with a more situated notion of literacy and numeracy in practice. In particular, drawing on linguistic theory of the kind cited by Herbert and Robinson, he challenges the common assumption of literacy planners that writing is simply 'spoken language written down', and highlights the value of a more practice-based and situated notion of literacy and numeracy learning. A significant contribution of this chapter is its recognition of a broad range of communicative practices, including particularly everyday numeracy practices, within which literacy is only one component: the 'new communicative order' will make increasing demands for knowledge such as this upon those offering programmes of support and development.

Anna Robinson-Pant's chapter 'Women's literacy and health: can an ethnographic researcher find the links?' likewise draws attention to the role of research in practical literacy and development work. From the standpoint of her own ethnographic studies as well as practical involvement in literacy programme in Nepal, she challenges the dominant assumption that has been almost universally accepted in developing countries that women's literacy is the key to improving a family's income, health and education. In Nepal, a successful women's literacy programme is considered to be one that raises a woman's awareness around health, nutrition and family planning, as well as simply improving her literacy skills. Research has thus focused on how to measure women's awareness of development issues and participation in development activities, commonly termed by aid agencies as 'empowerment'. This chapter aims to show, by contrast, how in-depth ethnographic research can help to explore more fully the links between women's literacy and development. Based on ethnographic research into two women's literacy programmes in Nepal, Robinson-Pant analyses the women participants' experiences of participating in literacy classes and interacting with professional literacy workers. The women's own perspectives on literacy and development are set against the planners' definitions of 'empowerment' and 'women's development'. Ethnographic research, she suggests, can help planners to take into account women's needs and perceptions when designing programmes, though aid agencies familiar only with a quantitative survey approach may encounter many hurdles. The chapter ends by looking at the process of introducing ethnographic research to an aid agency working in women's literacy and health. The challenges and constraints of using ethnography within a programme context are analysed. The introduction of an ideological perspective on women's literacy raised questions as to whether the aid agencies' agenda was to control or empower women through their literacy classes.

An original contribution of the chapter, however, lies in its reflective questioning of what it means to do ethnographic research in an applied context. Debate around the advantages of using ethnographic research in development policy and planning contexts has focused on the contribution that it can make to the developers' understanding: e.g., more in-depth analysis and insight into implementation issues, local meanings of concepts like 'literacy' and a wider perspective on 'evaluation' of projects (see Introduction to this book). There has however been far less discussion about what 'development' does to 'ethnography'. In other words, how does carrying out ethnographic research in a policy context differ from 'pure' academic ethnographic research? Robinson-Pant faces up to this issue through reviewing her own experiences of introducing an ethnographic approach to an American agency implementing literacy and health programmes in Nepal. As well as analysing the mechanics of conducting ethnographic research in an agency more used to traditional questionnaire-based surveys, she looks at the wider issue (addressed in the Introduction with respect to the New Work Order) of how far ethnographic research can be packaged and sold as a product to the developers.

Regie Stites' chapter 'Household literacy environments as contexts for development in rural China' presents a case study of precisely such problems entailed in relating ethnographic style micro studies of literacy in context to macro state policies on literacy and development. He documents literacy environments in two areas within a rural Chinese township: an outlying farming village and the township market centre. The case study compares and contrasts the material and social contexts for reading and writing in the two areas. Drawing primarily from data collected during visits to a hundred households and eight focus group interviews, the case study focuses attention on the literacy environment of the rural household as a context for the changes in literacy practices envisioned in state educational policy. Adult literacy work in rural China can be seen as part of the broader effort to diffuse central ideology and control into peripheral communities and in so doing to reduce the marginality of these communities. As more marginalised populations (rural women, rural and remote communities, ethnic and linguistic minorities) become the target for adult literacy education in China, the effectiveness and appropriateness of the goal of 'mass literacy' and the mass campaign style of literacy promotion are increasingly called into question. The general conclusion of the case study is that the literacy environment of the rural household has been largely untouched by adult literacy work. Although 'outside' literacy environments are being transformed in interaction with social, political and economic development, these 'outside' environments are generally the domain of men. With rare exceptions, rural women have limited access to these 'outside' literacy environments and thus have few opportunities to apply and develop the literacy skills and knowledge conveyed in the adult literacy curriculum. How an ethnographer may intervene in policy in such contexts represents a politically charged question that Stites' work helps us conceptualise if not resolve in more sensitive ways.

Shirin Zubair's 'Literacies, gender and power in rural Pakistan' provides further insights, in this case with respect to Pakistani communities, into actual literacy needs and practices. Despite large statistical surveys, she argues, little is known about how the socio-cultural and political structure of these communities may affect the literacy goals, practices and the significance of literacy itself. The use of ethnographic methods in this study was inspired by the work of contemporary literacy researchers like Heath (1983), Baynham (1995), Barton and Hamilton (1998) and Street (1984, 1995) who have argued that, in order to capture the diversity and complexity of various literacies in such underdeveloped communities, one needs to take account of the ideological issues and social practices that surround people's literacy practices. In this spirit, Zubair conducted ethnographic fieldwork in various phases between June 1996 and March 1998, in two adjoining villages in the Seraiki-speaking area of Southern Punjab, Pakistan, focusing on the lived experiences of thirty-five women. The study, she argues, fills a gap in the existing literature on women's literacy use in such contexts. Unlike the use of ethnography in development policy (Robinson-Pant, also in this volume), her interest in using qualitative, ethnographic approaches

100

stemmed mainly from a theoretical standpoint that was in contrast to the statistical studies available on literacy rates in Pakistani communities. Nevertheless, the findings of her research may feed useful insights into development policy and implementation issues by providing a detailed ethnographic description of how women use literacies to make meanings of their lives, and how power and identities are contested, challenged and negotiated discursively through literacy practices.

Her project initially aimed at building a profile of the literacy repertoire of the community as well as looking at individual trends among various groups. However, like other contributors to this volume, the conditions of fieldwork and the epistemological reflectivity entailed by a contemporary ethnographic perspective led her to change her focus. After the initial stages of fieldwork and data analysis, it became evident that the acquisition and uses of literacy were tied to the ideologies surrounding the expected gender roles in the community. Thus during the course of her research project, the questions changed from who read/ wrote what in which language to how women lived and used literacies, why and how their access to secular literacy was controlled by men and why these women aspired to literacy and education in a particular language. The ethnographic approach used in the research captured these conflicting ideologies and perceptions of literacies in the village community. For instance, whereas women's pre-occupation with literacy envisaged reflection literacy (Hasan 1996) as their target, men – like many development agencies – considered functional literacy would suffice. Hence, says Zubair, 'the uses and conceptions of literacy are caught up in a web of power dynamics of family relationships and genders'.

Another issue of a more methodological nature, that became pressing as she pursued her research, pertained to her own identity, her own role as researcher, a theme that runs throughout this book. As she notes, the issue of power dynamics between the researcher and the researched is crucial in social science research. As she says, Foucauldians and feminists have argued that social science is not a neutral inquiry into human behaviour and institutions. It is a way of exercising power and control over the less privileged and relatively powerless people. How does a researcher committed to local meanings and 'empowerment' but herself already enmeshed in webs of power handle these contradictions? Zubair uses her qualitative methodology – participant observation, case studies and focus groups – in an attempt to face up to these problems, by attempting to give her subjects a voice, thereby empowering them at least to some extent. Acutely aware of the problems involved in representing others through such accounts (see Chopra, this volume), Zubair struggled hard to empower her subjects by making her research methods more open, interactive and dialogic, adjusting her research tools to the villagers' own requirements and trying to deal with the subjects' agendas as well as her own: that is by negotiating and mediating with the subjects and sharing the knowledge she thereby acquired with the subjects who helped her construct that knowledge. The problem of finding a voice for themselves was the main issue identified by some of her subjects and she has endeavoured, but with a real sense of the difficulty of the project, to give a voice of their own to these women, these *silent birds* (in their own words) who have not been heard before. Acutely aware of the limitations of such a project, she argues in the spirit of the 'practical epistemologist' cited above, who never 'completes' a task but is always searching and questioning, that such a response to the dilemmas of 'empowerment' represents some kind of step beyond the simplistic assumptions of modernist 'development'.

It is with such tentative moves that the authors in this book hope to move forward, in ways that respect their subjects' integrity and life meanings but at the same time remain true to the standards of rigour and validity that inform the best of academic research. Whether they have succeeded will to some extent be measured by how far readers engage with the conversation they have inspired and go on themselves to offer further steps. We all look forward to engaging in that conversation.

5

LITERACIES, LANGUAGES AND DEVELOPMENTS IN PERUVIAN AMAZONIA

Sheila Aikman

Introduction

This chapter investigates the relationship between literacy and development in a bilingual society in the Department of Madre de Dios in south-eastern Peru, a region of lowland tropical rainforest bordering with Brazil and Bolivia. It examines different and contested development discourses and practices and the conceptualisations of and expectations for literacy embedded in them. The Harakmbut peoples are currently implementing two development projects, which are conceived within the discourse of the indigenous movement for self-determination. These projects, one concerned with establishing intercultural bilingual education in the primary school and the other an integrated sustainable development strategy are shaped by the Harakmbut people's aims for their self-development and by deteriorating political and environmental conditions pertaining in Madre de Dios. The projects have different implications for the sustainability and development of literacy practices in Harakmbut – a predominantly oral language – and Spanish.

Through an examination of Harakmbut historically situated experience of the development projects of church and state over the twentieth century the chapter seeks to construct an understanding of the Harakmbut approach to literacy which underpins their self-development strategies aimed at challenging these hegemonic agendas. This analysis sets the scene for an examination of literacy demands on the Harakmbut through their self-development projects, in which literacy is currently predominantly unproblematised and 'autonomous'.

The chapter first presents the theoretical approach taken then provides a brief introduction to the ethnographic and linguistic context. The discussion then moves to the heterogeneity of development discourses and practices in the Madre de Dios region and examines the two 'alternative development' projects which the Harakmbut are implementing through their representative indigenous federation. With the premise that motivation to develop literacy will occur when individuals have identified a need to engage in certain practices (see for example Rogers et al. 1999), two examples of literacy practices arising from the implementation of Harakmbut self-development projects will be examined. The chapter ends with a discussion of policy options for the Harakmbut and argues for the importance of utilising understandings of their current literacy practices derived from the ethnography to orient training and project development.

A theoretical approach to the development context in Madre de Dios

The approach here is to form an understanding of the development context in which Harakmbut self-development has arisen. In Latin America today modernity is seen as being very heterogeneous, with a wide range of actors working with partial connections and ambiguities. This highlights the incompatabilities of a range of conceptualisations and aims for development. Arce and Long (2000) write in terms of 'local modernities', which suggests a plurality of modernities existing together in time and space, and in dynamic interaction. Consequently, policies emanating from different ideological positions – government neo-liberal development and indigenous self-development – are being put into practice in shared spaces. Madre de Dios provides an example of this complexity and diversity where a blending and juxtapositioning of elements of different modernities and indigenous alternatives outside of modernity is taking place which challenge false polarities of modern and tradition (Arce and Long 2000). Similarly Harakmbut self-development, then, can be located not within a discussion of indigenous versus mestizo developments but in a locality, a region and a state where the modern and 'premodern' exist together contemporaneously (Kay 1989; Escobar 1995a).

The 1980s in Peru was a period of violence and growing poverty, while at the same time a fragile democracy was established. Democratic electoral processes co-existed with economic policies and neo-liberal development aims focused on economic growth and industrialisation, which had negative effects on the poorest sectors of the population (Yocelevzky 1996). The penetration through the 1990s of private and state enterprise to plunder natural resources, such as gold, timber and oil, to feed this development has further undermined the self-sufficiency of many of the poorest sectors. By the 1990s, the Harakmbut were sorely pressed by colonisation of their territory and depredation of their lands, and faced an uncertain future for their way of life, indigenous language and sense of Harakmbut cultural identity. The political landscape of Peru at the beginning of the twenty-first century promises no quick legislative solutions to the depredation of the Amazon and the recognition of indigenous rights, quite the contrary.

The political and economic deterioration of the 1980s, however, was accompanied by unprecedented forms of collective mobilisation and theoretical renewal in terms of the development of social movements and their analyses of modernity and postmodernity (Escobar 1995a). Social movements are seen as providing a new critique of the discourse and practice of development and are located at the intersection of the micro-processes of meaning production and macro processes of domination (Escobar 1995b). Escobar underlines that the analysis of social movements is not in search of grand structural transformations but for the construction of identities and greater autonomy through modifications in everyday practices and beliefs (1995b: 217). The Harakmbut's representative organisation, FENAMAD (the Federation of Natives of the Madre de Dios), is actively linked with a wider network of indigenous organisations at the Peruvian, Latin American and international levels. It is a social movement which unites indigenous peoples around the globe in their demands for recognition of rights to 'self-determination'. Harakmbut representatives have taken their demands for recognition of their ancestral lands to the United Nations Working Group on Indigenous Populations and support the draft Declaration on the Rights of Indigenous Peoples.

This analysis of development in Madre de Dios, is concerned with understanding the discourse of the indigenous movement and the way in which this is expressed in practice through the Harakmbut concept of self-development. The indigenous self-development discourse locates the struggle in the domain not only of production and economics, but also of meaning (Tucker 1999); it is a development based on social and cultural principles. As such it draws from indigenous knowledges and practices which challenge the hegemonic discourse and practices of neo-liberal economic development. Bonfil (1984) points out that it is not satisfactory to consider indigenous peoples in terms of one sub-culture in a larger more complex national culture because they are not part of the class system where the exploited look for alternatives within the dominant society. On the contrary, indigenous peoples have alternatives outside of this national system and define their legitimacy in terms of their own past and history of exploitation as indigenous people. Since the mid-1980s they have had their own indigenous representative organisation, FENAMAD, which has been developing experience and capacity in defending their rights as indigenous peoples nationally and internationally. The Harakmbut are, nonetheless, working with partial connections and ambiguities, and, taking a pragmatic approach to developing alternatives, are blending and juxtaposing elements of the modernities in which they participate with their indigenous values and meaningful cultural priorities. We are therefore concerned not only with development as a multiplicity of expressions of modernities, but with multiple realities and multiple views of development (Pottier 1993: 28).

Language and literacy in Madre de Dios

The Harakmbut-speaking peoples comprise seven groups and number approximately 1,800–2,000 people. The largest group is the Arakmbut who number some 1,200. Recent linguistic research indicates that Harakmbut is unrelated to neighbouring indigenous languages (Helberg 1996) and each group speaks a different dialect (Pozzi-Escot 1998). Until the introduction of the Spanish language through 'civilising' agendas from the 'outside', the Harakmbut had an oral tradition.

The communicative practices of the Harakmbut can be described in terms of the two languages which they use: Spanish is used exclusively in the inter-ethnic domain for communicating with non-Harakmbut speakers, while within communities communication is primarily in Harakmbut, that is, within families, between families and between members of the Harakmbut-speaking groups. As marriage between Harakmbut and non-Harakmbut increases – as has been slowly happening since 1980 – Spanish is being used more frequently than in the past. While children of mixed marriages usually learn and speak Harakmbut there are now instances in some communities where children are growing up as monolingual Spanish speakers with only a passive understanding of Harakmbut.[1]

The Spanish language is used as a lingua franca with and between settlers and colonists, though some of the latter may be Quechua first-language speakers. Spanish is the language of commerce, the legal system and the education system. Today, after several decades of sustained contact with the wider Peruvian society, the Harakmbut wear Western clothes, work gold, buy beer and in some cases employ highland workers as gold diggers. All but a few of the oldest generation speak Spanish and everyone under 50 years of age has attended some formal schooling, which is exclusively in Spanish, a situation which the bilingual intercultural project aims to change.

In order to understand the meanings and uses of literacy for the Harakmbut from their particular perspectives of the 'realities of development' it is important to understand the way in which different meanings of literacy and different literacies have been embedded in approaches to development, and how these have contributed to Harakmbut understandings of literacy today. As Street (this volume) discusses, the focus is on what literacy means in specific contexts and for specific groups of people. This raises such questions as: What do the Harakmbut consider counts as literacy? In what ways have they 'taken hold of literacy' (Kulick and Stroud 1993)? The question is not what impact literacy has had on the Harakmbut (Finnegan 1999), but what are the implications of the autonomous approaches to literacy taken by the dominant development discourses on Harakmbut literacy practices and expectations today.

The context in which the Harakmbut live and work is overwhelmingly oral but official documents determine to a large degree the nature of social interaction in development activities, and this permits an examination of the ways in which oral and written usage are part of one continuum. As Besnier (1999) notes, the spoken language provides literacy with a particular socio-cultural meaning and links it to ideological formations underlying local conceptions of the truth, the self. How do spoken and written language interrelate in the Harakmbut's social practices and project activities? Everyone brings different language practices and knowledge to a literacy event. Although, as Street (this volume) notes, an examination of literacy events can remain at the level of description, there is, nevertheless, a need for an examination of the practices brought together at key 'development events' in Madre de Dios. What is the nature of literacy mediation in such circumstances (drawing on work by Barton and Hamilton 1998 and Kelman 1999)?

Our approach will be to explore literacy as a situated practice, rooted in particular sets of power relations, ideological understandings and commonly accepted rules of behaviour (Heath 1999; Street 1999). How, then, do the Harakmbut use literacy for specific development practices and how can they ensure that 'literacy works for them' (Meek 1991)?

The potential contribution of ethnography

Commitment to an approach that examines alternative practices to the grand narratives of development means resisting the desire to formulate alternatives at an abstract, macro level and resist the notion that alternative understandings will develop in intellectual and academic circles (Escobar 1995a). Escobar (1995b: 221) insists that the idea that theory is produced in one place and applied in another is no longer acceptable practice; on the contrary, investigations of social movements provide examples of 'travelling theories' – a process of multiple conversations in a discontinuous terrain. This demands an ethnography which has moved beyond static descriptions of abstract idealised systems, and provides an intensive study of the local social arena (Giddens 1995) and which responds to development as negotiated, socially constructed, and a never-ending inter-action between many social actors (Pottier 1993).

This chapter is concerned with the expression and practice of a particular social movement, its articulation of an alternative development and the nature of the literacy practices it encompasses. Alternative developments are contextualised and have their own histories, which impact on the construction of conceptions of literacy and oracy. Constructing an understanding of this alternative develop-ment and the place of literacy involves constructing an appreciation of the com-plexity and contestations of literacies and developments (Arce and Long 2000). Ethnography provides the detailed contextualised information needed for an analysis of the Harakmbut's unarticulated assumptions and understandings of their needs and motivation for acquiring literacy and language skills. But there is another important need for an ethnographic approach which is linked to the nature of the relationship between the researcher and the researched. Where the researcher is engaged with current affairs and contemporary social and political issues, she can contribute towards the formulation of policy and the development of strategies (Ahmed and Shore 1995). This chapter aims to 'cross the divide' (Street, this volume) between academic and applied concerns, between theory and practice.

The fieldwork for this chapter is based on recent annual visits to the Madre de Dios region which have allowed me to work with many of the different Harakmbut peoples, but in particular with the Arakmbut of the Karene River.[2]

My ongoing ethnographic research with the Arakmbut since 1980 has examined processes of change and 'development' in relation to schooling, language and territory. Through this work I have tried to 'contextualise particular sets of recurring global issues' (Pottier 1993) and examine them as social constructs in an attempt to illuminate possible directions or strategies for Harakmbut self-development in areas of education and language use. Some of this writing has been directly produced under the auspices of FENAMAD as an input into indigenous policy making (Aikman 1992), and some as a contribution to discussions on Harakmbut bilingual education policy with indigenous leaders, linguists, anthropologists and NGOs working actively in this field in Peru. Other writing has had the aim of contributing to debates on indigenous educational practice and policy development at the national and international level (Aikman 1996, 1998, 1999a). Through an ethnographic investigation of the meaning of literacy for the Harakmbut embedded in their self-development, this chapter aims to contribute to a continuous questioning of the processes, assumptions and agencies involved in development and contribute some insights upon which the Harakmbut can choose to reflect in the course of their ongoing policy making and project implemention. As 'self-motivating actors capable of exerting their own influences' (Long and Van der Ploeg in Pottier 1993; see also Gardner and Lewis 1996) the Harakmbut are masters of their own self-determination.

Developments and literacy in the Madre de Dios

The Harakmbut peoples have no word for development. What an Harakmbut man and woman want out of life for themselves and their children is expressed in terms of new technologies and opportunities for sustaining or recuperating the quality of their lives, having enough to eat and making sure outsiders do not take resources which are essential for the community to continue as it always has done (Gray 1997). This is not to say that the Harakmbut are opposed to change. For them development comes from outside and can be either beneficial or destructive depending on the circumstances (ibid.). Since their first sustained contact at the beginning of the twentieth century, the Harakmbut have been on the receiving end of development agendas of the state, the church, individual entrepreneurs and multinationals. This section considers three agendas which are important for the Harakmbut peoples, the meanings they have constructed for literacy and for the future of their territories in the twenty-first century: Dominican proselytisation and 'civilisation'; Peruvian state development policies and Harakmbut self-development.

Missionary proselytisation – Spanish-language literacy as 'progress'

The Dominican missionaries who penetrated the Madre de Dios region in the early twentieth century to pacify and convert the 'natives' of the region believed that the indigenous peoples should be integrated into the state, rather than excluded from state-centred approaches to 'progress'. This 'indigenist' approach, based on difference in terms of cultural and socio-economic factors rather than race, was a challenge to the Peruvian state's racial and imperialist frame of thinking at the time (Gray 1997).

Expressed in terms of a 'conquest' (Rummenholler 1987), the Dominicans' mission encompassed not only the religious but also the social, cultural and moral lives of the indigenous peoples. The Dominicans aimed to accomplish their 'civilising' task through education and production (Misiones Dominicanas n.d.: 51). Through a process of 'de-education' the indigenous peoples would shed their savagery and unlearn and be rid of their values and beliefs, acquiring in their place, through 're-education', beliefs and values that the missionaries considered essential (Osende 1933: 228). The Harakmbut were coerced into adopting a sedentary existence, living in small nuclear family huts and becoming agriculturalists and pastoralists (at least temporarily) while leaving aside their communal houses and hunting and gathering practices. For the Dominicans, civilisation, or what they later called 'modernisation', was achieved through formal education, which prioritised literacy, because 'without Spanish the savage's soul is closed to the light [and] unable to enter fully into civilisation, religion and the life of the nation' (Sarasola 1931). In Madre de Dios, as in many other parts of the Amazon, the Spanish language and the evangelical message brought with them the enormous weight of Western civilisation (Castillero 1997).

The modernising state – from literacy as Spanification to biliteracy

Assimilation and integration have been the hallmarks of national policy towards indigenous peoples throughout Latin America, including Peru, for most of the twentieth century. Since the return to democracy in 1980, integration in Peru has involved the recognition of a hierarchy of rights, with individual rights and equal citizenship taking precedence over indigenous peoples' collective rights to territory and self-government (Gray 1997). Collective rights recognised in the 1970s and 1980s have been undermined in the 1993 Peruvian Constitution when the government unilaterally violated the principle of inalienability by ending prohibitions on the mortgaging of indigenous lands (Colchester and Gray 1998). Successive recent governments' vision of the rainforest has been as a national and social panacea for problems elsewhere in the country to be solved through agricultural colonisation of the Amazon as an unexploited resource (Walter 1987).

Schooling has been seen by government as an important means of in-corporating the indigenous population through the direct influence of a national (Spanish-language) curriculum. Early experiments with bilingual education in the Andes had an integrationist flavour and a transitional policy (Citarella 1990). In Madre de Dios, the Dominican missionaries established a school network (the

Educational Network for the Southern Peruvian Amazon – RESSOP) which still today runs many of the primary schools in Harakmbut communities where the national curriculum is taught through Spanish-medium teaching (Aikman 1994).

The articulation of schooling with Spanish-language literacy has continued to be a strong feature of education for indigenous peoples and in the 1960s a small group of linguists began to voice their concern that the language of schooling (Spanish) was confused with the aims of education and that school literacy was being seen as synonymous with 'Spanification' as if this was one single process (Pozzi-Escot 1998). They accused the Ministry of Education of uncritically treating Peru as a monolingual Spanish-speaking country. For the Harakmbut who attended either Dominican missionary or Ministry of Education schools, schooling has been and still means 'learning Spanish' (Aikman 1999a). By the 1990s state education was being condemned for being 'very very poor quality' (Iguinez 1995) and directly driven by a World Bank economic development model (Coraggio 1995).

After almost two decades of debate and government U-turns intercultural bilingual (biliterate) education (IBE) still has a presence within the Peruvian Ministry of Education. IBE is on the official agenda, although the monolingual Spanish educational practice continues for the vast majority of indigenous students. For the entire course of its existence, formal schooling has been synonymous with Spanish-language education and, moreover, 'knowing Spanish', whether written and/or spoken, has continued to be synonymous with being 'civilised', 'developed', 'modern' and Peruvian (Aikman 1999a). The Harakmbut experience of formal schooling since the 1950s has been that school is a place where children learn to read and write Spanish. In Madre de Dios, as in many other places, schooling promotes literacy, and, as many studies have shown, it promotes a particular type of literacy which is embedded in particular power relations (Heath 1983; Street 1995). Literacy is presented within this formal schooling environment as a set of neutral techniques to be mastered in order to access knowledge and skills which will 'modernise' and 'develop' the individual. Thus the education and development discourses of modernity in Madre de Dios have brought with them strongly defined constructions of literacy and what literacy can do for the Harakmbut.

Indigenous self-development

The Harakmbut want to combine the positive aspects of their own lifestyles, including ensuring secure access to their resources of meat, crops and gold, with the benefits accruing to the settlers living around them of access to clean drinking water, television and participation in the market economy. When the Harakmbut are not in agreement with a proposed outside development initiative, such as the building of a road through their land, they challenge the road because they see it as exploiting their lands and resources, while the colonists see this as opening up the area for communication and trade. In this way the Harakmbut are exercising their self-determination to promote their own alternative to mainstream development (Bonfil 1984; Escobar 1995b). The Harakmbut people's own vision of development, their self-development, is outside the culturally based idea of 'development' and its Western framework of progress and degeneration. Self-development for the Harakmbut does not consist simply of economic factors but covers all dimensions of indigenous life – social, cultural and political.

Gray (1997) describes how 'development', from an indigenous perspective, is frequently seen as negative because of its associations with political-economic state-oriented growth models or as the justification for the neo-colonial extraction of resources from indigenous territories. Yet this 'development' can also provide badly needed resources to protect and promote indigenous rights. Indigenous peoples have been discussing alternative development based in the ability of indigenous peoples to become self-supporting. Henriksen (1989) explains: 'The idea should not be one of privatisation of rural indigenous economies, but collective or community developments which are determined by the recipients who become the subjects of development.' Therefore, if new technologies or alopathic medicines can make life easier or cure new diseases, such as tuberculosis, they are welcomed, but the Harakmbut reserve the right to consent to their use or introduction (Gray 1997).

Similarly, the Harakmbut recognise the importance of Spanish for promotion of their self-development agenda and its key role in facilitating access to the provision of resources to protect and promote indigenous rights, such as an understanding of legal documents, lobbying ministries or negotiating with salesmen for fair deals. Spanish is the lingua franca not only of the Madre de Dios but of Peru and Latin America and is an official language of the United Nations. They hold the view that schooling provides them with Spanish and that their children have a right to schooling because it teaches them Spanish (Aikman 1999a). Thus they view Spanish literacy as autonomous.

The two development projects currently being implemented by the Harakmbut within their framework of self-development provide an illustration of Harakmbut self-development in practice: these are (1) Programme for Intercultural Bilingual Education (IBE) and (2) Territorial Consolidation and Sustainable Development Project. The next section looks briefly at these and the literacy practices embedded in them.

Intercultural Bilingual Education – formal schooling and Harakmbut literacy

The Programme for Intercultural Bilingual Education for the Madre de Dios, a joint Ministry of Education and European Union project (FORTE-PE), is financed by the European Union. It is a primary schooling project being co-implemented by FENAMAD and the Ministry of Education and is part of an Amazon-wide IBE programme aimed at establishing a new mode of basic education for indigenous children (ISPL/AIDESEP 1997). It focuses on training Harakmbut teachers according to a model based on indigenous conceptions of self-development and interculturalism and on an analysis of the history of relations between indigenous society and wider national society. It rejects a transitional approach to bilingual education where mother-tongue literacy is conceived of as merely a bridge to Spanish literacy and, on the contrary, emphasises an 'additive' approach (Baker 1996) valuing the mother tongue in its own right as a language of education and a language of cultural expression and transmission. It is a biliterate model of education and Harakmbut are currently being trained as linguists to begin the complex process of defining an orthography and producing written materials in the Harakmbut language.

This programme was developed and designed by the Inter-ethnic Association for the Development of the Peruvian Amazon, an Amazon-wide indigenous umbrella organisation. It developed out of demands for an education which respected indigenous children's heritage and built on the realities of the lives they led. Over a period of ten years indigenous professionals and non-indigenous professionals collaborated to produce the model for training and a new primary curriculum (ISPL/AIDESEP 1997). These curricula are based in principles of the indigenous movement and laid down in the document Committee on Indigenous Education (1998). This programme recognises intercultural bilingual education as a right.

In its conceptualisation and development in the northern Amazon, the IBE model challenges the former dominant structures and hegemony of formal education. However, in its implementation in Madre de Dios it is faced with a contradiction: it is to be implemented in collaboration with and through the education structure founded and controlled by the Dominican missionaries.

Territorial Consolidation and Sustainable Development – informal education and Spanish literacy practices

The project for 'Territorial Consolidation and Sustainable Development in Madre de Dios, Peru' is known locally as the 'Plan Karene'. It is funded by DANIDA and implemented by FENAMAD with support from the International Work Group for Indigenous Affairs (IWGIA), Copenhagen. The project came into being through a long process of community-level discussions and priority setting in the early 1990s by Arakmbut elders who were very worried about the destruction of their lands, and with it their livelihoods as hunters and gatherers. They drew on non-indigenous support to produce the project proposal, and for its implementation FENAMAD employs a team of specialists – some indigenous some not (see Aikman 1998).

The project has two main foci: territorial defence and economic sustainability based on self-sufficiency. The territorial component incorporates a strategy to decolonise Harakmbut land by strengthening its legally recognised boundaries, removing settlers through legal action and providing training in indigenous rights and Peruvian law. It is intended that the removal of colonists will set the conditions for the rejuvenation of a more efficient subsistence production and allow the Harakmbut to recover their former diversity of crops and sever a growing dependency on purchased foodstuffs. It is also supporting the sustainable production of forest products, which will promote a broad-spectrum economy and provide access to the regional market economy.

Now beginning its second phase, this project is preparing to focus on non-formal education in a range of areas including community organisation, territorial defence and small-animal husbandry in order to help the Harakmbut take on the challenge of self-development. An important component of this phase is the establishment of a council of elders to encourage and promote teaching and learning about the social, cultural and political dimensions of the Harakmbut way of life.

Both projects are formulated within the framework of the indigenous movement and Harakmbut self-development: the IBE project focuses on providing an alternative to hegemonic primary education which rejects Harakmbut knowledge and language; and the Plan Karene focuses on providing an alternative economic development based in an Harakmbut holistic conceptualisation of their productive activities within their cosmological system (Gray 1997). The response in the Harakmbut communities to each of these projects is, however, quite different. While the Plan Karene developed out of community participation and problem-setting and is addressing what Harakmbut see as their immediate concerns, the IBE programme has been developed elsewhere, albeit by indigenous organisations, and has as its goal long-term change. Furthermore, the members of the Harakmbut communities have complex relations with the school. Many Harakmbut welcome Harakmbut knowledge and language within the institution of the school, while others are wary of having a direct involvement with an institution which has hitherto been the domain of missionaries or mestizo teachers. Still others are concerned that bilingual schooling will lead to loss of status and prestige in the eyes of the wider Peruvian society and reinforce their 'otherness'.[3]

In the IBE project literacy has a strong role to play, both Spanish-language literacy and Harakmbut literacy. There biliterate nature of the schooling has been read as an integral part of the programme from its inception, and though the approach to intercultural education is highly theorised and interrogated, Spanish literacy and mother-tongue literacy still appear to be conceived as an 'autonomous' practice. For its part, the Plan Karene documents make no reference to language or literacy, neither of which has been identified as a specific issue for debate or area in need of investigation. The autonomous approach to literacy and languages which has been identified throughout the examination of developments in Madre de Dios has produced a situation where the nature of communications practices are 'invisible' factors in the development process. Yet, this is not to say that the Harakmbut do not participate in complex and demanding communication practices and literacy events.

Literacies for self-development

The Plan Karene is a project of FENAMAD, which comprises indigenous political leaders elected by constitutent communities. The project is implemented by two indigenous co-ordinators and a small team of specialists, some of whom are indigenous, some not. Project management and implementation require a range of literacy practices, for example report and agenda writing, planning meetings and project documents, accounting and administration, media dissemination of information, and myriad other activities associated with projects and accountability. The Plan Karene has no formal language policy; all literacy is in Spanish and meetings, visits and training usually take place in Spanish too, although, wherever possible, Harakmbut-speakers are used in an effort to incorporate monolingual women and elders into the project activities and promote ownership.

The members of the project team – co-ordinator, cartographer, lawyer, agronomist and anthropologist – act as mediators in their respective capacities to facilitate negotiations between the communities and colonists, Ministry officials and a range of bureaucrats, and deal with technical procedures. The Harakmbut community members bring specialist understanding to the project in a whole range of areas – the nature of their territory, cultural practices and values, flora and fauna, history and sprirituality. Together indigenous and non-indigenous work closely together, using the necessary combinations of oracy and literacy, to move towards the resolution of conflict and satisfaction of goals. The following are two examples of literacies integral to the project.

A legal literacy event

In August 1999 I was privy to a literacy event which brought together an Harakmbut elder, an Harakmbut university graduate working in the Plan Karene as a co-ordinator, and a group of Quechua migrants/colonists. The event took place on a beach where there was a discussion about land tenure and infringement of Harakmbut land rights by one of the colonist families. In the course of the event no texts were written or read yet the power of the written legal word underpinned all interaction, communication and decisions. The discussion centred around defined rights to the land enshrined in national legislation and indigenous versus colonist claims. The colonists were asked by the Harakmbut co-ordinator to provide the legal documentation as proof of their claim, which the colonists could not do.

The Harakmbut were adopting a 'legal literate strategy' for defending their lands, lands which they knew intimately, a landscape which contained their history and spirituality, a forest which had satisfied their physical and spiritual needs until national development policies had declared open season in it. After decades of trying to ignore colonists, followed by attempts to work in respectful collaboration, they had not succeeded in protecting the natural resources on which they depended. Now their strategy included utilising Peruvian legislation, although in the Madre de Dios the written law was rarely enforced and, however authoritative and forceful it sounded on paper, in practice it could be negotiated and ignored.

The indigenous project co-ordinator knew the law and its protocols, and he knew the rights of the Harakmbut and how they articulated with other laws, such as those concerning agriculture and mining. He also knew how to talk with the colonists, in particular how to avoid conflict and arguments, which can easily flare into violence in such encounters. Kelman (1999) in a different context discusses the way in which literacy mediators abbreviate the distance between the powerful and the less powerful. Here the co-ordinator was acting as a mediator between the elder whose ancestral territory was being destroyed and the Quechua migrant who was intent on eking out a subsistence living on what appeared to him to be virgin forest. The co-ordinator translated between languages (Harakmbut and Spanish) and also between discourses and cultural conventions.

In the process of defending their land the Harakmbut were learning about other aspects of the written legal word – that it is not 'written in stone'. However ponderous and definitive the Peruvian legislation may sound, it is subject to change. Changes brought about by decrees, suspension of the Constitution and the passing of a new Constitution turn the word of law into a quagmire of documents which contradict, annul, confuse and obfuscate the process of trying to use this means of protecting their territory. Whatever the written word states, the Harakmbut still have to face unrepentant settlers, aggressive and 'superior' colonists, drunk and aggressive tradesmen, and even threatening gold panners – and when the death threats come they are never written down.

Training in small-animal husbandry

A training programme in small-animal husbandry (chickens, ducks and guinea pigs) was a part of the early phase of the project designed to involve the women who mainly tend small animals around their houses. The women have tended hens and ducks for many years but disease wipes out the stocks at regular intervals and purchased medicines are beyond the means of the women. The project's non-indigenous agronomist visited the communities and gave advice to the women, including distributing medicines. He began preparing written manuals to support training for the women in constructing weather-proof hen houses, diagnosing chicken flu, and administering vitamins. Spanish-language manuals existed from other projects for the non-indigenous population in the region but in the end were not utilised in the Plan Karene because the target group (women) had low or no reading ability in Spanish. Moreover, in a social and cultural environment which is overwhelmingly oral, written manuals in either Spanish or Harakmbut were unlikely to be the women's preferred way of learning. A subsequent indigenous trainer has focused on spending informal time with the women and learning about the different local remedies which the women have been using and discussing together how to improve their success.

The use of literacy materials in training in this project needs to be subject to scrutiny. In an oral context which focuses on practical skills and knowledge with adult learners who bring to the situation a lot of experience, the use of written documents in Spanish may be severely limited. For training, such as in small-animal husbandry, the language and literacy needs of communities have to be carefully evaluated so that training activities are appropriate and support and learning are in keeping with the learning strategies of the learners. In short, an explicit consideration of language and literacy is necessary at the level of project planning.

But the analysis must go further and ask which literacy practices in which language? And, as the small-animal husbandry example illustrates, it must also ask: is literacy really necessary? Are there times and places where literacy may hinder rather than help? In a society where communication, knowledge, learning and teaching are oral practices, the value of literacies and the languages of literacy in self-development need to be carefully assessed. Here, in practice, Harakmbut self-development is challenging the relationship between development and literacy.

Conclusion

The Harakmbut people's objectives for self-development, as we have seen, are to strengthen their way of life through the protection of their traditional territory and the rejuvenation of their diversity of economic activities, all of which are deeply embedded in their cultural, social and spiritual practices. The Plan Karene addresses these objectives by prioritising an Harakmbut alternative to the development agendas being promoted by the state and the church and through current trends in global capitalism. Its strategies for achieving an alternative to development, nevertheless, are wide ranging and drawn from indigenous and non-indigenous society.

The Plan Karene demands a range of sophisticated literacy practices and a subtle analysis of context for an appropriate use of different languages at different times. It illustrates the importance of examining oral and literate practices as part of a continuum of communicative strategies and resources, which complement each other and are intimately intertwined in specific social events. An understanding of processes of mediation emerges as important for facilitating communication, especially in intercultural and multilingual contexts. What do different participants bring to a 'literacy event' and how do they participate?

The IBE project prioritises Harakmbut school literacy. The aims of this project are long term and are couched in a discourse of rights: rights to education in the mother tongue, to equal treatment of Harakmbut with Spanish in the school, to its equal status with Spanish and to its development in a written form. Mother-tongue school literacy as a right has the potential to raise the status of the Harakmbut language in educational terms but, as an 'autonomous' literacy, its contribution to self-development will remain limited. However, if the FENAMAD

IBE project can initiate a discussion and investigation of uses and demands for Harakmbut literacy or literacies outside the school, then it could be a powerful and valuable approach for the strengthening of an Harakmbut way of life.

At the beginning of this chapter questions were posed about what counts as literacy and how the Harakmbut have taken hold of literacy for their own uses. From ethnographic analysis, it appears that literacy is shrouded in unproblematised and 'autonomous' conceptions of literacy as a set of Spanish-language skills acquired in school through a pedagogic process that has no links with Harakmbut language, society or culture. Nevertheless, the Plan Karene provides examples of different contexts where Harakmbut of different age, gender and language ability tackle a wide range of literate and oral practices in Spanish. In what ways can the Harakmbut 'take hold of literacy' and use it to achieve their goals of self-development? Can the ethnography suggest ways to strengthen their abilities to succeed in this project of adapting, resisting and transforming literate and oral knowledges and practices to suit their own development?

The Plan Karene has the support of the Harakmbut as a grassroots-initiated project with which they identify. Its aims for the next phase of implementation are to focus on a diversity of training to provide Harakmbut with skills and knowledge to promote their self-determination. This will include training in more effective and efficient use of current resources such as forest produce, community organisation and how to utilise the native community management structure imposed by the state. Thus the Plan Karene provides a motivating context for training and learning at community level which will bring the Harakmbut into contact with an even greater range of literacies. At present the Harakmbut have no articulated awareness of the language and communication dimensions to the project, and no specific literacy strategy. Language and literacy training need to be part of a communication strategy developed in an understanding of the wider oral and literate communicative practices, the potential of mother-tongue literacy and the 'ideological' nature of language use.

In August 1999 FENAMAD held a series of community-level meetings to debate their priorities for Harakmbut self-development. They began by examining the main myth of their oral canon, Wanamey, and from it they distilled three pillars for their self-development: territory, culture and organisation. The Harakmbut language – a key to knowledge, the spirit world and reproduction – is the cornerstone of this self-development agenda. The Spanish language, both oral and written, will support the development process as the Harakmbut use what they consider useful and positive from outside development agendas and reject what they see as contrary to their goals. Ethnography can provide important insights into the shared spaces in which the Harakmbut blend and juxtapose elements of different modernities and articulate their indigenous alternatives to these. An ethnographic study can help define the underlying meanings and uses of literacy and language in the context of Madre de Dios and provide important insights for project planning and policy making for Harakmbut self-development. In this way ethnography may contribute a particular set of perspectives of the local social arena where development is a negotiated, socially constructed and never-ending interaction between many social actors. It is for those defining and implementing their own alternative development, such as the Harakmbut, to decide how to utilise the ethnographic data and produce a reflexive policy making based in practice.

Notes

1 For details of the Harakmbut linguistic ecology see Aikman 1999b.
2 I would like to the thank the Harakmbut and the leadership of FENAMAD for their continuing support for my work. I would also like to acknowledge the National Academy of Education/Spencer Foundation for the Postdoctoral Fellowship which funded my research in Madre de Dios in 1998 and 1999.
3 See Aikman 1999a for details of reactions to intercultural bilingual schooling in the community of San Jose.

References

Ahmed, A. and Shore, C. (1995) 'Introduction: Is Anthropology Relevant to the Contemporary World?', in A. Ahmed and C. Shore (eds), *The Future of Anthropology: Its Relevance to the Contemporary World*, London: Athlone.

Aikman, S. (1992) 'Investigaciones en educacion intercultural de los Harakmbut', preliminary report for FENAMAD, manuscript.

—— (1994) 'Intercultural Education and Harakmbut Identity: A Case Study of the Community of San Jose in Southeastern Peru', PhD thesis, University of London.

—— (1996) 'Language, Literacy and Bilingual Education: An Amazon People's Strategies for Cultural Maintenance', *International Journal of Educational Development* 15(4): 411–22.

—— (1998) 'Towards an Intercultural Participatory Approach to Learning for the Harakmbut', *International Journal of Educational Development* 18(2): 197–206.

—— (1999a) *Intercultural Education and Literacy*, Amsterdam: John Benjamins.

—— (1999b) 'Sustaining Indigenous Languages in Southeastern Peru', *International Journal of Bilingual Education and Bilingualism* 2(3): 198–213.

Arce, A. and Long, N. (2000) 'Reconfiguring Modernity and Development from an Anthropological Perspective', in A. Arce and N. Long (eds), *Anthropology, Development and Modernities: Exploring Discourses, Counter-Tendencies and Violence*, London: Routledge.

Baker, C. (1996) *Foundations of Bilingual Education and Bilingualism*, 2nd edition, Clevedon: Multilingual Matters.

Barton, D. and Hamilton, M. (1998) *Local Literacies: Reading and Writing in One Community*, London: Routledge.

Besnier, N. (1999) 'Orality and Literacy', in D. Wagner, R. Venezky and B. Street (eds), *Literacy: An International Handbook*, Boulder, CO: Westview Press.

Bonfil, G. (1984) 'Del Indigenismo de la Revolucion a la Antropologia Critica', in C. Junqueira and E. Carvalho (eds), *Los Indios y la Antropologia en America Latina*, Buenos Aires: Ediciones Busquedas.

Castillero, A. (1997) 'Las Barreras Linguisticas de la Evangelizacion', in J. Calvo Perez and J.C. Godenzzi (eds), *Multilinguismo y Educacion Bilingue en America y Espana*, Cusco: Casa Bartholome de las Casas.

Citarella, L. (1990) 'Peru', in F. Chiodi (compiler), *La Educacion Indigena en America Latina*, Vol. II, Quito: Abya-Yala/UNESCO/Orealc.

Colchester, M. and Gray, A. (1998) *From Principles to Practice: Indigenous Peoples and Biodiversity Conservation in Latin America*, IWGIA Document 87, Copenhagen: IWGIA.

Committee on Indigenous Education (1998) 'Our Children, Our Future', Draft Working Document presented to the UN Working Group on Indigenous Peoples, Geneva, July.

Coraggio, J.L. (1995) 'Intervencion', in V.E. Edwards and J. Osorio Vargas (organisers), *La Construccion de las Politicas Educativas en America Latina*, Lima: CEAAL/Tarea.

Escobar, A. (1995a) *Encountering Development: The Making and Unmaking of the Third World*, Princeton, NJ: Princeton University Press.

—— (1995b) 'Imagining a Post-Development Era', in J. Crush (ed.), *Power of Development*, London: Routledge.

Finnegan, R. (1999) 'Sociological and Anthropological Issues in Literacy', in D. Wagner, R. Venezky and B. Street (eds), *Literacy: An International Handbook*, Boulder, CO: Westview Press.

Gardner, K. and Lewis, D. (1996) *Anthropology, Development and the Post-Modern Challenge*, London: Pluto Press.

Giddens, A. (1995) 'Epilogue: Notes on the Future of Anthropology', in A. Ahmed and C. Shore (eds), *The Future of Anthropology: Its Relevance to the Contemporary World*, London: Athlone.

Gray, A. (1997) *Indigenous Rights and Development: Self-Determination in an Amazonian Community*, Oxford: Berghahn Books.

Heath, S.B. (1983) *Ways with Words: Language, Life and Work in Communities and Classrooms*, Cambridge: Cambridge University Press.

—— (1999) 'Literacy and Social Practice', in D. Wagner, R. Venezky and B. Street (eds), *Literacy: An International Handbook*, Boulder, CO: Westview Press.

Helberg, H. (1996) *Mbaisik: en la Penumbra del Atardecer*, Lima: Centro Amazonico de Antropologia y Aplicacion Practica.

Henriksen, G. (1989) 'Introduction', in *IWGIA Indigenous Self-development in the Americas*, Copenhagen: IWGIA Document 63.

Iguinez, M. (1995) 'Intervencion', in V.E. Edwards and J. Osorio Vargas (organisers), *La Construccion de las Politicas Educativas en America Latina*, Lima: CEAAL/Tarea.

ISPL/AIDESEP (1997) *Lineamientos Curriculares: Formacion Magisterial en la Especialidad de Educacion Primaria Intercultural Bilingue*, Iquitos: Instituto Superior Pedagogico Loreto/Asociacion Interetnica de Desarrollo de la Selva Peruana.

Kay, C. (1989) *Latin American Theories of Development and Underdevelopment*, London: Routledge.

Kelman, J. (1999) *Writing on the Plaza: Mediated Literacy Practices among Scribes and Clients in Mexico City*, Cresskill, NJ: Hampton Press.

Kulick, D. and Stroud, C. (1993) 'Conceptions and Uses of Literacy in a Papua New Guinean village', in B.V. Street (ed.), *Cross-Cultural Approaches to Literacy*, Cambridge: Cambridge University Press.

Meek, M. (1991) *On Being Literate*, London: Bodley Head.

Misiones Dominicanas (n.d.) *Alma de la Selva*, Lima: Misiones Dominicanas.

Osende, V. (1933) 'Observaciones sobre el Salvajismo', *Misiones Dominicanas del Peru* 15(79): 228–30.

Pottier, J. (1993) 'The Role of Ethnography in Project Appraisal', in J. Pottier (ed.), *Practising Development: Social Science Perspectives*, London: Routledge.

119

Pozzi-Escot, I. (1993) 'Reflexiones sobre la Politica Linguistica Peruana', *Amazonia Peruana* 12(23): 15–36.

—— (1998) *El Multilinguismo en el Peru*, Cusco: PROEB ANDES/ABC.

Rogers, A., Maddox, B., Millican, J., Newell Jones, K., Papen, U. and Robinson-Pant, A. (1999) *Re-defining Post-Literacy in a Changing World*, London: Department for International Development.

Rummenholler, K. (1987) *Tieflandindios im Goldrausch: Die Auswirkungen des Goldbooms auf die Harakmbut im Madre de Dios, Peru*, Bonn: Mundus Reihe Ethnologie 12.

Sarasola, S. (1931) 'La Educacion de la Mujer en Nuestro Colegio de Misiones', *Misiones Dominicanas del Peru* 13(62): 1–13.

Street, B. (1984) *Literacy in Theory and Practice*, Cambridge: Cambridge University Press.

—— (1995) *Social Literacies: Critical Perspectives on Literacy in Development, Ethnography and Education*, London: Longman.

—— (1999) 'Meanings of Culture in Development', in A. Little and F. Leach (eds), *Schools, Culture and Economics in the Developing World: Tensions and Conflicts*, New York: Garland Press.

Tucker, V. (1999) 'The Myth of Development: A Critique of a Eurocentric Discourse', in R. Munck and D. O'Hearn (eds), *Critical Development Theory: Contributions to a New Paradigm*, London: Zed Books.

Walter, C. (1987) 'El Uso Oficial de la Selva en el Peru Republicano', *Amazonia Peruana* 8(14): 61–90.

Yocelevzky, R. (1996) 'Introduccion: La Democracia en America Latina', in R. Yocelevzky (ed.), *Experimentos con la Democracia en America Latina*, Mexico DF: Universidad Autonoma Metropolitana.

6

ANOTHER LANGUAGE, ANOTHER LITERACY?

Practices in northern Ghana

Pat Herbert and Clinton Robinson

Introduction

Literacy implies the use of a language. This is entirely self-evident, though reports of literacy efforts have been written without reference to the language in which people have acquired their literacy competence (cf. Robinson 1992). In situations where there are several languages, the question of the language of literacy ought to be one of the first posed – all the more where some languages have a script, or a long written tradition, and others do not. Recent concern about the nature of different literacies points to the need to examine the place of language in differentiating between literacies. This chapter looks at evidence for the relationship between languages and literacies in the multilingual context of northern Ghana. After clarifying some terms and concepts, we present observed literacy practices, in an attempt to understand how multilingual usage by individuals and communities affects such practices. We conclude by asking in what ways languages, in this context, are determinants of different literacies.

Many definitions of literacy have been suggested, but there is no scholarly consensus. There has been a radical shift away from the dominant view of literacy as a neutral, technological skill – unaffected by social contexts, and bringing with it cognitive consequences for change – towards a broader view whereby material and social conditions determine the outcome (Verhoeven 1994; Street 1995; Triebel 1997). Street labels the earlier view as the *autonomous* model and the later one as the *ideological* model. He defines literacy in this model as 'a social construction not a neutral technology: it varies from one culture or subgroup to another and its uses are embedded in relations of power and struggles over resources' (Street 1984: 28).

For Street and those who subscribe to this latter model, the reference is not to *literacy*, but to *literacies* (Triebel 1997), or rather *literacy practices*. This concept is a development of Shirley Brice Heath's notion of 'literacy events' (1983), which focuses on what people do with literacy in their daily lives, rather than on what literacy does for them (cf. Barton 1994). In a literacy event, people communicate in everyday life using a mixture of oral and literate features, but the notion of literacy practices refers not only to the literacy event, but also to the ideas and constructions that people have of what is happening when they are involved in it. – e.g., what people think reading is, and what counts for them as reading (Baynham 1995; Street 1995).

Alongside the concept of literacy practices as social practices there emerges the notion of *multiple literacies*. In the dominant view of literacy, only 'school literacy' is defined as such, which perpetuates the notion of literacy as something done by an individual only. Yet many literacies are practised in communities (Street 1995; Prinsloo and Breier 1996). People have different literacies which they use in different domains of life such as home or school and which serve different purposes. A literacy can be imposed, as when one completes an official form, or it can be self-generated, as in the writing of a personal letter. Street (1995) and Barton and Hamilton (1998) distinguish dominant versus vernacular literacies, the former originating from the dominant institutions and the latter from everyday life. This raises the issue of dominance and marginalisation in literacy practices. Research of this kind has come to be known as the New Literacy Studies (NLS) upon which this chapter draws (Street 1995; Prinsloo and Breier 1996). We will consider, in the conclusion, how far the literacies we examine can be termed 'vernacular'.

The NLS have taken an interest in multilingual situations, particularly with regard to the literacy practices of multilingual individuals within their social context (Barton and Hamilton 1998). Up to the present, however, little work has been done in situations of high linguistic diversity (cf. Robinson 1994) – where distinct linguistic communities exist in the same geographical and social space, and where these communities, often numerically small, are in sustained contact with exogenous languages. This is the situation in many African and Asian countries with a colonial past. In such a context, literacy studies necessarily intersect with a sociolinguistic analysis, since the choice and use of languages, in both written and oral form, carry a very high level of social meaning (cf. Barton 1998).

Where individuals and communities habitually use a number of languages the key questions of sociolinguistic analysis are: Who uses which language, with whom, for what purposes, and in what circumstances? The same questions can be asked, *mutatis mutandis*, with regard to literacies. It is therefore essential in a multilingual environment to ask about literacies in particular languages. The sociolinguistic situation not only informs the analysis of literacy practices, but is a determining factor in their acquisition, distribution, use and social function.

Languages are frequently used in different domains, such as education, religion, family life and commerce: different literacy practices are often identified within a single social environment. It is therefore of interest to see which languages are used for written communication in each domain, and what mix of languages occurs (cf. Aikman, this volume). Street (1994:9) writes of 'groups of people whose primary identity is with local languages and literacies'. Language use always carries a symbolic function, indicating group membership, social cohesion and personal or corporate identity (Robinson 1996). The NLS argue a similar point for literacy practices – beyond the communicative impact, literacy practices symbolise and mediate social relationships, networks of solidarity and support, relative power/status differentials (Barton 1994; Barton and Hamilton 1998). Issues of identity emerge all the more strongly where linguistic diversity compounds the variety of literacy practices. Language policies, educational language use, language planning and the languages of the media all contribute to patterns of access to power and exclusion from it, thus playing a role in governance and participatory citizenship. However, issues of language are rarely, if ever, the sole cause of such patterns. Barton and Hamilton (1998: 229) make the same point about literacy, while cautioning that 'literacy can both support and subvert democratic endeavours: literacy is used in different ways, both to open up activities and to control them'.

Fishman (1991) shows how language is related to culture, particularly in the case of minority and indigenous languages; in parallel fashion, Street (1995: 115) makes the link between literacy and *the language-in-culture nexus*: 'Literacy practices are always embedded in oral uses, and the variations between cultures are generally variations in the mix of oral/literate channels.'

The concept of literacy practices as social practices highlights the way in which literacy as a linguistic occurrence is linked to its social context (Baynham 1995). However the complex relationship between culture and language may be defined, it is certainly observable that, where cultures differ, the oral and literate features of communication differ also.

This chapter takes as its starting point, therefore, the close connections and the shared analytical parameters of literacy studies and sociolinguistic investigation. This raises a set of interrelated questions.

Does this language-in-culture nexus show that where there is a different language or culture, there is also a different literacy? How far is language a determining factor in literacy practices? What kind of social impact is intended, or may result, from literacies in different languages? There is the issue of which language is used in the literacy practice, and whether this language is the official, regional or local language. These questions find an echo in Wright's analysis (this volume) of linguistically distinguished literacies in Eritrea. Along with these considerations emerge the political concepts of dominance and marginalisation. How was the literacy practice acquired – formally from the school, non-formally from the local literacy project or church initiative, or informally from relatives, friends? Who is using the literacy practice? In considering this, we can try to establish notions of identity, and what the practitioner construes from the literacy practice.

In this chapter we do not attempt to answer all these questions, which would represent a substantial research agenda in multilingual contexts. Rather, a simpler set of questions is addressed by discussion of the literacy practices in northern

Ghana: namely the choice of the language, the nature of the user and the purpose of the literacy practice.

It is important first to sketch the overall context of northern Ghana, particularly with regard to its linguistic realities, ethnic composition and educational setting.

Language setting

Ghana, like most African countries, is multilingual, with over sixty-three indigenous languages.[1] The languages of power are spoken by the dominant groups of the south. They were the first to have their languages written down, they were the first to have literature in them, in the late nineteenth and early twentieth centuries (Cole 1971; Hall 1983) and they were nearer to the trade centres when the first European merchants landed on their shores. This has given them educational, economic, socio-cultural and political advantages and, therefore, an advantage in the whole process of development. Most of the minority language groups reside in the rural areas in the north; some languages are spoken by thousands of people over a wide area, and others only by a few hundreds in a very limited area. Although these languages were initially recorded by linguists in the nineteenth century (J.T. Bendor-Samuel 1971), they have only been written down for use in literacy programmes during the last fifty years.

The official language of Ghana is English, the most widely used second language in the country: it is used in government, in commerce, and on formal or public occasions. It is also employed in formal education – beyond the first three years of primary education in the north – and at secondary level in the south, where regional languages such as Asante Twi, Fante, Ga and Ewe compete for national-language status. The latter were the only four regional languages to be recognised by the government in the 1950s and 1960s, because of the number of speakers and the existence of written literature such as the Bible. However, when the Bureau of Ghana Languages was set up in the 1970s and made responsible for the development of indigenous languages, more regional languages were recognised for use in the media, public functions and education. In the 1980s, the number rose to eleven (Cairns 1987) and now fifteen are recognised, namely Akan or Twi (in its three written dialects of Akuapim, Asante and Fante), Ewe, Ga, Nzema, Dagaare-Wali, Dagbani, Gonja, Kasem, Frafra, Ga-Adangbe, Buli, Kusaal, Sisaala.

Comparatively few of the English speakers have proficiency at university level because English is so rarely used across all speech domains. Generally, Ghanaians speak three or four languages, depending upon their communication needs. The local language remains firmly established as the language of the home and the community, in which personal, family and in-group matters are discussed and established.

Most of the local languages were formerly unwritten, and have been written down only within the last fifty years – chiefly by missionaries, but also by Non-

Governmental Organisations and by government entities. Literacy programmes have also been initiated in these languages; these are closely associated with Bible translation and Christian teaching, in the case of the missionaries, and are linked with broader education and development concerns on the part of NGOs and government departments. For example, the Bureau of Ghana Languages and linguists of the Bible Society were involved in the analysis and writing of Dagbani; Assemblies of God missionaries worked on the translation of the New Testament and set up literacy classes. Presbyterian missionaries with Dagomba pastors and writers provided literacy materials in Dagbani and set up a rural literacy project. SIL, a Christian-based NGO, set up a large-scale adult literacy project among the Dagombas, and facilitated more research on the orthography by discussion between all the previous linguists.

SIL has worked in Ghana since 1962 under a co-operative agreement with the University of Legon, in Accra, to analyse and write down unwritten languages, facilitate literacy projects and translate Scripture. Since 1980 this work has been carried out under the auspices of the Ghana Institute of Linguistics, Literacy and Bible Translation (GILLBT), a Ghanaian NGO. This NGO has been involved in researching and writing down most of the local languages in the north and central areas of Ghana and setting up large-scale literacy activities in those languages and in English for young people and adults (Hall 1983: 9; D. and M. Bendor-Samuel 1983: 4). Currently GILLBT works in twenty-seven local languages in the northern and central areas of Ghana.

The involvement of SIL and GILLBT in literacy activities, with their Christian motivation, raises the question of whether the resulting literacy practices are imposed, and whether they represent a narrow agenda. Much comment on SIL's work has been critical of its Christian nature and its Western (particularly North American) cultural background. From some ideological viewpoints, these two aspects have often been regarded as synonymous, thus obscuring the important interplay between them. While such considerations are significant in analysing and assessing SIL's work, more recent developments in SIL's perspectives and relationships have involved changes which remain to be documented. The Ghana situation illustrates some of these changes, which are taking place on a broader scale as well. Literacy activities were certainly linked initially with Bible translation; however, in the process of implementation particularly since 1990, it has become clear that literacy activities were relevant only in so far as they were linked with the broad range of communication needs in local communities. This led to a twofold commitment: on the one hand, to give precedence to community perceptions in planning literacy, and on the other hand to commit resources to literacy as such, funded and managed distinctly from translation work. These two commitments have led to the kind of analysis of literacy which this chapter presents.

Formal education is available in Ghana, with a 76 per cent enrolment rate in primary schools, but there is a big drop-out rate between primary and secondary education, such that secondary enrolment stands at 36 per cent (UNESCO

1995). Northern Ghanaians have a lower attendance rate at school, resulting in a lower degree of literacy and use of literature (D. and M. Bendor-Samuel 1983). National government literacy campaigns have given some people a second chance to become literate, but a national mass literacy campaign – launched in the 1950s under the auspices of the Department of Social Welfare and Community Development, using English as the medium of instruction – left some groups in the north, like the Konkombas, virtually untouched. The Experimental World Literacy Programme of UNESCO in 1973 used regional Ghanaian languages which are the common languages of local and regional markets, but failed to reach many of the northern groups because their own languages were not used (Langdon 1996).

UNESCO's 1998 estimate of adult literacy in Ghana in 1995 was 64 per cent, but the reality is that, in some of the ethnic groups, it is only 5 per cent or less. At present there is a large programme of non-formal, adult education (NFED) in the fifteen regional Ghanaian languages previously mentioned. Various NGOs, running non-formal literacy projects in the north, have different foci; e.g., School For Life, a Danish/Ghanaian NGO, focuses on shepherd boys and on boy and girl traders who have dropped out of school. In its literacy materials in Dagbani and Konkomba, School For Life incorporates Danish educational ideas.

An example of the effect of these various literacy initiatives may be seen in a particular ethnic group in the north-west of Ghana, the Dega. They have the opportunity to become literate in three different languages: in formal school at primary level they learn to be literate in Asante Twi, a regional language, and then, at secondary level, in English. If they drop out of school, they have the opportunity of joining either the government NFED programme, to become literate in Asante Twi, or the GILLBT literacy programme, for their own language, called Deg.

This chapter draws on data collected in the course of literacy consultations and training events in northern Ghana, as well as extended visits to particular language areas. The research is part of what Street (this volume) identifies as the 'task of making visible the complexity of local, everyday community literacy practices'. Much of the material was collected in unstructured interviews or by observation, and thus appears anecdotal in places; in recognising this we express the hope that this work may inspire other, more rigorously structured approaches to a greatly underresearched context.

Literacy practices in multilingual contexts

Subscribers to the dominant view of literacy talk of how literacy affects the learners. However, this idea has been turned on its head by the more recent notion that literacy is embedded in cultural practices: the question becomes how the learners affect literacy practices. Is their use of language integral to the effect they have upon the literacy practices? This section will examine literacy practices in a number of domains: religion, economic activities, meetings and personal life. The use of languages in these practices will be emphasised.

Religious literacies

Church denominations proliferate in Ghana and the language used in worship is dictated by which ethnic group spread the denomination. Speakers of Fante, in the south of Ghana, were the first to respond to the early expatriate Methodist missionaries; and wherever the Fantes have spread Methodism, Fante is used for worship. The Ashantes, also in the south, who speak Asante Twi, a dialect of Twi, spread Pentecostalism, thus Twi is used in the Pentecostal church even in the north. For example, the Dega who are Pentecostalists use the Twi Bible even though their own Deg New Testament has been translated and published. The Deg Seventh Day Adventists do the same. But in Tamale, the urban capital in northern Ghana – where local-language scriptures, songs and prayers are used in Baptist churches – there is a prevailing use of English in Bible reading, preaching and singing. American Baptists initiated these Baptist churches.

Ghanaians are deeply spiritual people. There must be a good reason why northerners of certain denominations continue to use southern languages, like Asante Twi and Fante, or English in their religious literacy practices. For the northerners these are the languages of power, of past conquerors, and they are participating in a powerful ritual addressing the most powerful being of all – God. Their own languages are minority languages, not even recognised by the government in some cases, therefore they are not suitable for this purpose. The Vaglas, for example, do not even use their own language in part of their tradi-tional religion, but a 'secret language' is used by those who lead the rituals for their god of death, Sigma; this 'secret language' is only used by the ritual leaders and is therefore a language of power.

Islamic practices centre around the reading of the Quran in Arabic. In the Quran (Koran) the Arabic word for 'read' is *qara'a* which 'also carried the mean-ing "recite by heart"' (Baynham 1995: 170). In the north of Ghana, it is a common sight to see children at the Quranic schools sitting and reciting by heart from the Quran. In many of the local Ghanaian languages in the north the root of this word has had its influence. For example, in Vagla the word to read is *karmi* (from Arabic *qurmi*), in Kusaal, *karim* (Ar. *qurim*) and in Dagbani, *karimbo* (Ar. *qurimbo*). This explains why many speakers of these languages perceive 'read-ing' as 'reciting by heart'. At an Islamic funeral celebrated by the Nafaanras of north-west Ghana, when it was time for the prayers to be said as part of the ritual, the ones praying had cards with the prayers printed in Arabic script. Each card was a portion of a certain book of the Quran that needed to be 'read'. Everything was recited or 'read' at the same time, so that the ones praying appeared to be reading the cards, but in fact, by the way the cards were held, it was obvious they were reciting from memory. An observer asked and was categorically told they were unable to read the text (personal experience). But they still needed the text because for Muslims the linguistic form of the Quran literally incorporates the word of God; the text is sacred and powerful in itself (Baynham 1995).

The following examples illustrate the complex interplay between the role of text, religious systems and existing beliefs. The inherent power of text is illustrated graphically in local practices, both Islamic and Christian, that go beyond the reading of the text. In northern Ghana, followers of Islam approach an imam for help: he writes the relevant prayer from the Quran on a slate with chalk and washes it off into a calabash. The supplicant then drinks the water. By swallowing the sacred text, they believe that they will receive a blessing.

The Deg paramount chief, a Roman Catholic, had his own way of judging a difficult case, for example when judging two people suspected of sheep-stealing. For each suspect, he took his Twi Bible, opened it at random and dangled a key on a piece of string above it. Then he lowered the key and whatever words it touched he read out. The words which contained an affirmative indicated the one who was guilty; a negative indicated innocence according to whose turn it was (personal observation).

What socio-cultural beliefs and practices do these religious literacies reveal? The 'attitudes to the Holy Books, such as the Koran, [and] the Bible show reverence for something semi-magical or charmed and a respect for wise teaching' (Langdon 1996: 42). A problem-solving approach to religion is common among Ghanaians whether they be traditionalists, Muslims or Christians. The Muslim example reveals the strong animist belief that ingesting a part of whatever has spiritual power transmits that power to the body. The example from the Deg chief reveals the strong belief in divination, common among Ghanaians. Often a chicken is used and the questions that are asked are framed in such a way that only the affirmative or the negative can be given. The chief substituted the Bible and the key for the chicken as instruments of divination to find out who had stolen the sheep, but the answer could only be yes or no. These semi-magical uses of sacred text may not reflect mainstream Muslim and Christian views respectively, but they do illustrate a significant difference between their view of text. The inherent power of the form of the Quran lends religious power to the ink; the Christian view of the Bible as directly applicable gives even a phrase or two the status of revealed meaning. The two practices differ in that, for the Muslim, the actual text or script is the word of God, so he swallows it, but for the Christian, the meaning of the text is the word of God, and he uses what it says.

Funerals, as much social as religious events, are one of the most important aspects of Ghanaian culture, and demonstrate particular literacy practices. The financial cost is huge in comparison to the amount of wealth that people possess; therefore, all who are invited to attend are expected to contribute to the cost. One of the most important participants at such a funeral is the person who keeps the accounts. The amounts and donors are recorded in English (in the classic school method) because it was at school that this kind of record keeping was learned; however, although most people use the English numerals, the amounts are laboriously called out in Deg, even though many of the Dega themselves have forgotten the larger numbers. In the funerals among the Kusaasi, the Dagomba and the Vagla, who are further north, there is a record made of the donors and amounts in English, but nothing is read out to the assembled mourners.

Why are these practices different and what is the social meaning behind them? For the more northern groups, it is a matter of mutual obligation that records are kept of the funeral contributions; recipients of contributions are obliged to do the same for others when they have a family funeral and are in need of support. However, the record is for the family, not necessarily for other participants in the funeral. For the more southern group, the Dega, the amount given is a matter of prestige and power. If a large amount is called out, the gathered assembly shows its appreciation in the volume of clapping and verbal affirmation. Therefore, the amounts are called in Deg for all to hear and understand.

Economic literacies

Literacy in English is one of the keys to salaried employment in Ghana. In a number of languages, however, local non-institutional literacy practices have economic implications. Outside the post office in Wenchi, in the Brong-Ahafo region, sits a man who will compose and type any letter for a certain amount of money – or indeed any document that one may wish typed. He will type it in English, though the customer may give the message orally in a number of languages: for example, Twi, Hausa, Ligbi or Nafaanra. Translation is therefore a key feature of this literacy practice. This man has been educated by a formal institution, but he sees no need to institutionalise his literacy practice; he has no office set up, with all that this entails, but simply sits on a chair outside the post office using his literacy for commercial advantage. Why does he only write in English? Possibly because he uses a roman script typewriter. However, Ghanaian languages are also written in roman script, though often with symbols unavailable on unadapted machines. The choice of language probably has more to do with the intended recipients, who are often officials and government departments.

There is a small rural press in the Brong-Ahafo region where they type and duplicate simple documents such as examination papers for the local schools, references for the school children, funeral cards to announce the dates and names of invited guests and other paraphernalia; there is a printing charge. This was an offshoot of the Deg literacy project, started by the literacy workers to acquire extra funds for themselves. Since the press is part of a Deg-focused project, the language used for local, cultural matters (such as the funeral cards) is Deg, because it denotes identity; but if the cards had been made by other ethnic groups in the nearby town, it would have been in Twi, the dominant regional language. Moreover, the typewriter has the special Deg characters added to it.

Although many northern Ghanaians would not be interested in literacy for economic gain, they have acquired numeracy from the lottery sheets that are available. A Dagomba watchman has been observed sitting and pondering over his lottery sheets, but has declined the offer of being taught to read and write.

Those who are literate in English have an opportunity to get paid work in the towns. However, there are limited opportunities for literates in the rural areas. The Deg paramount chief holds regular traditional council meetings with his sub-chiefs, and a secretary has to write up the minutes and reports in English for governmental use. Those who run small stores need someone who can write receipts and send letters to the towns to order goods. If there is a school, teachers are needed and the larger villages have an agricultural officer and veterinary assistant. These opportunities, of course, are all for English literates.

Meetings literacies

Barton and Hamilton (1998: 215) use the term 'meetings literacies' for literacies which are important for the running of organisations. An example of this is the way the committee of the Deg Adult Literacy project runs its Annual General Meetings. The committee and the majority of those who attend the meeting have become literate through the formal school system in English, the official language (Twi), and the regional language, and they have become literate non-formally in Deg through their own project. The literacy component at the AGM consists of the reading of the minutes and the construction of an agenda in English, as well as the reading aloud of financial and progress reports in Deg, and minute-taking in English. The interchange of literate and oral features that occur in such a meeting are usually in Deg. In contrast to this, the Dagombas at their quarterly literacy committee meetings write everything in English, but translate as they read it out into Dagbani. If a government official were to be present, the whole proceeding would be in English.

When all those present understand both languages and this is a formal occasion, why is there this language mix? The agenda and the minutes are official formalities to which nobody listens very much, but for which an official language has to be used as taught in school. The reports are what really matter; they communicate what has been happening in the project and they show financial accountability. The reports can raise many questions; so it is important not only to communicate, but also to allay any suspicion as to the real identity of the group as Deg people, and establish trust. This is done by the insertion of typical Deg discourse features, e.g., the use of proverbs, or referring to older people respectfully as 'my father' or 'my mother' or 'brother', even though this is un-natural in English. This is the kind of information that Gee describes when he refers to what is necessary to show that one is a 'real Indian' among American Indians (Gee 1996), and it is also why Fishman (1991) argues so strongly for linkages between language and culture.

Personal literacies

Some of the Dega have been educated formally and manage to find employment in the larger towns. One such, JM, got a good job and built himself a house in Tamale, which is mainly populated by Dagombas. Above John's front door is the legend *Deg Bie* which means 'Deg person'. Written in his own language, before linguists had even tried to analyse the language and write it down, this indicates that here, in the midst of an alien ethnic group, there lives a Deg family that wants to assert its identity. Similarly, proverbs in local languages are painted on bicycles, on passenger lorries and on houses. It is as though people are saying 'This is mine, and this is where I come from.'

Letters in the local language have been used by literate women in the Vagla area to preserve their privacy, to correspond with lovers without needing to ask other people to read them. This is in a society where adultery is heavily punished, therefore all liaisons must be kept secret.

Langdon writes (1996: 24) about the Konkombas, 'Controversial issues are handled in dialogue, and it is this practice which underlies essays and other written literature, which present arguments for and against a case, thus reproducing the oral decision-making process.' The Vaglas, in contrast, hate conflict, and so they use their literacy by writing letters to diffuse any controversial problems. When a group of literate Vaglas wanted to apologise, explaining their refusal to co-operate with their project manager in buying and selling second-hand clothes to help their literacy project, they wrote a letter explaining their point of view, but it was not in dialogue form.

Writing is perceived to be a respectful way of communicating, so a person wishing to ask for financial help or any other kind of help will use a letter and sometimes deliver it by hand. Envelopes have to be used because this shows respect. Many Ghanaians, when writing letters in their own language, will open and close them in ways that are culturally appropriate; e.g., the Dega will open a letter as follows:

to an adult woman: *N nya, Lolasom* – 'My mother, Lolasom'

to an adult man: *N mee, Noah* – 'My father, Noah'

To sign off, they will write:

N jage bono. Menee, he bie, Kofi. – 'I finish here. It is I, your child, Kofi.'

However, if they are writing to someone of another culture who reads English, they will write in the English way, 'Dear Lolasom', or 'Dear Noah', and finish appropriately, 'Yours sincerely', etc. If they are writing to someone who reads both Deg and English, they will open the letter in the Deg way and in Deg and then continue in English. Why do they do this? To the Dega, respect is one of the highest values; it must be expressed by referring to someone's status when addressing them and in the closing of a letter. The traditional way of closing a dialogue expresses cultural identity.

Individual multilingual literacies: an example

In a multilingual situation like that in Ghana, where people have the opportunity of being educated at the tertiary level, a person such as NA, a Deg, practises multilingual literacies. At his teacher training college in Navrongo, a Kasem-speaking area, he learned Kasem and became literate in it. His first teaching job was in an area where people spoke Vagla, a language related to his own, so he easily learned and became literate in that language. Now working in his own homeland in Brong-Ahafo, he reads the national newspaper in English at home; the Twi Bible in church; the Deg New Testament for his own personal devotions at home. He uses Twi, Deg and English for teaching; he studies for his General Certificate of Education 'A' levels in English in his spare time; and he writes letters in Deg, Vagla, Kasem, Twi or English to whichever correspondents are literate in those languages at home.

Between the oral and the written

Constructing meaning from graphic symbols is an early step to literacy. Where people make marks that are meaningful in a particular context, even though not using a representation of language as such, we observe something that may be called a literacy practice ('proto-literacy'?). The Vaglas have a very potent local beer, brewed from guinea corn, which is made by the women and sold in their houses. On entering these mud dwellings, one sees short, mostly vertical, lines scratched with a stick by women to remind them of beer debtors. These women are otherwise illiterate, but they can keep accounts by this simple method.

Other symbolic systems are used, though without text. Among the Dega, where strong male bonding is usual, friends who divert to different areas on their way to farm will expect to meet up with their friends at cross paths on the way home. If this does not happen, they leave sticks or grass in certain positions to show they have gone ahead or have gone somewhere else.

While walking along the paths in New Longoro, a village in north-west Ghana, one might see an egg lying on a path leading to the river – and a needle and a handkerchief lying with it. All are animistic symbols with significance to the people in the area. They could mean that someone was being cursed, or that there was a plea for fertility. Women in that area wear their clothes in a way that communicates a message to the observer; scarves are worn in certain ways to indicate that they have had a row with their husbands or their cloths are wrapped round them to indicate whether they are single or married. The relation between these semiotic systems and literacy begs the question raised by Kress (1998): what will literacy studies include and exclude in their research agenda? If anything, these practices show that literacy is one of several symbolic systems available for communication, embedded in cultural practices and determined by them.

The structure of written communication in Africa has been informed more by literacies of schooling in foreign languages than by the discourse patterns of oral practice in African languages. Attempts are being made, however, to reverse this trend. At school, the Dega learn how to write stories using English discourse features such as: 'Once upon a time' as an opening and 'They all lived happily ever after' as an ending. But when they write their own stories in Deg, they write in ways that have been passed down in their oral literature. The opening of the story begins as all Deg story-tellers would begin, '*Ya mole mola*', 'Let's tell stories', with the assumed oral affirmative response from the audience, and the closure is written following the oral model as well, '*Ya sa jegle jeg*' 'Let's dance and shake.' Integral to the text of these stories are Deg social values and social structures. To give instruction and advice, the Dega always embody it in a story. So, when a health worker wanted to advise his people about the dangers of AIDS, he wrote a story rooted in his own culture which incorporated the advice within it. This has proved more popular as a health book than those based on the factual, linear way of presenting health, modelled on English health books translated into Deg.

Conclusion

This chapter has placed an emphasis on local literacies in African languages, rather than looking at school literacy in languages of wider communication and its uses. These are generally better documented and, in the case of literacy in English, would be expected to show broadly similar patterns of use across ethnolinguistic groups in a particular country or region. A further research question remains, however, as to how far literacy practices in English differ among different linguistic groups in Ghana.

Are these local language literacies the 'vernacular literacies' defined by Camitta (1993: 228–9) as being the alternative uses of writing 'closely associated with culture which is neither elite nor institutional, which is traditional and indigenous to the diverse cultural processes of communities as distinguished from the uniform, inflexible standards of institutions'? In a multilingual environment, the use of the term 'vernacular' is also used to refer to language without reference to literacies. It is in this sense that the contributors to Tabouret-Keller et al. (1997) debate 'vernacular literacy' – they examine social, political and technical issues in the adoption of vernacular languages for the purposes of literacy. This is a related, though different, question but it is different from asking whether literacies and literacy practices are 'vernacular'. In this chapter, we have documented literacies in vernacular languages: does this necessarily mean they are 'vernacular literacies'? Clearly, the initial answer is no – since in the definition of vernacular literacies, language is not necessarily a component. However, from the evidence in this chapter, the use of vernacular languages (preferably local) results in literacy practices which show similarities to the vernacular literacies in the six overlapping areas of everyday life as defined by Barton and Hamilton (1998: 247–50): organising life, personal communication, private leisure, documenting life, sense-making and social participation. Thus we have noted the literacy reports written for the Deg literacy project's AGM which is a form of organising life; the love letters that the Vagla women want to keep private in their personal communication; and the Dagomba watchman who cannot read text, but in his leisure time reads numbers on his lottery card. Donors and donations were documented in the funeral practices of the Dega, the Kusaasi and other northern groups. An example of sense-making is NA's using his Deg New Testament for his private devotions. Lastly, a form of social participation is the participation of many northerners in their Islamic religious practices, in the Nafaanra funeral through the use of prayer cards that are 'read' or 'recited'.

The literacy practices cited from Ghana are rooted in everyday experiences and serve everyday purposes; they are informally and non-formally learned, not usually supported by formal institutions and – thus less valued, in northern Ghana – by the dominant cultures. As Barton and Hamilton (1998: 252) observed: 'different media are integrated; literacy is integrated with other symbolic systems, such as numeracy, and visuals; and different topics and activities can occur together'. This is evident in the 'meetings literacy' practised at the Deg AGM by the writing and then oral delivery of the progress reports, the accounting in the financial reports, and the general mix of oral and literate features in the discussion.

Does another language therefore mean another literacy? In terms of literacies defined by domain – religion, economic activity, etc. – each literacy is practised in different languages, and is somewhat different in each case. Do the differences depend on language? Probably not, at least not on language alone. Along with language differences go cultural patterns, made up of ancestral customs, historical antecedents, external influences and political forces. The resulting differences are carried and symbolised by particular languages, not caused by them. Thus differences of Deg and Dagbani religious literacies have more to do with differences of Christian and Islamic influences, and with external forces associated with them, than with difference in language. On the other hand, the use of personal literacies in local languages for reasons of privacy is common across language boundaries.

Literacies in local languages in Ghana contrast with literacy in English, much more than with each other. This bears out the sociolinguistic situation, prevalent across Africa, where the former colonial languages have been the means of elite formation and political power. However, literacies in local languages are in daily use at the grassroots level; this speaks of the importance of local identity and local communication patterns. Local people are using literacies for their own purposes and in the languages they want to use – a hopeful sign in a continent where other people's agendas have dominated for too long.

Acknowledgements

Part of this chapter first appeared as 'Another Language, Another Literacy? Evidence from Africa' in *Written Language & Literacy* 2(2) (1999): 247–66. The editor would like to thank John Benjamins publishers and also William Bright, editor of *WLL*, for their kind permission to adapt the article for the present book.

Note

1 The thirteenth edition of *Ethnologue: Languages of the World* (Grimes 1996: 274) lists and names sixty indigenous Ghanaian languages. Current research, based on more recent SIL linguistic surveys, reveals that the number is more likely sixty-three and may be more. If non-indigenous languages are taken into account (English, Hausa, etc.) then the number rises to seventy-three.

References

Barton, D. (1994) *Literacy: An Introduction to the Ecology of Written Language*, Oxford: Blackwell.
—— (1998) 'Is Literacy Studies Reinventing Sociolinguistics?' Paper presented at Sociolinguistics Symposium 12, London, 26–28 March 1998.
Barton, D. and Hamilton, M. (1998) *Local Literacies: Reading and Writing in One Community*, London: Routledge.
Baynham, M. (1995) *Literacy Practices: Investigating Literacy in Social Contexts*, London: Longman.
Bendor-Samuel, D. and Bendor-Samuel, M. (1983) *Community Literacy Programmes in Northern Ghana*, Dallas, TX: SIL.
Bendor-Samuel, J.T. (1971) 'Niger-Congo Guru', in T.A. Sebeok (ed.), *Current Trends in Linguistics*, Vol. VII, The Hague: Mouton.
Cairns, J.C. (1987) 'Ghana Literacy Assistance Program: Mid-term Evaluation', unpublished report.
Camitta, M. (1993) 'Vernacular Writing: Varieties of Literacy among Philadelphia High School Students', in B. Street (ed.), *Cross-Cultural Approaches to Literacy*, Cambridge: Cambridge University Press.
Cole, D.T. (1971) 'The History of African Linguistics to 1945', in T.A. Sebeok (ed.), *Current Trends in Linguistics*, Vol. VII, The Hague: Mouton.
Fishman, J.A. (1991) *Reversing Language Shift*, Clevedon: Multilingual Matters.
Gee, J.P. (1996) *Social Linguistics and Literacies: Ideology in Discourses*, 2nd edition, London: Taylor & Francis.
Grimes, B.F. (1996) *Ethnologue Languages of the World*, 13th edition, Dallas, TX: SIL.
Hall, E. (1983) *Ghanaian Languages*, Ghana: Asempa.
Heath, S.B. (1983) *Ways with Words: Language, Life and Work in Communities and Classrooms*, Cambridge: Cambridge University Press.
Kress, G. (1998) 'Literacy and the Challenges of the Contemporary Period: Consolidating the Items for a Working Agenda', Paper presented to the Annual Meeting of the British Association for Applied Linguistics, Manchester, 10–12 September 1998.
Langdon, M.A. (1996) 'The Place of Mother-Tongue Literacy in Social Development in Three African Contexts', Unpublished MA thesis, Reading University.

Prinsloo, M. and Breier, M. (eds) (1996) *The Social Uses of Literacy: Theory and Practice in Contemporary South Africa*, Amsterdam and Johannesburg: John Benjamins and SACHED Books.

Robinson, C.D.W. (1992) *Language Choice in Rural Development*, Dallas, TX: International Museum of Cultures.

—— (1994) 'Where Minorities Are in the Majority: Language Dynamics amidst High Linguistic Diversity', *AILA Review* 10: 52–70.

—— (1996) *Language Use in Rural Development: An African Perspective*, Berlin: Mouton de Gruyter.

Sebeok, T.A. (ed.) (1971) *Current Trends in Linguistics*, Vol. VII, The Hague: Mouton.

Street, B. (1984) *Literacy in Theory and Practice*, Cambridge: Cambridge University Press.

—— (1994) 'What Is Meant by Local Literacies?', *Language and Education* 8(1&2): 9–18.

—— (1995) *Social Literacies: Critical Approaches to Literacy in Development, Ethnography and Education*, London: Longman.

Tabouret-Keller, A., Le Page, R.B., Gardner-Chloros, P. and Varro, G. (1997) *Vernacular Literacy: A Re-evaluation*, Oxford: Oxford University Press.

Triebel, A. (1997) *Cognitive and Societal Development on Literacy: A Report on the State-of-the-Art of Research on Literacy*, Bonn: DSE (Deutsche Stiftung für Entwicklung).

UNESCO (1995) *World Education Report*, Paris: UNESCO.

—— (1998) *World Education Report*, Paris: UNESCO.

Verhoeven, L. (ed.) (1994) *Functional Literacy: Theoretical and Educational Implications*, Amsterdam: John Benjamins.

7

LITERACY AND THE MARKET

The economic uses of literacy among the
peasantry in north-west Bangladesh

Bryan Maddox

Introduction

The dominant characterisation of the landless peasantry in Bangladesh and elsewhere in Asia is of illiteracy. By very definition the peasantry are regarded as illiterate, and poverty and illiteracy are commonly treated as synonymous terms. This is true both in academic discourse and in popular culture. For example, in her article 'Can the Subaltern Speak?', Gayatri Spivak, argues for the heterogeneous nature of the subaltern subject, but nevertheless equates the peasantry with illiteracy (1993: 78, 79). Likewise, Thomas Eriksen, in his introductory reader in social and cultural anthropology, argues that 'Peasants (and other "traditional peoples") . . . usually master no information technology other than the spoken word' (1995: 195). This is also the norm in characterisations of rural life in the popular press (for example, see Sainath 1996). Within the political culture of Bangladesh, illiteracy is regularly evoked as 'the' barrier to economic and social progress, and this dominant ideology is largely shared by the rural poor themselves. Such a negative characterisation continues despite the fact that since the 1970s political changes and social movements in Bangladesh have successfully acted to increase access to education in rural areas (within the government and non-government sector). This process has accelerated since the 1980s with the development of locally based non-formal primary and adult education. This community-based education has largely been developed within the NGO sector, and together with innovative systems of saving and credit (such as those of the Grameen Bank) represents significant development success stories.

One of the implications of these changes is that, since the 1980s, large numbers of people (adults and children) who would previously have been excluded are gaining access to education. This means that it is no longer acceptable simply to equate poverty with illiteracy. We must recognise the existence of '*subaltern literacies*' in order to have a better understanding of the uses of literacy among the rural and urban poor (see Maddox, forthcoming). This chapter therefore explores an alternative view. Based on ethnographic fieldwork in the north-west of Bangladesh, it examines the alternative idea of the 'literate poor' and in particular the economic uses of literacy among the peasantry. The chapter concludes by briefly looking at the possible implications of these ideas for adult literacy programmes.[1]

The research was conducted in and around Nilphamary, a small town in the north-west of Bangladesh. Like many other parts of the country, the economy of the area is dominated by agricultural activity, and the town acts as both a local market and a district centre for government and non-government institutions (see Hartmann and Boyce 1983). The town itself developed in the early 1900s as an administrative centre on the railway line between Calcutta, Silliguri and Darjeeling. Under British colonial rule in the 1800s, this was an area of extensive indigo cultivation, and there is some feeling locally that the name Nilphamary may be connected to indigo, as 'nil' means blue, the colour of indigo.[2] After independence and partition, the railway connection with India was broken, and the area is therefore somewhat isolated economically by the political boundary with India to the north, and by distance from the large economic centres to the south. Nevertheless, the area is heavily influenced by the political and economic activity of the capital city, Dhaka. The town itself is split into two main centres of activity, one associated with the state apparatus (such as court, land registry, school and hospital), and the other associated with the bazaar. The town also acts as a centre of religious activity and contains two large mosques and a Hindu temple.

Working lives – the market

The vast majority of people in the area around Nilphamary earn their living from the agricultural sector. As in other parts of Bangladesh there is a high polarisation in terms of land ownership, with a large landless (or semi-landless) peasantry and a small number of wealthy landowners (Ahsan 1989; White 1992; Rashid 1995).[3] Land and labour are perhaps the most significant commodities in the rural economy (see Datta 1998).

A salaried job is very rare among the peasantry. Most people in rural areas of Bangladesh either share-crop, rent land, or sell their labour to more wealthy farmers in return for cash or food (Datta 1998). This situation often involves complex relationships of obligation and debt. For example, during the time of our research, following the floods of 1998, many men sold their labour in advance in return for cash, and this indebtedness had implications that lasted for several months. Such indebtedness works to the advantage of large landowners who are very reliant on wage labourers at times of harvest and planting.

These 'market' principles are the dominant features in production. Although most rural people spend their lives involved in agricultural work, few are able to consume what they produce. Crops are mainly grown for sale for cash rather than for direct use or other types of exchange. The main cash-crops in the area are rice, wheat, tobacco, potatoes (other crops include turmeric, onions, spinach and garlic). The agricultural cycle produces periods of unemployment and hunger between planting and harvest, and is prone to uncertainty because of competition for work, price fluctuations (of the local, national and international market), and climatic factors (such as floods). The peasantry therefore also relies on a diverse range of economic activities throughout the year. These include such activities as fishing, livestock rearing, homestead gardening, rickshaw pulling and shop-keeping. A study by Hossain (1995) suggests that such activities can amount to 85 per cent of the income of landless families (Hossain cited in Osmani 1996). This highlights the importance of market activities in people's lives.

Although women tend not to buy or sell produce in public spaces such as the bazaar, they nevertheless play a significant role in economic production. Much of their work around the relatively private domain of the homestead involves livestock rearing, homestead gardening and work such as looking after children and cooking (Wilson-Moore 1989; Kabeer 1994). Women also do much of the post-harvest grain-processing, including work in the fields after harvest, and this work is rarely paid with cash. While women produce goods for sale (such as goats, cows, hens, ducks, eggs, vegetables) their work is often regarded as low status, and is in a sense rendered invisible, as it is male members of their family (including male children) who sell their produce for cash at the market (Wilson-Moore 1989).

Cash is much sought after in the rural economy as a means to buy household commodities such as staple foods, medicine, seeds and fuel. Poor peasant families, for example, will rarely eat livestock or large fish but are more likely to sell them for cash. The staple diet of the rural poor includes relatively few of these 'expensive' items, and normally is restricted to foods such as rice, lentils, chilli and salt (see Kabeer 1994). At times of need people make use of social networks (especially kin-based networks) to obtain credit, and the poorer sections of the population are normally indebted to some degree. Credit and debt are pervasive features of rural life. As well as borrowing from friends, kin and money-lenders, credit is available from NGOs and is nominally linked to investment in income-generating activities.

Literacy and the market

Bangladesh is a multi-literate country. Bangla, as the main spoken language in Bangladesh, is the dominant literacy in terms of political and economic life. It is associated with the language movement of the 1950s and the war of independence from West Pakistan. It is also the form of literacy that is most commonly used in economic activity in rural areas. In contrast, Muslims in Bangladesh use Arabic (script and language) almost exclusively for reading the Quran and other religious texts. The use of Arabic (and occasionally Urdu) for religious reading is widespread in Bangladesh, and the Nilphamary area has an extensive system of maktab and madrasa schools. Bangla and Arabic literacies could not be more different. Arabic is primarily thought of as a sacred script and is associated with the word of the Prophet and God; it is rarely written down except in religious contexts. In Street's (1984) example of maktab and commercial literacies in an Iranian village, people were able to adapt religious uses of literacy for economic purposes. In contrast, there is little or no exchange between religious uses of Arabic script and its economic use in Bangladesh. However, as the Arabic numerals used in Quranic texts are also used in Bangla, this aspect of religious literacy may be transferred to other economic contexts. Bangla language and script is used extensively as a language of economic and political activity as well as in education, newspapers and literature. It is also used widely in Hindu religious literacies. English plays a comparatively minor role in Bangladesh compared to the situation in India. It is used for some commercial and professional activity, in some newspapers, and as the lingua franca within the international NGO community. There are also several minority languages spoken by tribal groups (adivasis), some of whom use their own scripts such as with Chakma and Mandi (see Timm 1991).[4]

Within Muslim peasant communities of the Nilphamary area, both Arabic and Bangla literacies are considered to be necessary, interdependent and 'functional' for both economic and spiritual well-being. In our research area, Arabic reading was linked with religious gain (and the Arabic word *foyda*), whereas Bangla literacy was more associated with economic gain (*labh*). The teaching in adult literacy classes largely follows a secular agenda based on Bangla literacy. However, in our research we found that most women, and a few of the men attending the literacy classes could read Arabic for religious purposes having previously learned from family members or at the local maktab (religious school). These people nevertheless considered themselves to be illiterate. It is hardly surprising that the peasantry rarely uses the Bangla term for literate (*shakkor*). Although the term is used in NGO literature (and primers), few of the people that we spoke to even claimed to know its meaning. Other terms indicating degrees of social status and learning are more frequently used.

Bangla literacy, for economic purposes, plays an integral role in the economic life of the peasantry in Bangladesh. Its use is widespread and central to economic and cultural institutions and the practice of daily life (rather than being peripheral or 'marginal', see Goody 1968: 5). Although the oral culture and face-to-face relationships are highly valued, literacy plays a part in nearly all forms of economic activity, and those people who are not able to do so directly must make use of mediators. Most forms of property in Bangladesh are regulated and given legitimacy by the state. The inheritance and sale of land and livestock (goats, buffalo and cows) require payment of tax and involve official documentation. Around the bazaar in Nilphamary the stall-holders (with few exceptions) use literacy for record keeping and calculation. This is also the case with the vast majority of the shopkeepers who run *mudi* or *golmal dokan*, the small neighbourhood shops in the town and surrounding rural areas. In market activity, many small stall-holders work on the basis of borrowing and repaying money each day, and because this credit (*baki*) plays an important role in daily economic activity, many economic transactions involve literacy use for both calculation and record keeping.[5] In rural areas many people also buy basic goods (such as oil, paan, salt, tea and cigarettes) on a credit basis with their local shops. These forms of economic literacy involve the fusion of literacy and numeracy in practice. In our research work with adult literacy groups we found that these literacy practices were much valued by both male and female learners. These types of economic literacy involve a vocabulary and form that is quite different from that of the literacy primer (which is largely based on discursive texts and development messages and maintains a separation of literacy and numeracy). The literacy associated with economic calculation and record keeping involves particular types of written text, practice and vocabulary. It is useful here to note that literacy is not simply 'spoken language written down', but involves particular types of language, form and genre (see Cope and Kalantzis 1983; Halliday 1996). In comparison with the extensive vocabulary of the literacy primer, these types of activity make use of a select and relatively limited vocabulary, not all of which is present in the primer.

The two example texts (Figs. 7.1 and 7.2) were written by people who previously attended adult literacy classes and who were applying their new literacy and numeracy skills in their economic life. The texts were written in notebooks of the type that are commonly used for such purposes and are widely available. Figure 7.1 is the text of a farmer. It is written in the form of lists, and its purpose is largely for record keeping and calculation. Like most economic uses of literacy it involves a fusion of literacy and numeracy. This text is a record of agricultural spending such as diesel fuel (used for a water pump), fertiliser and rice seed. Elsewhere in his notebook are records of household spending and money owed to wage labourers for work in rice transplanting. Figure 7.2 is the text of a woman who keeps a record of household spending on food. She uses such records in discussions with her husband and to gain power in financial decision-making within the household. The top line includes the day and date of the record. The vocabulary used is relatively short and relates to commonly used food items. In our research we met several women who keep records, of both household spending and agricultural activity.

One of the distinctive features of this type of literacy (and numeracy) use is the low social status attributed to it. Many of the people we spoke to during the research who used literacy in this way on a daily basis did not regard themselves as literate. Such practices are often hand-written on small scraps of paper (or cigarette packets) and small notebooks kept in the top pocket of men's shirts, or kept hidden away inside the home. During our research we found it useful to describe these practices as 'micro-literacies'. This emphasises both their size and invisibility, and draws on a parallel with 'micro-ethnographic' approaches (see Bloome 1993; also Barton and Hamilton 1998).[6] These practices contrast with the higher-status and more socially visible forms of literacy practice and accounting of the larger businesses (see below). The element of secrecy and privacy associated with these micro-literacy practices may be because these texts often

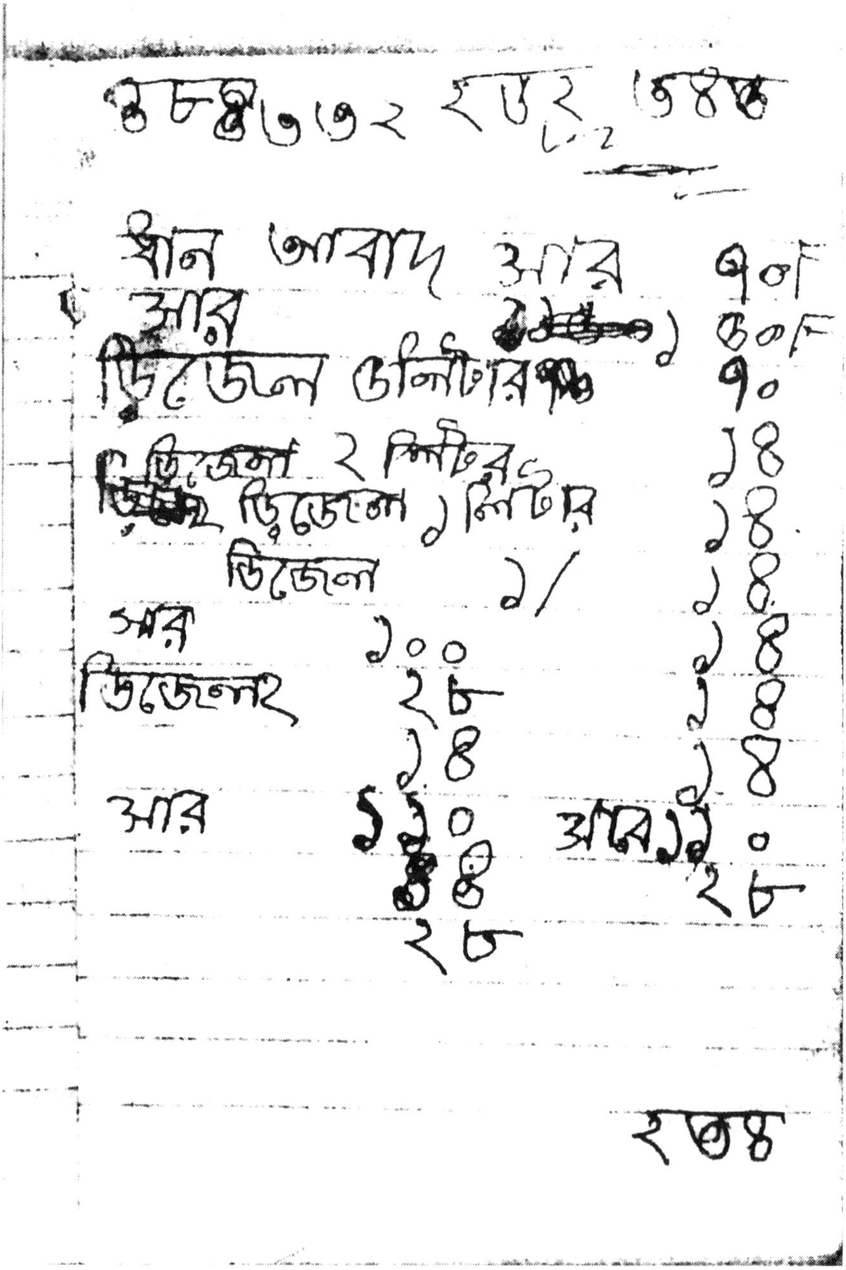

Figure 7.1 *Hishab* (accounts): a farmer's record keeping. © Bryan Maddox

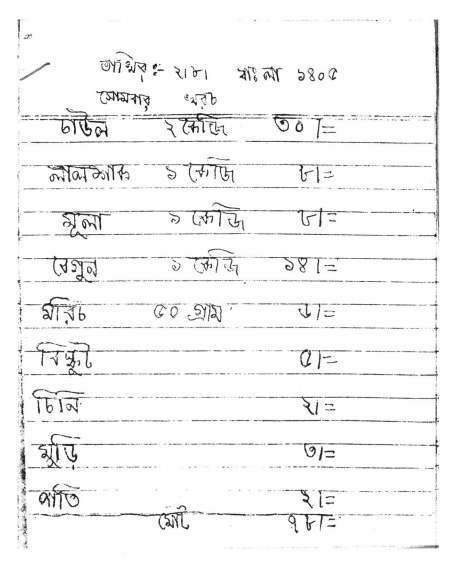

Figure 7.2 Managing poverty: a record of household expenditure. © Bryan Maddox

relate to economic (and therefore private) activity, but are often carried out in crowded public spaces such as the bazaar. In the case of women's literacy (both religious and economic), this is normally carried out within the privacy of the home. These distinctive features of the economic literacy practices mean that it is easy to gain the misleading impression that there is a dearth of written materials and practice in the bazaar and rural areas, and this is particularly so for outside observers.

The low-status economic literacy practices and texts of the workers and peasantry are quite different from those of the middle and professional classes and in many cases would not, in themselves, qualify people to be counted as literate. Such terms tend to be reserved for high-status groups in society (e.g., *bhadralock*). In other words this is not simply a debate about literacy use, but also relates to the status and representation of literacy use in and between social classes. This contrasts with the idea that literacy is a 'universal' skill that is devoid of class specificity, and has implications for understanding the role of literacy in economic and social development.

Literacy and the bazaar

This discussion can be further illustrated by looking at literacy and numeracy use within the Nilphamary bazaar. As Goody (1968) noted, many ethnographic studies fail to give due recognition to the role of literacy within a group or society, and this is also true of anthropological studies of market activity and the bazaar (see for example Geertz 1979; Fanselow 1990).

Geertz, for example, in his study 'Suq: The Bazaar Economy of Sefrou' (1979) pays little attention to the uses of literacy within that economic domain. It is clear within his account that literacy activities do take place within the Moroccan 'Suq' bazaar (he mentions scribes, letter writers and written contracts), but these remain on the margins of his highly detailed and descriptive account. Geertz is interested in the 'flow of words' within the bazaar (p. 99), but these are spoken words. The role of book-keeping and written calculation remains relatively unexplored in his account, even though he emphasises the pervasive role of credit in the bazaar (p. 223; see also Fanselow 1990: 260). This is somewhat surprising considering his Weberian approach to the market (see Weber 1978, 1992).

In his discussion of economic practices such as 'the qirad, or what is called in the Western tradition, the commenda' (Geertz 1979: 133) it becomes clear that literacy had been used extensively in written contracts for long-distance caravan and maritime trade (pp. 135, 136, 238). Such practices are often described as important in the development of both economic and literate traditions (see Clanchy 1979; Goody 1986, 1996). However, the discussion remains marginal to the main thrust of his argument that emphasises orality. The lack of recognition of written texts and practices is unfortunate, as Geertz's study may have usefully explored and tested some of the more theoretical ideas about the role and impact of literacy on culture, economy and society.

The academic literature on literacy and economics tends to be dominated by deterministic or 'autonomous' (in Street's sense) theories about the 'impact' of literacy on the economy. These theoretical positions have often become institutionally embedded, and appear as implicit assumptions within economic and educational policy (for example, see Windham 1999). Such approaches oversimplify the role of literacy in economic development. For example, in Max Weber's theory, rational book-keeping and the separation of family and business accounts were a small part of a much wider and detailed explanation of the development of capitalism in Europe, and yet literacy is still evoked as the route to economic 'take off' (see Weber 1992). Such deterministic approaches emphasise formal relationships between literacy and economic development without giving sufficient attention to more substantive questions of culture, political economy and the actual uses of literacy (Graff 1979). The same can be said for statistical approaches that aim to plot relationships of correlation and causality between 'literacy' and other social indicators such as health. Such approaches tend to make a fetish out of both literacy and the market.[7]

The Nilphamary bazaar provides a good opportunity to examine the economic uses of literacy within a specific institutional and cultural context. As in other Bangladeshi towns, the economic activity in Nilphamary takes place in clearly demarcated domains. Each type of produce has its own location. Inside the bazaar there are separate areas for the sale of vegetables, grain, meat and household goods. Large agricultural items (such as water pumps), as well as medicines, electrical goods and books are sold outside the bazaar along the town's main street. Literacy, in the form of advertising and shop-front signs is conspicuously visible throughout the town and the bazaar. This includes a large illuminated sign advertising cigarettes, and advertisements for large multinational companies such as Singer and Pepsi. There are also several printers' businesses located on the main street. No live produce is sold within the bazaar. Livestock (such as cows, goats, hens and ducks) are sold at the twice-weekly market, the *haat*. The *haat* attracts artisans selling baskets and matting, clothing and locally made agricultural implements. During market days the town is full of people (mostly men), and the teashops and rickshaw pullers do a brisk trade.

Like the religious and economic texts discussed earlier, the economic uses of literacy and numeracy in the bazaar have distinctive features in terms of both social class and genre. They are mostly associated with record keeping and calculation, unlike the dominant social constructions of literacy. This can be illustrated by looking at the uses of literacy and numeracy within the fish market.

The fish market is situated along one edge of the bazaar. There is one small covered area where imported fish are sold, but the majority of fish sellers set up their stalls each morning on either side of a busy road. The road itself is used by people carrying goods to market, bicycles and rickshaws, as it is the main route

145

to several villages. But since very few cars or lorries use this route they present no problem for the fish market. Fish are normally carried to market in baskets that are supported over people's shoulders with a wooden pole.

During the monsoon season (July to October) much of the local area is flooded and many rural farmers turn to fishing for their livelihood. This includes fishing at night using lanterns. At this time the market is filled with small stall-holders, and the price of fish is relatively low. Later in the year the water begins to recede and fishermen begin to rely on catches from small rivers and 'tanks'. Tanks (*pukur*) are large man-made ponds used for hatching and growing fish. The more wealthy farmers and businessmen who own tanks drain them several times a year using diesel pumps. At these times fish will often be distributed among local men and boys who will sell them at the market on behalf of the tank owner. This is done on a credit basis. As the fish are graded and separated into baskets for sale they are weighed and distributed to the people who will sell them. At this point written note is taken of fish distribution, and the owner is paid in cash for the fish later in the day (see Figure 7.3).

There are also a few businessmen who import fish, own several tanks and employ fish sellers on a wage labour basis. These fishermen can afford to buy ice for storage, but other fishermen must sell their produce while it is fresh, even if that means staying at the bazaar late into the night. This means that on any one day, there will be fish sellers at the bazaar selling fish under quite different economic circumstances. Some will be selling fish that they have themselves caught, others will be selling on a credit basis and returning a proportion of their income to the tank owner, or running small businesses buying from fishermen and selling at a profit. Finally there are the wage labourers who are selling fish but are paid in cash on a daily rate. Most of these people selling fish are involved in literacy and numeracy although in many cases it does not appear to be the case.

Like many other goods in the bazaar, fish sales are not based on fixed prices but are negotiated between the seller and buyer. Fish are nominally sold by weight (kg), but there is normally some room for negotiation. The price varies throughout the year depending on availability and demand, but profit margins often depend on the ability of the fish seller to strike a good bargain. While much of this bargaining involves mental arithmetic it also involves written calculation (and in the case of the more wealthy stall-holders, the use of calculators). Literacy is also used for calculation of profit margins and noting down sales made on credit arrangements. However, literacy use is not homogeneous among the fish sellers. It depends on their educational background and on their position within the market. For example, most of the people who are employed to sell fish by businessmen will keep detailed (and visible) ledgers of their sales so that their employer can monitor sales. If these salesmen are not able to keep their own ledgers they rely on other people to act as literacy mediators (these include people employed as accountants and also family members as helpers). In contrast, the people selling fish that is purchased from tank owners must keep their

Figure 7.3 Literacy mediation in market activities. © Bryan Maddox

own records in order to calculate and to try and maintain profit margins (this is not always achieved successfully). Finally, people selling fish they themselves have caught do not necessarily require written records to calculate profit margins or to show to an employer, but they may want to note down fish sold on credit. Some people keep notes and make calculation and keep records on small scraps of paper that are kept hidden in their top pockets. Other people use literacy in a more obvious way using large, well-ordered ledger books. What is relatively rare in the bazaar and in other types of rural economic activity is the non-use of literacy.

Adult literacy programmes

Our research highlights the possible value of adult literacy and numeracy tuition that is geared to the economic uses of literacy. Most adult literacy programmes in Bangladesh are based on Freirean ideas of social analysis and consciousness raising (see Freire 1972). Such approaches are valuable in legitimising social change and stimulating solidarity, as well as providing information, but they often lack an analysis of the wider uses of literacy. Rather than helping people to engage with existing literacy practices they tend to introduce a model of literacy based on discursive texts and development messages. Such a curriculum inevitably lacks some of the basic curriculum and knowledge that is used in everyday economic activity (for example, words such as total, income, expenditure and writing of the day, date and calendar months).

The primer curriculum also tends to separate the teaching of literacy and numeracy, when these are fused in economic literacies. During our research with adult literacy groups, male and female learners tended to prioritise calculation and record keeping over other forms of literacy activity (see Figure 7.4).

Most literacy primers encourage reading of relatively long texts containing development messages, whereas the economic uses of literacy centre on writing short lists and a fusion of record keeping and calculation.

It could be argued that teaching such economic uses would be restrictive and tend to reinforce current social inequalities. The idea of a 'universal' type of literacy skill is that it can be applied in all the life situations that are appropriate.

There are clearly more uses of literacy than the economic ones, for example letter writing is an important use of literacy in rural areas. However, it may be that teaching based on the economic uses of literacy would provide a meaningful foundation upon which people can develop their skills. In this sense it could be regarded as 'situated' learning (see Lave and Wenger 1991; Barton et al. 1999). In highlighting the class-specific patterns of literacy use it becomes clear that the 'universal' skills advocated in many literacy programmes are based on a model of literacy that is quite different in form and content from the literacy practices of the peasantry. An understanding of the economic uses of literacy may therefore have implications for issues such as the application and sustainability of learning.

Figure 7.4 Literacy and numeracy fused in daily life. © Bryan Maddox

Conclusion

The economic uses of literacy are a pervasive feature of Bangladeshi society. However, the economic literacy and numeracy of the type discussed above tend to be undervalued by politicians and development planners. They remain low status and marginal in relation to the dominant forms and constructions of literacy as *shakkor*, and yet they are perhaps the form of Bangla literacy that is most relevant to the intended beneficiaries of adult literacy programmes.

With the continued success of formal, non-formal and adult education in Bangladesh a much greater proportion of the rural peasantry will have access to education. However, it is likely that formal and deterministic theories of literacy and economy will not be suited to understanding the social and economic impact of such changes, nor are they suited to the development of sensitive frameworks for evaluation. A more situated analysis of the use and possible economic impact of literacy in Bangladesh would involve recognition of the particular socio-cultural and economic factors in people's lives.

Notes

1 This chapter is part of a larger piece of work forthcoming. The research was supported by an ESRC studentship, and was conducted during ten months of fieldwork between October 1997 and May 1999. I am grateful to Talat Mahmud who worked with me throughout the field-based research. Many of the ideas expressed in this article are the

result of our work together, although Talat cannot be held responsible for my views presented here.

2 The indigo cultivation was highly exploitative, and based on forced labour. On the colonial indigo trade in Bengal see Guha (1974), and Rao and Rao (1992).

3 I have used the term 'peasantry' here in a broad generic and inclusive sense. There is, of course, considerable debate about definitions of the peasantry, and there is not space within the chapter to examine this debate in detail (see Wolf 1966; Shanin 1971). As the people described in this chapter are involved simultaneously in a number of different economic activities ('modes of production'), I can see no advantage here in describing (or separating) their class position in terms of a rural proletariat or artisan class. In this sense I am using the term 'peasantry' in a similar way to the Bangla term 'krishok-sromik' (farmers and workers).

4 This 'multi-literate' situation is by no means unusual. For example, see Scribner and Cole's (1981) description of the uses of Vai, Arabic and English literacy in Liberia.

5 See Doronilla (1996: 119) for a similar description of literacy and numeracy use in a Philippine market economy.

6 There are parallels here with 'vernacular literacies' as described by Barton and Hamilton (1998). Barton and Hamilton argue that vernacular literacies are often associated with low status and secrecy.

7 For a detailed discussion of literacy and fetishism see Skaria 1996. Carrier (1997) provides a good analysis of the market idea in Western culture.

References

Ahsan, E. (1989) 'Ownership and Control: Land Acquisition, Fragmentation, and Consumption in Rural Bangladesh', *Urban Anthropology* 18(3).

Barton, D. and Hamilton, M. (1998) *Local Literacies: Reading and Writing in One Community*, London: Routledge.

Barton, D., Hamilton, M. and Ivanič, R. (eds) (1999) *Situated Literacies: Reading and Writing in Context*, London, Routledge.

Bloome, D. (1993) 'Necessary Indeterminacy and the Microethnographic Study of Reading as a Social Process', *Journal of Research in Reading* 16(2): 98–111.

Carrier, J. (ed.) (1997) *Meanings of The Market: The Free Market in Western Culture*, Oxford: Berg.

Clanchy, M. (1979) *From Memory to Written Record*, Cambridge, MA: Harvard University Press.

Cope, B. and Kalantzis, M. (1983) *The Powers of Literacy: A Genre Approach to Teaching Writing*, London: Falmer Press.

Datta, A.K. (1998) *Land and Labour Relations in South-West Bangladesh*, London: Macmillan.

Doronilla, C.M. (1996) *Landscapes of Literacy: An Ethnographic Study of Functional Literacy in Marginal Philippine Communities*, London and Hamburg: UNESCO and Luzac Oriental.

Eriksen, T. (1995) *Small Places, Large Issues: An Introduction to Social and Cultural Anthropology*, London: Pluto Press.

Fanselow, F. (1990) 'The Bazaar Economy or How Bizarre is the Bazaar Economy Really', *MAN* 25: 250–65.

Freire, P. (1972) *Pedagogy of the Oppressed*, London: Sheed & Ward.

Geertz, C. (1979) 'Suq: The Bazaar Economy in Sefrou', in C. Geertz, H. Geertz and L. Rosen (eds), *Meaning and Order in Moroccan Society*, Cambridge: Cambridge University Press.

Goody, J. (1968) *Literacy in Traditional Societies*, Cambridge: Cambridge University Press.

—— (1986) *The Logic of Writing and the Organisation of Society*, Cambridge: Cambridge University Press.

—— (1996) *The East in the West*, Cambridge: Cambridge University Press.

Graff, H. (1979) *The Literacy Myth: Literacy and Social Structure in the Nineteenth Century City*, New York: Falmer Press.

Guha, R. (1974) 'Neel Darpan: The Image of a Peasant Revolt in a Liberal Mirror', *Journal of Peasant Studies* 2: 1–46.

Halliday, M.A.K. (1996) 'Literacy and Linguistics: A Functional Perspective', in R. Hasan and G. Williams (eds), *Literacy and Society*, London: Longman.

Hartmann, B. and Boyce, J. (1983) *A Quiet Violence: View from a Bangladeshi Village*, London: Zed Books.

Hossain, M. (1995) 'Rural Income and Poverty Trends', in *1987–1994: Dynamics of Rural Poverty in Bangladesh*, Dhaka: Bangladesh Institute of Development Studies.

Kabeer, N. (1994) *Reversed Realities: Gender Hierarchies in Development Thought*, London: Verso.

Lave, J. and Wenger, E. (1991) *Situated Learning: Legitimate Peripheral Participation*, Cambridge: Cambridge University Press.

Maddox, B. (forthcoming) 'Subaltern Literacies: Writing, Ethnography, and the State', PhD thesis, King's College London.

Osmani, S.R. (1996) 'Living Standards in Bangladesh: The Last Two Decades', Conference paper, London University, December 1996.

Rao, A. and Rao, D. (1992) *The Blue Devil: Indigo and Colonial Bengal*, Delhi: Oxford University Press.

Rashid, S. (ed.) (1995) *Bangladesh Economy: Evaluation and Research Agenda*, Dhaka: Dhaka University Press.

Sainath, P. (1996) *Everybody Loves a Good Drought: Stories from India's Poorest Districts*, Delhi: Penguin.

Scribner, S. and Cole, M. (1981) *The Psychology of Literacy*, Cambridge, MA: Harvard University Press.

Shanin, T. (1971) *Peasants and Peasant Societies*, Harmondsworth: Penguin.

Skaria, A. (1996) 'Writing, Orality and Power in the Dangs, Western India, 1800's–1920's', in S. Amin and D. Chakrabarty (eds), *Subaltern Studies*, Delhi: Oxford University Press.

Spivak, G.C. (1993) 'Can the Subaltern Speak?', in P. Williams and L. Chrisman (eds), *Colonial Discourse and Post-Colonial Theory*, London: Harvester Wheatsheaf.

Street, B. (ed.) (1984) *Literacy in Theory and Practice*, Cambridge: Cambridge University Press.

Timm, R.W. (1991) *The Adivasis of Bangladesh*, London: Minority Rights Group.

UNESCO (UNDP) (1997) *Basic Education for Empowerment of the Poor*, Bangkok: UNESCO, Asia-Pacific.

Weber, M. (1978) *Economy and Society*, Berkeley: University of California Press.

—— (1992) *The Protestant Ethic and the Spirit of Capitalism*, London: Routledge.

White, S. (1992) *Arguing with the Crocodile: Gender and Class in Bangladesh*, Dhaka: Zed Books.

Wilson-Moore, M. (1989) 'Women's Work in Homestead Gardens: Subsistence, Patriarchy and Status in Northwest Bangladesh', *Urban Anthropology* 18(3–4): 281–98.

Windham, D. (1999) 'Literacy and Economic Development', in D. Wagner, R. Venezky and B. Street (eds), *Literacy: An International Handbook*, Boulder, CO: Westview Press.

Wolf, E. (1966) *Peasants*, London: Prentice-Hall.

8

WOMEN'S LITERACY AND HEALTH

Can an ethnographic researcher find the links?

Anna Robinson-Pant

Introduction

Debate around the advantages of using ethnographic research in development policy and planning contexts has focused on the contribution that it can make to the developers'[1] understanding: e.g., more in-depth analysis and insight into implementation issues, local meanings of concepts like 'literacy' and a wider perspective on 'evaluation' of projects. There has however been far less discussion about what 'development' does to 'ethnography'. In other words, how does carrying out ethnographic research in a policy context differ from 'pure' academic ethnographic research? This chapter looks at the question through my experiences of introducing an ethnographic approach to an American agency implementing literacy and health programmes in Nepal. As well as analysing the mechanics of conducting ethnographic research in an agency more used to traditional questionnaire-based surveys, I look at the wider issue (addressed in Street's Introduction regarding the New Work Order) of how far ethnographic research can be packaged and sold as a product to the developers.

Women's literacy and health: researching the links

In the southern Indian state of Kerala, where literacy is universal, the infant mortality rate is the lowest in the entire developing world – and the fertility rate is the lowest in India.

(UNICEF 1999: 8)

Literacy has been seen as the key to development, and particularly in the context of women's and girls' education, as the means of improving family health. Research on the links between women's literacy and health has been dominated by a quantitative approach where the emphasis is to prove statistical correlation between women's literacy and macro indicators of development, such as child mortality, fertility rates or life expectancy (e.g., Cochrane 1982; Le Vine 1982; Le Vine et al. 1991). Such studies provide an overview for policy makers working at a national or international level, but do not give any insight into how or why such a link between literacy and health may exist. What is surprising about so many of these studies is also how readily correlation is taken as causality, as if significant correlation automatically indicates a cause–effect relationship (Wagner 1995). Even the reliability of such statistics has been brought into question, since government literacy rates are often based on self-reported literacy or use statistics based on enrolment rates of girls at school, rather than adult women's literacy (Bown 1990).

In the last decade, researchers have begun to realise the limitations of the above approaches in terms of policy formulation and planning for women's literacy/health programmes. Turning their attention to the 'almost un-researched subject of the impact of adult women's literacy' as opposed to school girls' literacy (Bown 1990), there has been a recognition that more qualitative methodologies are needed to explore why and how women's literacy may be linked to health outcomes. A major new direction, influenced by participatory development paradigms like PRA (Participatory Rural Appraisal),[2] has led to studies of how women themselves perceive literacy and the links with development (Bown 1990; Stromquist 1990; Rogers 1992; Yates 1994; Robinson-Pant, forthcoming). Researchers have challenged the top-down approach of literacy planners, suggesting that women's empowerment, rather than the usual 'efficiency' approach (Moser 1993) – of raising literacy in order to lower fertility rates – is a more appropriate goal for programmes linking women's literacy and health.

Whereas earlier research was influenced by economists and statisticians, more recently the work of anthropologists, psychologists and sociologists has led to what has been termed an 'ideological' or social view of literacy (Street 1994). Anthropologists studying the meaning and uses of literacy in various cultural contexts have questioned assumptions behind quantitative research approaches to literacy/health: that there is a 'great divide' (Goody 1968) between orality and literacy or between literacy and illiteracy, literates and illiterates. Qualitative and ethnographic research conducted in various countries (e.g., Street 1984, in Iran; Kell 1994, in South Africa; Yates 1994, in Ghana; and Robinson-Pant 2000, in Nepal) has led to deeper understanding of how people 'take hold of literacy' (Kulick and Stroud 1993) in specific contexts. These studies share an understanding of literacy not just as a technical set of skills, but as social practices that take place differently in different situations and move away from the question of the 'impact' of literacy (see Introduction).

Though academic researchers have moved towards an 'ideological' approach, many development agencies still adopt an autonomous research approach for evaluating the impact of their literacy programmes. In Nepal, for example, agency staff commonly use a questionnaire to evaluate how women's behaviour changes as a result of participating in literacy courses or how literate women differ from 'illiterate'. Empowerment has been analysed through asking women to answer yes/no to a range of questions, such as 'do you make decisions about household expenditure?' or 'do you think you could convince your husband not to take a second wife?' (Leve et al. 1997). The scores have been used to show the impact of literacy on women's lives, particularly in relation to family planning and health practices. Such research has sometimes revealed puzzling relationships or correlation: for example, that control groups of women who did not participate in development programmes had increased in decision making power over a year, as compared to literacy class participants (Burchfield 1997), or that women living far from a health post gained greater health knowledge in classes than those living near to health facilities (Smith 1997). Recognising the limitations of such questionnaire-based research even on its own terms, a few agencies have started conducting in-depth studies on literacy programmes.

It was in this context that I was approached by an American aid agency[3] to develop a research project looking at the links between women's literacy and health in two areas of Nepal. An integrated adult literacy/health education course had been used for several years in Nepal as an entry point for family planning and health activities which were the Agency's main area of work. Their aim was to 'find out how literacy course interventions get translated into women's health-seeking behaviors (if they do) so as to know how to strengthen programs or change programs to make these effects greater' (from Agency proposal). Analysing the kinds of linkages between literacy and health through qualitative research – rather than simply finding statistical correlation – was intended to lead more directly into programme recommendations. The findings were to be shared at the Agency's annual conference in Washington, with the idea of expanding the literacy/health strategy to other developing countries. On my part, having just completed academic research for my PhD on a similar topic, I was interested in the opportunity to introduce an ethnographic approach to this policy context.

Designing the research project: challenging assumptions

Though both the Agency and I shared the aim of conducting qualitative research into the links between women's literacy and health, we soon discovered that we had very differing assumptions about qualitative research and about literacy programmes. Issues arose around how research should be carried out, the overall objective of research in relation to policy and the place of literacy in development programmes. The process of challenging these assumptions was not one-sided – i.e., me, the ethnographic researcher transforming conventional evaluation procedures within the Agency – but involved a dialogue as to how I should adapt ethnographic research approaches to take account of the Agency's needs and perspectives. Analysing both the product (the findings of the research) and the process of challenging each other's assumptions, this chapter examines how far the compromise reached was effective.

The Agency's assumptions around literacy and research were characterised by the view of knowledge as 'commodity . . . measured as though it was inert . . . and judged for "quality" as though it were just another commercial product' (Street, this volume, p. 5). In this case, the package of 'knowledge' referred both to the research findings and to the health/literacy intervention which was being evaluated, a course based on a primer rather than a 'real literacies' approach (Rogers et al. 1999). An attention to the 'selling environment' (Street, this volume, p. 3) meant that a key concern was around how the research was to be packaged. The Agency needed ten succinct findings that could be presented as slogans or pictures on overheads at their conference in order to 'sell' the approach to other countries. The literacy/health course was assumed to be a neutral technical package that could be evaluated in terms of its impact, rather than in relation to the differing literacy and health practices of the groups participating in the programmes. Working from a deficit model that women needed a certain package of literacy and health skills to improve their health, the Agency believed it was just a question of evaluating whether the women had been sold the right package.

The Agency's views of qualitative research were conditioned greatly by the desire for tangible, measurable results. The original research proposal was based on assumptions from quantitative research experience: the 'health-seeking behaviour' of forty literate women was to be compared with that of forty illiterate women (the control group) through a formal test of their health knowledge. Interviews on their reproductive health would be conducted, using the 'lifeline method', where women place objects (leaves, flowers, etc.) on the ground to represent key events in their lives (marriage, children, adoption of family planning). Since the main audience of the research was to be in Washington, I was hired as a Nepali-speaking expatriate to produce the final report in English, though the actual fieldwork was to be carried out by a team of Nepali researchers. The research process and the product (my report) could, the Agency assumed, be separated out and conducted by entirely separate teams. I selected four women who had been working with communities using PRA methods, rather than established researchers, in the hope that their communication skills would enable them to pick up new ethnographic methods. The research timetable allocated very little time for analysis or debriefing with the field team, in the assumption that findings could be collated more readily than tables of statistics.

Though I disputed some of the Agency's assumptions around literacy and research concepts, I was left with the challenge myself of how to adjust an ethnographic approach to fit within the objectives and constraints of a development agency. In particular, I had to view my role as more detached from the fieldwork – being primarily training, advising and analysing others' findings. I also had to work out how to make ethnographic research findings immediately accessible to busy policy makers. The most difficult dilemma was, as it turned out, around what to do if the research failed to find linkages between literacy and health which the Agency could sell in Washington!

Integrating an ethnographic approach:
the research process

I was struck by the conflict of interests in the Agency's original research proposal. Although the approach was to be qualitative, the intention seemed still to be to prove the equation '*acquiring literacy skills = changed health practices*'. Whereas I had assumed we would be more interested in why or how literacy and health were linked, the emphasis was similar to a traditional quantitative study collecting evidence that literate women were more healthy. Terminology such as 'control group' implied that any differences identified between the two groups (literate and illiterate) would be due to the literacy class alone. Observation was also narrowly confined to the classroom, rather than including literacy and health practices in women's everyday lives.

In discussion with the Agency, I questioned whether there would be a divide within the community between literate and illiterate, suggesting that it might be problematic to decide who would be classed as 'literate'. I tried to expand the scope of the research by extending the equation above into: '*Does participating in this literacy class = increased health knowledge = changed health behaviour?*' The objective of the study became not to prove the equation (i.e., the impact), but to understand the links (=) and the conditions under which the equation may or may not make sense. For each part of the equation, there were other factors to bring into the picture which were not considered in the Agency's original proposal:

- *literacy class*: we needed to look at all the elements as a process, rather than simply evaluating the reading and writing: i.e., the literacy curriculum, the group as a social support, the facilitator (and her characteristics), the supervisor and his/her role.
- *health knowledge*: we needed to include other sources of information as well as literacy classes (e.g., radio, specific health training courses, friends, relations, the 'diffusion' effect from previous class participants, local health workers).
- *changes in health behaviour*: we needed to include the other factors that influence participants' behaviour, apart from health knowledge, e.g., accessibility to health services, reliability of health services, resources, power relations within the household, professional behaviour and attitudes of health workers.

By introducing a more complex and holistic view on the process of participating in a literacy/health class, I hoped to move away from simply identifying whether a woman participating in the class had adopted more family planning devices. In any case it was unrealistic to expect to observe behaviour change within the three-month course period, as suggested in the original proposal. The new strategy made more distinction between literacy and education (which were used synonymously by the Agency), between the health education and the literacy skills. Since women participating in classes could not be regarded in isolation, particularly in regard to family planning decisions, we proposed including some men in research activities. The Agency however were adamant that this was not a 'gender study' and that, since it was a women's programme, we should focus on their views only. They were also unwilling to abandon the idea of a control group, though we changed the criteria from 'literate/illiterate' to class participants/non-participants.

Regarding research methods, I felt too that assumptions and methods from quantitative research had shaped the overall strategy. For example, though focus group discussions were the key tool for investigating the significance of literacy in women's lives and linkages with health behaviour, direct questions similar to questionnaires were provided, such as, 'What difference does it make to women to be literate?' As noted in Street's Introduction, it is often meaningless just to ask people directly about 'literacy', as has been the practice in many agency surveys. Class observation proposed by the Agency was around noting simply whether or not the facilitator followed the steps in the guidebook, rather than capturing the richness of interactions between women and facilitator. By structuring focus group discussions around visual activities (e.g., mobility mapping, decision making maps), we aimed, however, to document the conversations that took place between participants. Class observation was widened not just to include evaluation of teaching techniques (steps followed) but to take notes of interactions, particularly on health topics. Ethnographic observation conducted outside the classrooms would enable us to analyse how women used literacy in their everyday lives and how health workers interacted with women visiting health posts or clinics. The conceptual tools of 'literacy events' and 'literacy practices' (see Street's Introduction) were key to this kind of ethnographic observation and analysis.

The research strategy worked out was thus a compromise in terms of my own ideas of an ethnographic study and the Agency's assumptions about what constituted policy-directed research. We retained the control group, the formal health test (though asked questions orally) and the exclusive focus on women as research subjects. However, the original proposal was widened to include more ethnographic observation of a range of activities and to make questioning less direct through visual methods. Concepts such as the divide between literate/ illiterate were challenged, and more distinction made between literacy, education and health education. By unpacking terms such as the 'literacy class' (being a group structure, literacy, health education, etc.), we aimed to explore the relationship between literacy classes and health behaviour as a process, rather than simply to evaluate whether or not a woman had changed her behaviour as a result of the three-month course. As I discuss later, what I failed to challenge, by focusing only on the level of methods, was our overall ideological differences: the Agency's underlying belief that they had the power to give women better health.

What did an ethnographic approach contribute?

Before analysing how an ethnographic research approach was affected by being used in a development context, I will look briefly at our specific findings around the Agency's literacy/health intervention.

An understanding of what goes on in literacy classrooms

The detailed accounts of classes observed over a week gave an 'inside' view which previous Agency evaluation reports (based on quick visits over a wider geographical area) had lacked. Though the course was intended to be for women of reproductive age, it turned out that many classes consisted only of young children, boys as well as girls, since their parents saw it as an efficient alternative to the local primary school. The curriculum focusing on family planning and AIDS presented great problems when classes were under-age or when the facilitators were young and inexperienced. As this extract from the researchers' field notes shows, the young facilitator in Magla (Terai district, on Indian border) relied on her mother and supervisor for help with discussion:

> The facilitator opened the course book and read thoroughly the 'Sudeni' [traditional midwife] chapter without asking anything to students . . . But the students were also quite used to this so they followed the lesson as the facilitator read. After the facilitator finished she kept silent, just looking at all students, then she smiled.
>
> The facilitator's mother first was sitting near to the asst. supervisor, then came and asked a student to vacate the place for her. She sat just beside her daughter and whispered to her. But the facilitator did not react. She kept silent but her mother insisted that she question the students. Maybe the facilitator did not understand. After this Asst. Supervisor began questioning. The facilitator's mother was the only student to answer all Mr. Jha's questions. Again the supervisor asked the students to read the chapter. During reading, the facilitator remained silent, looking down at the mat.[4]

What emerged in this class was that the facilitator preferred teaching the reading skills, and left her mother and the supervisor to take over discussion of health topics. Even then, health information tended to be presented as a message or slogan to memorise, rather than an issue for discussion. In most of the classes observed, young facilitators usually overcame their lack of confidence or embarrassment by treating the lesson as a technical exercise in decoding letters. Overall, there was far more emphasis on the literacy instruction than on discussion of health topics. The exception was where a health worker ran the class and related the issues to women's own experiences:

Today the lesson is 'Sudeni' [Midwife] . . . Most of them seemed interested especially, one Mayadevi, who is a Sudeni herself. Most of the
young girls were interested in listening to what Mayadevi had to say
interesting regarding her work . . . Two ladies in the corner were re-
membering the time of their delivery and how the Sudeni was asking
for a sari [as a gift] at the time of delivering a son.

(Researchers' notes, Khatiya class)

The facilitator's age, position and experience greatly determined how far the
classroom became a forum for discussion of health matters and who chose to
attend. In looking at the two contrasting districts chosen for field research, language was another key issue affecting health education which emerged through
class observation. The course book was written in Nepali, though in the Terai
area women spoke only Maithili, a language closer to Hindi. These classes
varied greatly according to how far the facilitator was familiar enough with
Nepali to mediate between the course book and the Maithili-speaking students:

When the facilitator said 'Garbatti' [pregnant woman] and the women
interrupted again saying she did not pronounce it properly, she said
'agarbathi' [incense stick] instead of 'garbati'.

(Magla, field notes)

Language difficulties like this (confusing 'incense stick' with 'pregnant woman'!)
led the facilitator to treat the reading passage as a decoding exercise, rather than
reading for meaning. In Terai classes, the participants and facilitator spoke and
tried to write in Maithili, even though the book was in Nepali:

Throughout the class, both the participants and the facilitator were
talking in Maithili. Even the answers they wrote to the questions were
in Maithili. Whenever the participants did not understand the meaning
they asked the facilitator to do it.

Most of the participants found writing in Maithili a real problem.
Some of the participants were writing half the sentence in Maithili and
half in Nepali.

(Magla, field notes)

Surprisingly, the language issue was not mentioned by participants or facilitators
when describing the problems they faced at the classes, but the researchers
in Dhanusha felt that both health content and literacy skills were considerably
harder to pick up, because of learning in a second language. Both classes in
Udayapur (hill district) were taught entirely in Nepali, since all the women were
Nepali-speaking. The researchers' detailed observations thus gave the Agency
staff a picture of the classrooms – what actually took place varied so widely,

according to the facilitator's characteristics, the class composition and the language groups.

An insight into everyday literacy and health events

The field researchers' observations centred more on formal health centres and places where they knew they could observe literacy events (e.g., village shop, library), rather than informal spontaneous events, largely because of the limited period of fieldwork. Though the assumption had been that women needed literacy skills to visit health posts or clinics, we found they did not even need to sign their names. They were however presented with prescriptions or 'receipts' at certain health posts, which they would take straight to the pharmacist to read. Though there was no need for the women to read – 'the prescription given by the Maternal Child Health Worker, no one reads, just holds it as a note' (researchers' notes from Khatiya) – the researchers felt that women might have more control over the process if they could read the papers they carried.

More surprising was the fact that very few health workers kept or used written records of patients. The private clinics in particular made no note of patients seen and treatments given (Garain clinic in Magla justified this by saying that people feel shy to have their name in records) and could not give the last week's record. The *dhamis* (traditional faith healers), though they took no written notes, could recall very accurately exactly who they had seen over the last week and why. Only the government health post staff kept a detailed register of patients, but not separate case records: the register was seen as an administrative requirement rather than a necessary tool in consultation. A health worker at Bakhola explained that she kept regular records of pills and condoms dispensed, because she had to produce evidence of two new family planning users each month to satisfy Red Cross rules for payment of her salary.

'Literacy' was thus found to have a different meaning from that assumed by our researchers: reading and writing for women using health posts was not perceived in functional terms as a need but was associated with identity and confidence. One woman who could not sign her name described herself as a 'thumb stamp person' (researchers' notes). The health staff too did not view record keeping as useful in consultation, but more as an administrative requirement necessary for ensuring their salary.

It was in everyday observation that the researchers picked up on the 'ideological' dimension, associated with the literacy class and with literacy events in the community. In particular, they noted the 'gendering' of literacy practices (Rockhill 1993) which differed greatly between and within areas. Small libraries (often in a tin trunk held at a village shop) were used widely by women in the hills: rather than borrowing books about health issues, they were particularly interested in books on women's legal rights. Conversely, the libraries in the Terai districts (consisting often of religious and fiction books) were used exclusively by men and school children because they were under the control of male elders, whose houses were considered inaccessible to married women. In this area, the researchers commented: 'we did not see any women holding any sort of committee meeting: even a puja [religious] committee was all male, it seems'. The kind of literacy required for committee meetings was associated with the male, public domain, and women were aware of being excluded from many of these literacy practices through their restricted mobility. The literacy class was thus perceived as more of a threat in this area than in the hills: 'An old lady pointing at us said, "they are here to spoil our daughters and daughter in laws, teaching them about family planning and how to fight at home with their mother-in-law"' (researchers' notes, Khatiya). In Terai Muslim communities in particular, there was strong resistance to the family planning messages in the literacy course.

'Literacy' therefore held very different meanings for the groups involved – whether health workers, women in literacy classes or male village elders. Whereas some Terai communities saw the health education as a threat (and this affected how the course book was taught in classes), hill communities saw literacy as more functional, enhancing women's committees or access to libraries. In both areas, however, women themselves associated literacy (particularly signing their name) with a new identity. What was also striking was how many women spontaneously wrote letters to the field researchers at the end of their stay – as if demonstrating their new roles as 'literate' women. The letters followed the genre of the course book, advising the researchers to keep healthy and eat green vegetables![5] The Agency's idea of a written examination at the end of the course also turned out to be very different from the women's. They worked collaboratively, even in the test, meaning any weight we might have given to individual scores was meaningless. Both these observations on new literacy practices being introduced by the Agency raised issues around how to evaluate the course formally.

Links between class participation and health behaviour

The linkages between participation in literacy classes and health behaviour turned out to be far more complex than imagined by the Agency: we could not produce a generalised list. Throughout the research process, we had received visitors from Washington and communications insisting that everyone there was anxious to hear whether we had 'found' the linkages! Though the health test had suggested that participants had greater health knowledge scores than non-participants in some areas (though both were equally knowledgeable about family planning), their health-seeking behaviour was quite similar, indicating that health knowledge was not the key factor in deciding whether or not to adopt new practices. The assumption behind the literacy/health course had been that women needed more information about family planning and child health in order to change their behaviour. Detailed lifeline interviews showed a very complex picture in relation to how health decisions were made. Rather than demonstrating women's lack of awareness, the interviews revealed a catalogue of poor health services, inadequate family planning counselling, husbands' or in-laws' opposition to family planning and the low value attached to the birth of a girl which forced women to keep trying for a son.

Many women described the feasting that took place at the birth of a son, and others commented, 'can anyone be happy seeing a daughter?' (describing the birth of their first child) and 'whatever the sons earn, the daughters take away in dowry'. Decision making around family planning needed to be seen as a more complex situation than simply a woman persuading her husband (as the literacy primer assumed). Often the relationship with in-laws and the felt need to produce sons meant that women themselves were ambivalent towards family planning or that even their husbands could not take a lead. For example, when Nirmaya's husband went secretly for a vasectomy, his mother shouted at her, the wife:

> They became angry with me. They wanted to have more sons. They used to say to me 'one son is like one eye; two sons means two eyes. So you have to give birth to another son'. After hearing my parents' words, I felt angry with my husband. But my husband convinced me that my daughter is also a son.
>
> (Nirmaya, Bakhola non-participant)

Women interviewed showed how their desire for sons reflected their own insecure position. For example, Sarita (class participant) had a third daughter, at which point her husband left her to migrate to India:

> Her husband was broke, they didn't have more land and she thinks to survive and arrange the third daughter's marriage is not a joke in the Jha community. She has to pay a lot of dowry along with a lot of money to her son-in-law before engagement.

The analysis showed that the adoption of family planning was not just around awareness of the benefits of small families (the message in the literacy course) or the availability of services, but needed to be seen in the context of economic concerns (such as whether a woman can still work after sterilisation or the side effects of pills or depo injections that made women less efficient workers) and social structures, such as the complex network of decision makers in an extended family. Above all, the fact that a daughter was seen as a liability was a value that had been internalised by women and affected their attitudes towards family planning.

So how did the literacy/health class affect these decisions? In focus group discussions, women analysed sources of health information (including the literacy class) according to criteria selected by themselves. They valued the class because it took place every day and gave specific technical information in a focused intensive way, unlike their neighbours, who were said to be their main source of health information and advice. Rather than using literacy skills from the class in certain practical situations, many women felt they had gained confidence from learning to write their names in place of giving a thumb stamp. This confidence and new identity helped them, not just in public places, but at home where they felt able to argue their case with other family members. The health information from the class also enabled them to argue more strongly for changes within the household, like taking children to a government health post instead of to the faith healer.

The literacy class did not appear to change or challenge women's attitudes: those who said they used family planning or took children for vaccinations were already convinced of its value. Those who continued to use the faith healer or a combination of health services gave good reasons for their decision, such as the inefficiency of government clinics: 'I do not rely on the health post because the medicines are always out of stock there' (Devi of Magla); 'The health post never provides medicine and vitamins properly, so why is it there?' (Rani of Khatiya).

As a social structure, the class did not create new bonds between the women but strengthened existing bonds and existing divisions. Where there were already strong ties or 'unity' (the women's words), the classes were more successful and if the women were part of other groups (e.g., income-generating groups), they felt the class helped them to have more 'discipline' (meeting on time and regularly).

The ethnographic data overall revealed that the links between class participation and health behaviour were around gaining confidence and, to some extent, health knowledge, but that women's attitudes towards new health practices were affected much more by information from family and friends and their own position/relationships in the community and household.

Suggestions for programme implementation

The complexity of the situations around health decision making suggested that no single intervention would be appropriate and that the current intervention (literacy/health) had very different meanings and linkages with health behaviour in the two districts of the study. Observation of classes gave an insight into how the course worked in differing situations, particularly in regard to language. The analysis pointed to new possibilities for the course: the women said they were familiar with the family planning messages given in the book and that what they preferred most was the technical health information. This seemed to be the first time Agency staff had looked in detail at the course book (because we were now concerned with how the content related to women's attitudes and behaviour) and they were surprised at the lack of technical information it contained, for example about contraceptives. The ethnographic data above all revealed problems in programme implementation which had never been previously reported: that young facilitators were unable to handle the content of the course and that classes were full of young children rather than older women. There was a need for greater monitoring and supervision of the programme, as well as for literacy/ health interventions which were targeted at a wider population and used a variety of teaching approaches or course materials.

A critique of conventional research into literacy/health

The methods used in the fieldwork and the problems faced highlighted the limitations of traditional questionnaire-type surveys that have looked at the links between literacy and health. The researchers' informal observations of people's behaviour where they stayed revealed a great difference between what people said they did (the basis of most questionnaire research) and what they actually did. One of the health workers lived in dirty conditions and her child was vomiting worms, yet she was very active in health education work. These contradictions again indicated that changing attitudes or behaviour is not simply a matter of providing knowledge or literacy skills.

Decision making proved to be one of the hardest areas to investigate. Our findings showed how unreliable question/answer formats (often used in literacy/ health research in Nepal) would have been. In focus group discussions, the researchers asked women to list decisions commonly made in their families and to indicate against each kind of decision (e.g., sending children to school, going to the hospital) whether women and men participated in discussion and who made the final decision.

In Bakhola, this activity took place first with the research manager present. Women listed the following kinds of decisions, saying that they were able to discuss all of them with their husbands:

- family planning
- selling and buying of animals and land
- market
- marriage
- budget
- dhami (faith healer)
- meeting
- hospital (NGO clinic, health post, private clinic)
- school (send daughter)
- literacy class

They said that they made the final decision themselves for going to the literacy class, going to a meeting, going to hospital or the *dhami* and for sending daughters to school. After the course, they felt they were more strongly taking decisions about whether to take children for vaccinations and treatment and taking pills or depo injection themselves.

However, later the story turned out to be quite different:

With the project manager present, the women said they participate in all decisions as they said they wanted to show well in front of our supervisor. Afterwards they laughed and said, if we tried to make these decisions (like attending a meeting), our husbands would break our legs! Due to this confusion, we collected up all the slips and did it all again. This time the results were as follows:

- meeting – they cannot decide to go, only if the husband agrees
- Family Planning – said strongly they can decide on their own.
- we can give force to send daughter to school
- hospital – we can decide to send children but we need money
- we can sell small things without husband agreeing (vegetables etc.).
     (Quoted from the researchers' comments at debriefing session)

This example showed how any findings in this sensitive area needed to be regarded as possibly biased towards portraying a better picture than the reality. It was essential to analyse the data around decision making from the individual lifeline interviews in order to put the focus group discussion in a wider context. Our experience illustrated the dangers of using any one method in isolation – whether a questionnaire or PRA mapping.

A contribution for better or worse?

I have implied so far that these ethnographic findings were a positive contribution in revealing a more complex picture of classroom teaching, research processes and the meanings of literacy and health in the communities studied. However, the experience of using an ethnographic approach in this policy context left me far more ambivalent about the usefulness of the research. As a result of the negative picture that emerged of this particular literacy/health programme, our research report was initially not allowed into a public arena. In terms of programme development, the complex research findings that had emerged made it impossible to find a simple technical 'fix' (as was assumed through literacy/health classes as an entry point) or even to determine whether the Agency should continue to fund literacy classes as part of their health programme.

On a personal level, I was left feeling how difficult it was to change attitudes: not rural women's, but the policy makers' and planners' in Washington. I felt that the Agency had not taken on board the implications of adopting an ethnographic approach. They had chosen to follow a qualitative approach, assuming the findings would provide a straightforward answer to the question they posed: do literacy/health interventions lead to improved health behaviour? My initial worry had been around the practical constraints of carrying out ethnographic research with inexperienced researchers and a limited time scale, plus the dilemmas of integrating this approach into a traditional research proposal. However I now see that my first task should have been to tackle the issue of how the study was to be used, to ensure that the Agency understood and accepted the ideological implications of carrying out this research. Changing to an ethnographic approach was not simply a technical question of how to collect better data, but implied a decision to take a more holistic approach to programming and possibly completely change overall direction. The complex analysis that emerged through ethnographic research meant that piecemeal, incremental changes to the programme were inappropriate in this case and left the Agency with a dilemma that they had not anticipated.

What did the policy context take away from ethnographic research?

I too was left with an unresolved question: could the research process we had all participated in actually be considered to be 'ethnography'? Did it really differ from other qualitative research or PRA? Although I had set up many of the research activities and trained the field researchers in observation techniques and note taking, I was struck continually by the contrast in approach between this and my own academic research in Nepal. It was not just a question of time or intensity of fieldwork, the usual constraints named in relation to policy-oriented ethnography, but more around analysis, reflexivity and construction of the text.

Though the field researchers had documented the 'meanings' of literacy held by differing groups and individuals, the analysis of 'how these meanings are constructed' (see Street's Introduction) was missing. In other words, their field notes focused at the level of literacy 'events', such as reading a record card at a health post, rather than analysing the broader concept of 'literacy practices'. They tended to produce a list describing the many literacy events observed in the communities. Attempts to generalise were in numerical terms similar to PRA or quantitative studies – how many people saw the literacy class as a threat or how many health workers signed a record book – rather than at a conceptual level.

By contrast, my own academic research had aimed to develop general concepts through relating my specific findings to wider theoretical frameworks. The field researchers only had this theoretical framework through my brief training sessions, so related their findings primarily to the existing programme and the Agency's evaluation requirements. The concept of 'literacy events' is not only easier to use and understand, but links very clearly to defined interventions that can be determined and controlled by a development agency. 'Literacy practices' by contrast has a less direct link with policy, and the ideological dimension of analysis could be seen as producing more problems than benefits for developers. I recognised that by working in a policy context, I too had been pushed towards emphasising the aspects of ethnographic research that were more amenable to policy makers – such as describing literacy events where the Agency could have a potential role.

The study report also presented problems about genre, which I had not faced in an academic context. The Agency required a very brief report, though the ethnographic data consisted of lengthy detailed descriptions from the researchers' field notes. Although these could be summarised as points on a table, I felt that the ethnographic evidence was essential to understand the concepts. In the end, a seven-page summary report was condensed into ten slogans and pictures on overhead slides. This made the results instantly accessible, but denied the complexities of the processes we had documented. The statistical data, consisting of scores on the health knowledge test presented as graphs, received more attention than the rest of our findings. The Agency thus focused on data that were comparable with those from a quantitative-type survey, choosing to ignore the fact that the sample size and selection were not so representative in our research and made the statistical data questionable. The analysis of ethnographic data required more time to read and did not present such a simple picture.

Though the main body of the report came close to what I considered ethnography, I was aware of being less 'reflexive' about our roles as researchers. The genre of a development report with the neutral, objective voice of the 'developer' shaped the ethnographic analysis to such a degree that I felt the text read more like a PRA evaluation, with voices of participants, but with no indication as to how the researcher had shaped events or findings. Since the prime audience did not share my theoretical background, I felt that a reflexive report would have been misinterpreted in the policy context as suggesting a lack of confidence in the validity and reliability of our data.

Both the Agency research and my own academic ethnographic research were policy oriented, but the former being also sponsored and owned by policy makers had made a great difference to my role as researcher and the research objectives. Whereas within my own research, I had the freedom to change or reinterpret my research questions as the study progressed, I lacked the flexibility in the policy context to announce suddenly that we had been asking the wrong question! Though more relevant and useful findings emerged that led away from the equation, does literacy class participation = improved health behaviour, we could not change the research 'package' that the Agency had effectively bought. For me, this raised doubts about whether the research could still be labelled 'ethnographic' – the role that I adopted was essentially that of a developer, in contrast to my own academic research, where I had been able to critique the development discourse from outside. The bounded nature of the Agency-sponsored research imposed not only limits on the time taken and the number of words used, but the position and questions that the ethnographer could ask.

Conclusion

While writing this chapter, I have felt that it does not belong in this book, perhaps because – unlike the other ethnographic researchers included here – I have started, rather than finished, with a developer's (as compared to an ethnographer's) perspective on literacy. To ask what are the links between women's literacy and health is essentially a question posed by a policy maker rather than an ethnographer. For me, this question dictated, rather than guided, the kind of research carried out for the Agency in Nepal. The research report was a less reflexive and in-depth text than academic ethnographic studies, with findings more clearly bounded by policy constraints and concerns. From the Agency's point of view, the research did not give the answer hoped for (that the particular literacy programme led to improved health behaviour) but provided much strong evidence of problems in implementation that could not be ignored.

Though ethnographic approaches can be packaged and sold to developers, my experiences suggest that the research may not be effective on either party's terms if ideological differences between 'developers' and 'ethnographers' are not addressed early on in the process. The issue is around the developer's task, which is usually seen primarily as initiating change in people's behaviour (a catalyst) – an aim which is disputed or ideologically unacceptable to many ethnographers who wish to remain observers of change that is happening irrespective of their actions. Many of the ethnographers in this book present research that increases our understanding of literacy practices and local 'meanings of literacy', which other people (the developers) will then 'judge' and act upon (see Introduction). By contrast, my experience of conducting ethnographic research within a development agency shows the difficulty of combining the roles of both developer and ethnographer. *Designing and conducting* ethnographic research in a literacy policy context is far more problematic than *making use of* ethnographic findings from academic research projects for informing policy.

Acknowledgements

I have quoted from field notes written by Laxmi Khadka Sen, Nirmala Thapa, Rashmi Sharma and Shakuntala Thapa, whose research activities contributed greatly to this chapter.

Notes

1 I am using Hobart's terms 'developer' (meaning both Northern and Southern development workers) and 'developed' (referring to the local 'target' communities) (Hobart 1993).
2 'PRA can be described as a family of approaches, methods and behaviours that enable people to express and analyse the realities of their lives and conditions, to plan themselves what action to take, and to monitor and evaluate the results' (Chambers and Blackburn 1996: 1).
3 Referred to as 'the Agency' from now on. The field work took place over four weeks in Dhanusha on the Terai, near India (in Magla and Khatiya) and in Udayapur in the Eastern hill region (Griban and Bakhola). Names of places and people quoted have been changed in this chapter.
4 All quoted extracts are from field notes written by the four researchers, Laxmi Khadka Sen, Nirmala Thapa, Rashmi Sharma and Shakuntala Thapa. While two of the re-

searchers took notes in English, two preferred to write in Nepali, then translated into English.

5 Example of a letter sent to the researchers in Udayapur, translated from Nepali:

> Dear Sisters,
> My greetings to you. Every day I send you greetings. We are well here and I hope you are well too. I want to say one thing – that all pregnant women should eat green vegetables and fruit – papaya, mango, jack fruit, pumpkin, carrots. Pregnant women should be eating more nutritious food than usual.
> Your poor sister,
> Kumari Thakur

References

Bown, L. (1990) *Preparing the Future: Women, Literacy and Development*, ActionAid Development Report No. 4, London: ActionAid.

Burchfield, S. (1997) 'An Analysis of the Impact of Literacy on Women's Empowerment in Nepal', Harvard Institute for International Development, March 1997.

Chambers, R. and Blackburn, J. (1996) 'The Power of Participation: PRA and Policy', *IDS Policy Briefing*, Issue 7, August 1996, Sussex: IDS Publications.

Cochrane, S.H. (1982) 'Education and Fertility: An Expanded Examination of the Evidence', in G.P. Kelly and C.M. Elliott (eds), *Women's Education in the Third World: Comparative Perspectives*, Albany: State University of New York Press.

Goody, J. (1968) *Literacy in Traditional Society*, Cambridge: Cambridge University Press.

Hobart, M. (1993) 'Introduction: The Growth of Ignorance?', in M. Hobart (ed.), *An Anthropological Critique of Development: The Growth of Ignorance*, London: Routledge.

Kell, C. (1994) 'An analysis of literacy practices in an informal settlement in the Cape Peninsula', unpublished dissertation, University of Cape Town.

Kulick, D. and Stroud, C. (1993) 'Conceptions and Uses of Literacy in a Papua New Guinean Village', in B.V. Street (ed.), *Cross-Cultural Approaches to Literacy*, Cambridge: Cambridge University Press.

Le Vine, R.A. (1982) 'Influences of Women's Schooling on Maternal Behavior in the Third World', in G.P. Kelly and C.M. Elliott (eds), *Women's Education in the Third World: Comparative Perspectives*, Albany: State University of New York Press.

Le Vine, R.A., Le Vine, S.A., Richman, A., Uribe, F., Correa, C. and Miller, P. (1991) 'Women's Schooling and Child Care in the Demographic Transition: A Mexican Case Study', *Population and Development Review* 17(3).

Leve, L., Leslie, K.D. and Manandhar, U. (1997) 'Takukot-Majh Lakuribot, 10 Year Retrospective Literacy and Empowerment', Kathmandu: Save the Children USA.

Moser, C. (1993) *Gender Planning and Development: Theory, Practice and Training*, London: Routledge.

Robinson-Pant, A.P. (1997) 'The Link between Women's Literacy and Development', unpublished DPhil thesis, University of Sussex.

—— (2000) 'Women and Literacy: A Nepal Perspective', *International Journal for Education and Development*.

—— (forthcoming) *'Why Eat Green Cucumber at the Time of Dying?': Exploring the Link between Adult Literacy and Development*, Hamburg: UNESCO Institute of Education.

Rockhill, K. (1993) 'Gender, Language and the Politics of Literacy', in B.V. Street (ed.), *Cross-Cultural Approaches to Literacy*, Cambridge: Cambridge University Press.

Rogers, A. (1992) *Adults Learning for Development*, London: Cassell.

Rogers, A., Maddox, B., Millican, J., Newell Jones, K., Papen, U. and Robinson-Pant, A. (1999) *Re-defining Post-literacy in a Changing World*, London: DFID Research Report 29.

Smith, C. (1997) 'Women's Acquisition of Literacy Skills and Health Knowledge in Nepal: A Comparative Study of Non-formal Education Approaches', EdD dissertation, University of Massachusetts.

Street, B. (1984) *Literacy in Theory and Practice*, Cambridge: Cambridge University Press.

—— (1992) 'Literacy Practices and the Construction of Gender', in T. Ingold (ed.), *Encyclopaedia of Anthropology*, London: Routledge.

—— (1994) 'What Do We Mean by "Local Literacies"?', in D. Barton (ed.), *Sustaining Local Literacies*, Special Issue of *Language and Education* 8(1&2).

Stromquist, N.P. (1990) 'Women and Illiteracy: The Interplay of Gender Subordination and Poverty', *Comparative Education Review* 34(1): 95–111.

UNICEF (1999) *The State of the World's Children 1999*, New York: UNICEF.

Wagner, D.A. (1995) 'Literacy and Development: Rationales, Myths, Innovations and Future Directions', *International Journal of Educational Development* 15(4).

Yates, R. (1994) 'Women and Literacy: Functionality and the Literacy Process in Apam, Ghana', DPhil thesis, University of Sussex.

9

HOUSEHOLD LITERACY ENVIRONMENTS AS CONTEXTS FOR DEVELOPMENT IN RURAL CHINA

Regie Stites

Introduction

For the past five decades, government and party officials in the People's Republic of China have made 'work to eradicate illiteracy' (*saochu wenmang gongzuo*) a national priority. To achieve this goal, a series of mass literacy campaigns have been organised with the purpose of extending basic education and literacy to all of China's diverse communities and peoples. In the 1990s, the principal target populations for anti-illiteracy work have been rural women and inhabitants of China's most remote areas and underdeveloped regions, many of whom are members of non-Han minority groups. Adult literacy work in rural China can be seen as part of the broader effort to diffuse central ideology and control into peripheral communities and in so doing to reduce the marginality of these communities. This is the dominant rationale for the central government's promotion of 'mass literacy'. Yet, even at the level of central policy, recognition of the variety and complexity of the forms and functions of literacy (multiple literacies in Street's sense, see Introduction, this volume) is built into China's mass literacy curriculum. That curriculum is conceptualised as a balanced mixture of 'cultural', 'ideological' and 'technical' content roughly corresponding to the application of reading, writing, and quantitative knowledge and skills in the contexts, respectively, of formal schooling, politics and work. This tripartite conception of literacy also corresponds to the Chinese state's goals for social, political and economic development (see Stites and Semali 1991). Schooling rural Chinese women in cultural, ideological and technical literacies is seen as vital to the achievement of the complex aims summed up by the phrase 'socialist modernization with Chinese characteristics' (Stites 1995). However, central goals for mass literacy are poorly matched to the diversity of local literacy practices. This chapter presents a case study of literacy environments in two areas within a rural

Chinese township, Dahu: an outlying farming village and the township market centre. The study compares and contrasts the material and social contexts for reading and writing in the two areas. Drawing primarily from data collected during visits to a hundred households and eight focus group interviews, it examines the literacy environment of the rural household as a context for the changes in literacy practices envisioned in state educational policy. My general conclusion is that adult literacy work in Dahu has had very little effect in transforming the literacy environment of the home in ways that would create a social space for young women to engage actively in reading and writing.

In nearly all the homes I visited in Dahu I found people who, if perplexed about my reasons for being there, were still willing to listen to my curious questions and to answer them thoughtfully and sincerely. Yet there were also times during the fieldwork when I was very annoyed and frustrated by the apparent eagerness of my informants to provide the 'correct' response to a question. I was also embarrassed by their discomfort and diffidence at times when they clearly did not know what the 'correct' response should be (cf. Chopra, this volume, for a similarly reflexive account of relations between researcher and researched). But in most cases it was quite easy to discern where the 'correct' answers ended and more personal replies began. For example, whenever I encountered someone who said that they were illiterate I would ask them whether being illiterate had caused any hardships for them. The immediate response to this question was almost always that the life of an illiterate was 'bitter' (ku). However, when I would ask for examples of the sorts of problems that had come up because of their inability to read, most people were slow to answer. A fairly common response to this question was that being illiterate made it difficult to go to new places. One man told me that he was afraid to go to the city to shop or do business because he would not be able to read the names of stores or work units and would have trouble finding what he was looking for. On several occasions women told me that they were afraid they might get lost if they went into the city by themselves. Yet, when I asked if this prevented them from going to the city, they most often laughed as if I was asking a very stupid question and said that they seldom had any reason to go or that they always went in the company of others.

The answers that people gave to my questions about the hardships of illiteracy very often pointed to the embarrassment of being publicly recognised as an illiterate. Paulo Freire tells the story of an encounter with a Brazilian peasant who, when shown pictures of an Indian hunting with a bow and of a peasant, like himself, hunting with a gun, pointed out that only the peasant could be considered an illiterate. When Freire asked him why that was so, the peasant replied that to be illiterate you must live 'where there are letters and you don't know them' (Freire 1985: 14). For the most part, even the residents of China's most remote and inaccessible regions live in places 'where there are letters'. China, like India and other countries described in this book, possesses a highly literate culture. Yet, in any society there are spaces where literacy matters less and where being unable to read or write may very well be as inconsequential as being tone deaf or unable to whistle a tune. The language of China's central government policy on anti-illiteracy work often conveys an image of the state as a paternalistic purveyor of knowledge and culture to 'culturally impoverished' (*wenhua qiong*) regions (rural and remote) and populations (women and minorities) of the country (see, for example, Li Hui 1989). Ethnographic studies of 'literacy practices' (see Street, Introduction, this volume) have highlighted the ways that schooled literacies transform and often subordinate existing local communicative repertoires (Heath 1983; Street 1984, 1993). In this sense, anti-illiteracy work in the Chinese countryside can be seen as the latest phase of a long historical struggle to extend the reach of the state (Shue 1988; Woodside 1992). In China, as elsewhere, the standardisation and control of languages and literacies has been an important support for extension of state control in the Chinese periphery (Stites 1999). In a sense, the unschooled adults I met in Dahu were only illiterate when they ventured out of the relatively private spaces of the household and village. Today, in the context of the rapid development of the local society and economy those spaces are shrinking. State-sponsored adult anti-illiteracy classes in the various villages of Dahu are in part an effort to aid villagers in their adaptation to the changes going on around them. But these classes also serve another purpose, that of extending the reach of the party/state and sweeping away those peripheral spaces where illiteracy once mattered very little.

The research setting

Dahu Township is located in the mountainous interior of Fujian province on the south-east coast of China. In the early 1980s the dismantling of the Dahu Commune and the return of land to individual households led to a rapid diversification of the local economy and tremendous social and political changes. I collected field data in Dahu Township (*Dahuxiang*) during the 1990 anti-illiteracy campaign in the farming village of Yaotian and in the market centre villages Kengyuan and Dahu (two of the three contiguous villages that comprise the township centre). In 1990, the vast majority of residents were engaged in agricultural production on family-owned lands. During the period of study (June to December 1990) official estimates counted 1,033 adult illiterates between the ages of 15 and 40 in a total adult population for this age group of 8,884. More than 90 per cent of those counted as illiterate were women. At the start of the research period, seventeen evening *saomangban* ('illiteracy eradication classes') were being conducted in eleven of the eighteen administrative villages that comprised the township. There was a total of 246 students enrolled in these classes. With the exception of one teenage boy all of these students were women or teenage girls.

During a rare break in the annual cycle of agricultural work (from 12 to 26 October), I was able to visit forty-eight households in Yaotian. Between 27 October and 6 November, fifty-two households were visited in Kengyuan and Dahu, two of the three villages that make up the market centre. During the same period of time as the household surveys, eight focus group interviews were organised and carried out in Yaotian and in Kengyuan. Focus group interviews were conducted with a small group of unschooled women, a group of women with some schooling, a group of men with elementary school education, and a group of men with at least a junior middle school level of education in each village. There were six to ten participants in each focus group plus a discussion leader and recorder. I led the discussion in the men's groups. No men participated in the women's groups which were led by my wife and a local, female research assistant.

In some ways I felt a strong connection with the residents of Dahu. I know from my own experience growing up in a small farming community in the American Midwest what it is like to live far from a society's centres of knowledge and power. On the other hand, my status as a foreigner and my association with local leaders and teachers put me clearly in the camp of the state and its local agents. This perception of my role in the community was dramatically obvious during my household survey. In order to be able to visit people in their homes and talk with them informally about their reading and writing skills and habits, I was obliged to set up a rather formal procedure of being escorted around the village by local leaders. In the village of Yaotian, for example, I was nearly always accompanied by the village doctor, a research assistant from the Yongan Health Education unit, another research assistant from the Provincial Health Education Institute, and assorted others representing the village, township, regional and provincial political, medical and educational hierarchies. The answers that people in Dahu gave to my questions about the meanings and values of literacy must be interpreted within this context.[1]

Literacy environments in Dahu

In my analysis of settings for reading and writing activities in Dahu Township I found it useful to distinguish between the private space of the household on the one hand and public spaces such as the school, the worksite, the market and the street (cf. Zubair, this volume, on gendered accounts of such distinctions). The 'outside' environments for reading and writing practices in the outlying village of Yaotian were much less rich and varied than those in the market centre villages of Kengyuan and Dahu. The household literacy environments in the two villages were similar and in both cases were not conducive to active engagement in reading and writing.

Many of the unschooled adults I spoke with in Dahu told me that the only time they experienced difficulties as a result of their inability to read and write was when they 'went out' (*qu waimian*). Likewise, I was often told during my household survey that members of the household who could read and write only did so 'outside' (*zai waimian*). Out, of course, is a relative term and the meaning it had in each of the above contexts was somewhat different. In the first instance, 'going out' referred primarily to trips to public places such as the market and shops, or to Yongan (the closest city) or points beyond. In the latter instance, 'outside' usually referred to the workplace, school, reading room or other local social spaces beyond the household. The second sense of 'outside' highlights the fact that schooled adults (mostly men) in Dahu found themselves 'outside' of the household as a matter of course in pursuing their daily routines while unschooled adults (mostly women) only went 'out' on rare and exceptional occasions.

It was thus not surprising that 'outside' was the place where most of the reading and writing events I observed in Dahu occurred. My analysis of literacy practices in Dahu identified four major categories of settings for reading and writing outside the household. The first of these in terms of the amount and frequency of reading and writing that these sites facilitated on a daily basis were those within the 'cultural' category. This category includes formal educational settings such as the schools as well as informal learning and informational centres such as libraries, reading rooms, bookstores and the post office. The settings which came next in order of amount and frequency of literacy events were grouped within the 'political' category. This category includes the rooms used by various government and party organs as offices and meeting rooms. The third type of 'outside' settings were those in the 'vocational' category. This category includes the offices or worksites of various industrial and commercial enterprises as well as a range of collective and private shops and small businesses. The final category of 'outside' settings is collectively referred to as the 'street'. This category includes all open-air public spaces. The fields, orchards and forests of Dahu were not included within any of these categories of 'outside' settings for reading and writing activities because of the extreme rarity of reading and writing events in these settings. This is not to say that literacy is irrelevant to agricultural, horticultural or forestry work. It is simply a reflection of the fact that, judging from my observations and interviews, whatever reading and writing was done in support of or in connection with these activities was not done in the field.

Outside settings for reading and writing in Yaotian

The main setting for reading and writing events in Yaotian was the village elementary school. Like all the outlying administrative villages in the township, Yaotian had its own elementary school. This school was housed in two fairly new one-story buildings at the top of a small hill just west of the Yaotian village centre. The two school buildings faced one another across a yard about 20 metres wide. This space served as a play and assembly area for the school children. The Yaotian school had one class of children for each of the six grades of elementary school. Each class had its own room and each building contained five classrooms. The extra classrooms were used as office space for the teachers and principal, for storage of school supplies, and as a nursery for preschoolers. On weekday evenings the third-grade classroom was also the setting for the village evening school anti-illiteracy class. There were several problems with this arrangement. One was the problem of squeezing adult-size bodies into child-size seats and desks (both physically and psychologically discomfiting). A second problem had to do with the relatively poor lighting (two unshaded lightbulbs hanging from the ceiling) and the fact that the blackboard was actually black paint on a plaster wall (making it hard to see anything written upon it). The third problem was the fact that in an area of highly dispersed settlement such as Yaotian, finding one's way to the school from the more remote hamlets it was meant to serve was virtually impossible in the dark.

The only other setting in Yaotian that fitted within the educational category was the village reading room located in the building housing the government and party branch offices in the village centre. This reading room was open in the evening and held a collection of periodicals and books, some of which could be borrowed. Yaotian had once had a post office but this was no longer operating in 1990.

Beyond the village primary school and reading room the main settings for reading and writing in Yaotian were in the political category and included the rooms used as offices and meeting rooms by the village mayor and the village party branch as well as other administrative and collective organisations within the village such as the local women's federation and the local fire-protection committee, etc.

There were relatively few vocational settings for reading and writing activities in Yaotian. Essentially there were three types that fitted into this category, a mechanical repair shop, the office of the brick factory and shops. The most numerous type was the small shops (*xiaomai bu*) which sold just about anything that villagers might need on a regular basis. Typically these were housed in one room and carried a wide variety of daily-use items such as canned food, school supplies, soap, alcoholic and non-alcoholic beverages, and a variety of hardware items.

The final outside setting for reading and writing in Yaotian was the 'street'. There were two areas in Yaotian that might be considered as 'street' environments. One was the space between the long three-storey brick building which housed the village government and party offices and the village auditorium at the centre of Yaotian's principal village. Although residents of the upper end of the village often passed this way *en route* to the main road to the market centre, there were no shops or other reasons for pedestrians to gather or linger there. Another area of the village which might be considered a street environment was the intersection of the main road to the market centre and the lane which led off that road to the Yaotian village centre. There were several shops scattered along the main road near this intersection, but the area was more of a highway than a street. At both the intersection and the village centre, however, there were bulletin boards and walls used for painted or posted messages. Just outside the village health station on the wall of the village government building there was a small 'propaganda wall' (see below) where announcements and public education materials were posted. A similar notice area faced on to the main road near the intersection but this one appeared to have been unused for quite some time.

All eighteen administrative villages in Dahu Township had at least one 'propaganda wall' (*xuanzhuan lan*). In Yaotian, the space of wall reserved for this purpose next to the entrance to the village health station was used by a variety of agencies to inform, reward or entertain members of the community. On the streets of urban areas of Fujian, display boards containing the latest copies of newspapers were common. It was not unusual to see a dozen or more men standing together and reading these papers. The propaganda wall in Yaotian and other rural villages was a pale reflection of these urban public reading walls. No crowds of men gathered to read on the 'street' in Yaotian as they did so naturally in places like Fuzhou and Yongan, and to a lesser extent even in the Dahu market centre (see below). In the evening, when residents of Yaotian were most likely to have the leisure to gather in the village centre, the absence of street lighting made it impossible to read any of the notices on the propaganda wall.

In general, very little reading and writing took place in the shops or in the street in Yaotian. Although my data are limited, it seems reasonable to assume that most reading and writing in the village occurred within the context of activities at the school, in the village reading room, and at the various official and commercial worksites in the village. I discuss the home as a setting for reading and writing in a separate section below.

Outside settings for literacy in the market centre

The 'outside' settings for reading and writing events in the immediate vicinity of the two market centre villages of Kengyuan and Dahu were markedly richer and more diverse than those in Yaotian. As noted above, educational settings such as the local school and reading room were the sites for most of the reading and writing activity in Yaotian. This was also the case for the market centre villages, but unlike Yaotian the market centre also contained a large number and variety of political and vocational settings for reading and writing.

At one end of the market centre's main street was a four-storey office building which housed the township government and party offices. Based on the level of activity I witnessed on my many visits to various offices in this building, I would be willing to hazard a guess that this building alone was the setting for a greater number and variety of reading and writing events than all of the 'outside' sites in Yaotian combined.

At the opposite end of the street from the township government and cultural centres was the local branch office of the Agricultural Bank. Other privately owned businesses along the main street of the market centre included several dressmaking shops, a book rental shop and many hair salons.

Compared to Yaotian, the market centre contained a greater number and wider variety of settings for reading and writing within the educational category. It was within this domain that Yaotian's status as periphery and the relative centrality of Kengyuan and Dahu was most apparent. Next door to the township government building was the cultural centre which housed a library (with a circulating collection of roughly 2,000 volumes) and meeting rooms used for a wide variety of recreational and educational activities. At the top of a broad set of steps ascending the steep hill just behind the cultural centre was a very large and impressive auditorium which in recent years had served primarily as a movie theatre but still occasionally hosted large meetings. Just down the main street and next to an agricultural supplies store was the local branch of the New China Bookstore (a single room with roughly a hundred titles for sale). At the opposite end of the main street near the bank and the Central Primary School was a small privately owned book rental shop with at least twice as many titles as available in the bookstore. Book rental stalls were common in China in 1990. The main stock of such stalls was picture books – illustrated stories with short texts that could be read in one sitting. Most of the customers at the Dahu book rental shop seemed to be young men, though the owner reported that many young women (from the middle school) also rented books. The Dahu Post and Telegraph Office was located on the branch of the road that eventually led to Yaotian. A little further along this road were the Dahu Medical Centre and the Yongan Number Seven Agricultural Vocational Technical Middle School.

The market centre also had a relatively large number and variety of settings for literacy events within the vocational category. The immediate vicinity of the market centre contained several large industrial enterprises including the spar mine and processing plant, a textiles factory and a plastics factory. These enterprises each had at least one building with offices for their engineers, accountants and managers as well as numerous and diverse worksites for skilled and semi-skilled labour.

The settings for literacy events within the street category were also relatively more dense in the market centre than in Yaotian. An open-air market ground was located just opposite the township government building, and agricultural markets were held here every fifth day. Market days attracted large numbers of people from outlying villages to the market centre. They came to buy and sell meat, produce and small craft items in the market itself, to shop in the stores nearby, to visit one of several barber shops or beauty parlours, or simply to catch up on township news and see friends and relatives from other villages.

The main street of the market centre provided a much richer literacy environment than the 'street' areas of Yaotian. The walls lining the main street of the market centre were literally covered with writing. On both sides of the gateway to the government/party office compound there were large walls each of which was covered with text in large characters. This gate was also adorned with sign boards for all the government and party organs housed in the compound. Just beyond the gate to the north there was another billboard-sized area used for the posting of policy notices and other public announcements. Public health and family planning posters had been hand-painted on spaces of wall between shops at several points down both sides of the street. In addition a banner made of a chain of metal plates was strung above the street and bore a message exhorting the residents to achieve higher levels of productivity.

Facing the street just across from the entrance to the market and in front of the cultural centre was a long glass-fronted display case filled with posters and other visual written displays. This was the township 'propaganda wall' (*xuanzhuan lan*), a much larger and more elaborate display than its counterpart in Yaotian. The Dahu Township propaganda wall functioned as a sort of bulletin board and community newspaper reporting upcoming local social events (dances, performances, contests) and then posting reports and pictures of these events afterwards. While I was in Dahu, one section of the wall was taken up by a group of photos and accompanying text recording a recent song and dance meeting at the local cultural centre. This seemed to attract the most attention from people walking by who would often point out people they knew in the pictures. Another section of the display case was reserved for health and hygiene education. The display that I saw in this section consisted of three poster-sized pieces of paper covered with text in characters about one-inch high. These characters were written with a brush and were aesthetically pleasing, a fact which the artist pointed out to me with some pride, but the running script style used was a relatively difficult one to decipher. In the many times I passed the wall I never saw anyone reading this section.

The home literacy environment

Differences in the outside environments for reading and writing between Yaotian and the market centre villages of Kengyuan and Dahu were much greater than differences in the literacy environments of the households in these three villages. In all three villages the printed word was clearly in evidence in every household that I visited but the forms and quantity of literacy materials that I found in the majority of household compounds were not suggestive of high frequency or intensive reading and writing activity. Very few households in any of the villages kept books or other reading and writing materials in the house other than those used by school children. Yet the walls of the houses of even the least educated members of the community were covered with the written word.

Although there were great differences in size and quality of the structures in which the residents of Dahu made their homes, there was also a good deal of similarity in the form and function of the rooms which made up a family domicile. The basic plan discernible in both new and old houses and in the homes of both the relatively wealthy and relatively poor households consisted of three types of living spaces. The ideal pattern for a house in Dahu Township would have the following features. At the front and centre of the house there would be a relatively large room opening on to a front terrace or courtyard. Normally, when someone was home the large doors to this room would be kept open. This would function as the public space of the house where guests could be welcomed and given tea. The contents and structure of this type of room reflected its role as the household's public face. In the homes of more traditional families the back wall of this public room might hold a family altar above which decorative or ritual scrolls would be hung. Buddhist households might hang a picture of Guanyin, the Goddess of Mercy, in this spot. Christian families might put up a poster bearing scriptures and the sign of the cross on this wall. The majority of families, however, used this wall as a display area for decorative scrolls (pictures of the God of Longevity were very popular), Chinese New Year or wedding inscriptions, and/or informational posters available from various agencies. These posters carried practical advice and policy on a variety of topics ranging from forest management to the control of swine disease. The furnishings of the front room would normally be sparse and might consist of plain wooden benches or, in the newer and nicer homes, padded chairs and sofas. The television set was usually in the front room as was the stereo/radio if the family owned one.

The second type of space in houses in Dahu was the family bedrooms. These rooms were usually located to the side of, behind or above the front room and often were accessible only through the front room. In the older wood-frame homes these rooms generally had very small windows and were dark and poorly lit. In homes with active readers and writers the bedrooms were usually also the place where books and other reading materials were stored, sometimes on open shelves, but more often in closed cabinets. The amount of reading and writing that could take place in a bedroom would, of course, be limited by the number of people sharing the room and the availability of space and light.

The final type of space in houses in Dahu comprised various work rooms where cooking and other household work (including animal raising) took place. These areas of the house were primarily the domain of women who did the cooking and the bulk of the other household chores. Literacy materials in this part of the house were rare and confined to an occasional decorative or informational poster or perhaps a calendar.

In addition to these three types of spaces within houses it is important to consider the use of adjacent outdoor spaces. In some older houses the bedrooms and kitchen/work areas formed the extensions of a U-shape and thus flanked a courtyard opening out from the front room. Weather permitting, this courtyard would function as an extension of the family's living and work space.

Overall, the standard house type in Dahu was not conducive to reading and writing activity. Only the bedroom areas of the house were both private enough and furnished in a way that might allow for sustained reading and/or writing. But homes which actually had sufficiently well-lit bedrooms with tables or desks suitable for reading and writing were exceptional and rare. It is not surprising that homes in Dahu were generally not designed as places to read and write. Yet to varying degrees, reading and writing were part of the home life of almost every family in Dahu. The nature and extent of actual and potential reading and writing activity in the home setting were important concerns for my exploration of local literacy practices because of the fact that the women of Dahu spend the majority of their time working in or near the home. The home was the primary, if not only, setting in which women who acquired reading and writing skills in anti-illiteracy classes would have opportunities to put those skills to work.

Literacy materials in the home

One of the purposes of the household survey was to give me an opportunity to see the inside of as many homes as possible in Dahu in the short time I was able to stay there. While talking to members of each household about their reading and writing activities I also was able to see the material evidence of these activities. It was not uncommon to find someone engaged in some form of reading or writing task as my party and I entered the household compound. These chance observations were a valuable source of information and corroboration of things I had been told about reading and writing habits and practices.

As I have stated above, most of the reading and writing activity in Dahu occurred in contexts outside of the home. In light of this fact it is perhaps not surprising that my household survey uncovered relatively few reading and writing materials in the majority of households. The only type of literacy material that was found in every house I visited comprised various sorts of writing as decoration on the walls of the front rooms. These wall decorations can be grouped into three general categories: traditional, informative (posters and calendars) and honorific.

The traditional category includes the ubiquitous 'paired banners' (*duilian*), two lines of verse written in large characters and hung on doorposts, vertical support timbers, or walls. Also in this category are one-line verses (*hengpi*) which are hung horizontally above doorways or between paired vertical banners. The most common times for the hanging of *duilian* and *hengpi* in a home were the Chinese New Year celebration, when a member of the household married or celebrated an important birthday (such as the sixtieth), or when the house was newly constructed. The text on these banners consisted of a rather limited set of standard verses which have traditionally been considered appropriate for particular occasions and places in the household. Like some forms of classical Chinese poetry, the verses of standard paired banners are formulaic and are made up of balanced lines. This balance is achieved by having equal numbers of characters in each verse and by the use of various cohesive devices, including tone patterning and textual cohesion. The paired banners may each contain four, five, seven, eight, ten, eleven or more characters. Textual cohesion is often achieved through the inclusion of numbers, directions or seasons in each of the paired verses.

A look at one example of a paired banner celebrating the New Year will illustrate the typical features of the paired banner verse. This paired banner verse has seven characters per line. The first line of characters is '*dong lai zi qi xi lai fu*'. The second line reads '*nan jin xiang guang bei jin cai*'. These characters are written vertically with a brush on strips of paper and then hung side by side with the first line on the right. The parallel structure of the text is revealed clearly when a literal character-by-character translation is made as follows: 'east comes positive life-force west comes fortune'; 'south enters auspicious light north enters wealth'.

This translation also reveals the talismanic quality of the paired banner. Good fortune, prosperity, longevity and happiness are the constant recurrent messages of the paired banners.

It is difficult to say how often or by whom the paired banners and horizontal banners that decorate the interior of homes in Dahu were actually read. What is certain is that very few members of the community were capable of recognising or comprehending the meaning of every character that the banners contain. Fewer still were capable of producing these banners, since this requires mastery of the skill of calligraphy with the brush (*mao bi*) as well as knowledge of the rules of the genre. In other words, the ability fully to comprehend and/or produce these banners was not likely to fall within the range of literacy skills possessed by an adult neo-literate. On the other hand, every adult in the community was fully aware of the broader meaning and functions of wall banners, whether they could read the characters in them or not.

The paired and horizontal banners that hung in every household were sometimes produced by someone in the household but more often they were commissioned or purchased ready-made from someone in the village. For some older and better-educated men in the township the production and sale of these items could be a welcome supplement to the household income. However, I did not discover anyone in Dahu who might be considered a professional scribe. In Yongan, on the other hand, I encountered three men each of whom operated a full-time scribal business. I was also told that banners could be purchased in the village market of Dahu around the time of the Chinese New Year when the demand for banners would be at its peak.

The final category of literacy materials found hanging on the walls of homes in Dahu were those which I have described as belonging to the honorific category. Materials in this category included certificates that had been awarded to members of the household or to the household as a whole. One of the most common examples of this type of certificate was the 'three good student' awards given to school children who were exemplary in their study habits, work habits and morality. These award certificates were printed forms, very much like a diploma in size and substance, which were usually framed and hung in a prominent position in the public sections of the house. Other awards that might be similarly displayed included the 'five good family' (*wuhao jiating*), 'model worker' (*laodong mofan*) and 'specialist household' (*zhuanjia hu*) certificates.

The materials in the honorific category were all similar in that they consisted of printed forms upon which a name could be written. The purpose of these materials was clearly to honour and reward those who received them and they were thus placed in a position in the home where they could be read or at least noticed by visitors. I know that some of the unschooled mothers I interviewed were aware of the significance of the 'three good student' (*sanhao xuesheng*) certificates given to their children because they proudly pointed these out to me when I asked about the children's educational attainments.

The presence of reading materials such as books, magazines and newspapers was less obvious in the households of Dahu than printed materials on the walls. Indeed, a little more the half of the people I interviewed told me that their home did not contain a single such item. In some cases I was not able to verify by observation whether this was actually the case, but judging from what I was able to observe it seems plausible that these households did not contain more than an occasional newspaper, magazine or book. Many homes that were otherwise devoid of reading materials did regularly buy or subscribe to the *Television News* (*Dianshe bao*), a weekly one-sheet tabloid that contained the listings for television and radio programmes along with articles on related topics. This was an indication more of the level of television viewing than of time spent reading. It was quite clear that more people had a television in the home than had a collection of books, magazines or newspapers. In Yaotian, thirty-two of the forty-eight households owned at least one television set and those households that did not own a set were most often next door to one that they could and frequently did watch. Only nineteen households had any adult member who read books, magazines or newspapers (other than the *TV News*) at home.

In the market centre, the situation was not much different. Exactly half of the households I covered in my surveys of Kengyuan and Dahu reported that they had no reading materials in the home other than children's schoolbooks and an occasional copy of the *TV News*. On the other hand, only eight of the fifty-two households did not have a television set on the premises and four of these said that they watched television regularly elsewhere.

Reading at home seemed to be a fairly rare event in most households that I visited in the course of my survey. Thus there was not a great deal of variety in the sorts of reading materials found in the homes. Eleven households reported having newspapers in the home and another ten households had at least one member who regularly read a newspaper outside the home. Only two households in Yaotian were willing and able to have newspapers and magazine subscriptions. These were the first two households I visited on my survey and they turned out arguably to be the most literate households in the village.

There were both a greater variety and number of newspapers found in the homes of those included in my survey of Kengyuan and Dahu. More than half of the households in the market centre survey, thirty-two out of fifty-two, reported having at least one adult member of the household who regularly read at least one newspaper. Nineteen households reported that newspapers were read in the home. As in Yaotian, reading a newspaper was something that most people did away from home and the most likely spots for reading one were the office or the reading room at the cultural centre.

Books like magazines were fairly rare in homes in Yaotian. Only eight households contained home libraries of more than a few volumes and another eleven reported having a few or several books in the house. The remaining twenty-nine of the forty-eight households in the survey had no books in the home. The kinds of books kept at home by residents of Yaotian were mostly described to me as literature (*wenxue* or *xiaoshuo*) or as technical books (*keji zhishi*). Of the eight households that contained more than four or five books, six had collections of mostly technical books and the remaining two had mixed collections of technical books and literature. On the other hand, in the households that reported having one to several books in the home, these books were in nine of eleven cases literature. One resident of Yaotian told me that he had a collection of more than two hundred books (all technical) in his home and I was shown a collection of at least that many books in one other household. The other relatively large household collections of books ranged from a dozen to fifty or so volumes. The village reading room, the only public collection of books in the vicinity, has a circulating collection of about twenty volumes.

In the market centre also I uncovered relatively few large household libraries. There were only thirteen households that reported having more than several books in the home. Another eleven households reported that they had one to a few books at home. A little more than half of the households included in the market centre survey (twenty-eight) reported that they had no books in their homes. In contrast to Yaotian, the households with relatively larger collections of books in the market centre villages were more likely to have literature in their collections than they were to have technical books. Four households reported having relatively large collections of books that were exclusively literature. Another six households had mixed collections of literature and technical books and only one household had a home library that was exclusively composed of technical books. As in the Yaotian survey, those households that reported having a few books in the home most often had literature (seven out of eleven). The relatively high level of interest in literature in the market centre is also reflected in the composition of the more the 2,000-volume circulating collection housed in the Dahu Cultural Centre. I was told by a library worker that more than three-quarters of this collection was comprised of literature with the other quarter being made up of technical books and school texts.

Conclusion

As can be seen from the foregoing descriptions of literacy environments and literacy practices in Dahu, the 'cultural', 'political' and 'vocational' content of the Chinese adult literacy curriculum corresponds to different local literacy events (settings, purposes, materials, and participants in reading and writing activities). The correspondences between the curriculum and local literacy events are relatively strong in 'outside' literacy environments and relatively weak in the typical household. This is not surprising given the fact that the adult literacy curriculum is designed to support increased engagement in literacy events (especially political and work-related literacy events) outside of the household context. Increasing the participation of rural women in politics and in non-agricultural production (and at the same time lowering fertility rates) are key goals of the Chinese modernisation drive. The fact that the adult literacy curriculum corresponds very little to the literacy environment of the rural household creates problems for rural development.

The choice of Dahu Township as the setting for a case study of rural Chinese anti-illiteracy work in the International Year of Literacy, 1990, was a fortuitous one in several respects. Fujian Province shared characteristics with both the most advanced and the most backward regions of China. It had enjoyed the benefits of a rapidly growing and diversifying economy fuelled by open access to foreign markets and foreign investment through its coastal ports and industries. At the same time, the rugged interior of the province for the most part remained remote and underdeveloped. Dahu Township was situated at the crossroads of these two sides of Fujian. The township as a whole had prospered from the development of external markets for its mineral and timber resources and from the development of enterprises in the market centre. But this development and prosperity had not been distributed evenly across the population and regions of the township. Relatively remote agricultural villages such as Yaotian have lagged behind the market centre villages of Kengyuan and Dahu in occupational opportunities and income, and in levels of literacy and educational attainment. In all areas of the township, men were increasingly able to find non-agricultural employment but occupational options for women remained extremely limited. In many respects, centre and periphery were both present within the borders of Dahu Township.

The highly centralised nature of Chinese political organisation and the cellular structure of Chinese rural society have tended to reinforce imbalances in levels of literacy and educational attainment between the city and the country-side and between the politically integrated and the politically marginalised seg-ments of Chinese society. Although mass literacy campaigns had been part of the radical extension of the reach of the state into the countryside in the early years of the People's Republic, the expansion of the Chinese polity and the diffusion of literacy did not erase regional, occupational and gender gaps in levels of literacy.

One thing that economic diversification has not changed, and shows no sign of changing in the near future, is the imbalance between male and female literacy levels. Political, cultural and economic forces all contribute to the repro-duction of gender inequities in literacy in rural China. The evidence from Dahu reinforces this general picture of gender bias in the allocation of educational opportunity and in the division of labour in the rural community and household.

The description of literacy environments in Dahu revealed two levels of im-balance in the local patterns of literacy practices. First, there was a difference between the literacy environment of the home and of settings 'outside' of the home such as public spaces and worksites. These outside settings provided a far more conducive environment for reading and writing than did the home setting. This finding is important primarily because of the fact that women, who comprised nearly all of Dahu's adult literacy students, spent much more time working at home and much less time in 'outside' settings than did men. Second, there was also a clear difference in the quality of settings for literacy between the peripheral village of Yaotian and the market centre. These differences in the quality of settings for reading and writing were also reflected in smaller quantities of materials available for use in homes as opposed to 'outside' settings and in Yaotian as opposed to the market centre.

Although in official literacy statistics China appears to be making steady and impressive progress in its 'anti-illiteracy work', the gaps and contradictions between the modernising literacies envisioned in the adult anti-illiteracy curriculum and the lived experience of literacy practices and literacy environments in Chinese rural communities and homes will prevent China from achieving the goal of 'eradicating illiteracy' any time in the foreseeable future. Part of the problem is the goal itself. As Paulo Freire (1985: 7) has noted, the negative slant of the phrase 'eradication of illiteracy' suggests a naive concept of illiteracy as something that can be destroyed like a weed or contained and controlled like an epidemic. In any society, to be 'literate' entails far more than the possession of basic reading, writing and computation skills and to be considered 'illiterate' implies far more than the simple lack of these skills. Illiteracy is an index of social marginality – an attribute of those farthest removed from active engagement in the national economy and polity. This chapter and others in this volume have provided ethnographic accounts of the interactions between 'dominant' and 'vernacular' literacies (Street 1993, and see Introduction, this volume) and the rural development education programmes designed to transform local literacy practices. The case of Dahu is just one example of how multi-levelled and complex these interactions can be. The modernising message of anti-illiteracy work in Dahu – supported by compatible messages conveyed in other media such as television broadcasts, calendar art, etc. – was evident in the residents of Dahu's changing beliefs and attitudes about the value of literacy. The social spaces in which literacy once mattered little were shrinking. Although women in particular still had little opportunity and felt little need to read and write in the course of their daily lives and work, they had come to believe that literacy (as represented in the anti-illiteracy curriculum) would make their lives better.

Notes

1 In one exceptional but telling case, the sudden appearance of my entourage caused one woman we visited to panic. Ignoring my pleas to not go to the trouble of offering us tea she seated us in the front room and then rushed out to prepare the tea returning just long enough to carry in the tea tray and serve us. While she did this I tried to ask her about her family and their education. Instead of answering she turned to the member of the village party branch who was with us and asked what she had done wrong. He told her that we were conducting a 'social investigation' (*shehui diaocha*), an answer that only served to intensify her anxiety. Once finished serving the tea she again vanished to another room. After some uncomfortable moments and shouted requests for her to return she hesitantly edged back into the room just long enough to recite an account of the academic achievements of her sons, both of whom had graduated from senior middle school. My escorts had become very familiar with the sorts of questions that

I was asking in each household and they began to give me answers to these for this household. In the meantime I was trying to establish some rapport with the increasingly distraught woman, a task made doubly difficult by my strangely accented Chinese and her refusal to make eye contact or speak directly to me. As she became more and more elusive my hosts became more demanding of her, virtually ordering her to speak to me. Eventually, I insisted that they let her go and we moved on to the next household.

References

Freire, P. (1985) *The Politics of Education*, South Hadley, MA: Bergin & Garvey.

Heath, S.B. (1983) *Ways with Words: Language, Life and Work in Communities and Classrooms*, Cambridge: Cambridge University Press.

Li Hui (1989) 'Illiteracy Threatens Modernization', *Beijing Review* 1: 7.

Shue, V. (1988) *The Reach of the State: Sketches of the Chinese Body Politic*, Stanford, CA: Stanford University Press.

Stites, R. (1995) 'Limits to the Effectiveness of the 1990 Anti-illiteracy Campaign in Promoting Literacy among Women in a Rural Chinese Community', *International Journal of Educational Development* 15: 381–99.

—— (1999) 'Writing Cultural Boundaries: National Minority Language Policy, Literacy Planning, and Bilingual Education', in G.A. Postiglione (ed.), *China's National Minority Education: Culture, Schooling, and Development*, New York: Falmer Press.

Stites, R. and Semali, L. (1991) 'Adult Literacy for Social Equality or Economic Growth? Changing Agendas for Mass Literacy in China and Tanzania', *Comparative Education Review* 35: 44–75.

Street, B. (1984) *Literacy in Theory and Practice*, Cambridge: Cambridge University Press.

—— (1993) 'Introduction: The New Literacy Studies', in B. Street (ed.), *Cross-Cultural Approaches to Literacy*, Cambridge: Cambridge University Press.

Woodside, A. (1992) 'Real and Imagined Continuities in the Chinese Struggle for Literacy', in R. Hayhoe (ed.), *Education and Modernization: The Chinese Experience*, Oxford: Pergamon Press.

10

LITERACIES, GENDER AND POWER IN RURAL PAKISTAN[1]

Shirin Zubair

Pakistan has one of the lowest rates of literacy in the world. The disparity is acute between male and female literacy rates as well as between urban and rural populations. The adult literacy rate, among the lowest in the world, is even lower for females in rural areas. According to UNESCO (1991), male literacy rate was 47.3 per cent, and female literacy only 21.1 per cent. It is interesting to note that the literacy information available on rural Pakistan is largely based on statistics which fails to provide an insight into the actual uses and conceptions of literacy among its users.

Contrary to popular perceptions, the rural population in Pakistan – including women of all ages and backgrounds – is keenly interested in education. When a Non Formal Education (NFE) programme for females was launched in the Punjab through NGOs, no reluctance or hesitation was noticed among older, married women and grandmothers to sit together with younger girls in the same class (Alam 1993). The information available on literacy in Pakistan is mostly in the form of statistical data based on records of primary school enrolment and census surveys. It would be relevant to indicate that the question on literacy in Pakistan censuses is often worded differently. For example, in the 1972 census it was enquired whether a person could read and write with understanding whereas in the 1981 census the question was whether a person could read a newspaper and write a simple letter (Population Census Organisation 1981). There is little knowledge available about the actual literacy needs and practices in Pakistani communities. Even less is known about how the socio-cultural and political structure of these communities might affect the literacy goals, practices and the significance of literacy itself in these communities. An understanding of specific literacy needs and skills along with an awareness of the specific contexts in which they are learnt and used are important in designing and implementing literacy programmes to make them meaningful to the community members' lives.

Theoretical framework

Street (1998) argues that research indicates literacy practices to be developing and spreading in more complex ways, while the oversimplified government discourses reductively focus on falling standards and lack of literacy skills. He suggests that a possible bridge is the new approach, which views language and literacy as social practices and resources rather than a set of rules formally and narrowly defined. Drawing upon Street's ideological model (1984, see Introduction to this volume) of literacy, this chapter looks at literacy practices as part of broader gender roles which relate to power in the family, home and community.

Literacy practices and literacy events

Baynham (1995) defines literacy practice as 'a concrete human activity', involving not just the objective facts of what people do with literacy, but also what they associate with what they do, how they construct its value, and the ideologies that surround it. The concept of practice is linked to subjective elements in literacy practices. It involves the attitudes of people – what people think about what they do. It also involves the concept of values (Barton and Padmore 1991; Barton 1994); it focuses on the subjectivity and agency dimension of practice. Heath introduced the concept of literacy event as: *any occasion in which a piece of writing is integral to the nature of the participant's interaction* (1983: 386). Instead of one monolithic way with literacy, typically defined as school's way, close study of the ways in which people work with written texts in ordinary everyday settings shows up striking differences in ways of taking and making use of literacy, sometimes at odds with mainstream definitions of literacy.

Thus it has been observed in the recent literature on literacies that the qualitative case-study method is most suitable to illuminate literacy practices in multi-literate individuals and communities, since in these communities, concepts such as *identity, power* and *ideology* acquire far more significance as compared to a mono-literacy context (Horsman 1987; Rockhill 1993; Hartley 1994; Saxena 1994; Baynham 1995; Besnier 1995; Prinsloo and Breier 1996). Applying this perspective to study people's literacy practices in various communities, anthropologists and social linguists have carried out ethnographic studies (Heath 1983; Street 1984; Horsman 1987; Rockhill 1993; Besnier 1995; Barton and Hamilton 1998) using relatively unstructured methods to focus on the function and meanings of literacy/ies in the lives of their subjects. Hence, the use of ethnographic methods in this study was inspired by the work of contemporary literacy researchers like Heath (1983), Street (1984, 1995), Baynham (1995) and Barton and Hamilton (1998) who have argued that in order to capture the diversity and complexity of various literacies in such underdeveloped communities, one needs to take account of the ideological issues and social practices that surround people's literacy practices.

189

Ethnographic data

Data for this chapter come from ethnographic fieldwork carried out in various phases between June 1996 and March 1998, in two adjoining villages in the Seraiki-speaking area of Southern Punjab, Pakistan.[2] The present ethnographic study fills a gap in the existing literature on women's literacy use, focusing on the lived experiences of thirty-five women. Unlike the use of ethnography in development policy (Robinson-Pant, this volume), my interest in using a qualitative, ethnographic approach stemmed mainly from a theoretical standpoint in contrast to the statistical studies available on literacy rates in Pakistani communities.

Nevertheless, the findings of my research may feed useful insights into development policy and implementation issues by providing a detailed ethnographic description of how women use literacies to make meanings of their lives, how power and identities are contested, challenged and negotiated discursively through literacy practices.

In this ethnographic study, I am more concerned with attempting to understand what actually happens (see Street's Introduction to this book) in this community – what are the meanings and uses of literacies for the village people – than with development policy. In order to achieve these objectives, I have struggled hard to empower my subjects by:

1   making my research methods more open, interactive and dialogic, adjusting my research tools to the villagers' own requirements
2   trying to deal with the subjects' agendas as well as our own, i.e., negotiating and mediating with the subjects.
3   sharing the knowledge with the subjects who help us construct that knowledge (adapted from Cameron et al. 1992).

My project initially aimed at building a profile of the literacy repertoire of the community as well as looking at individual trends among various groups; however, after the initial stages of fieldwork and data analysis, it became evident that the acquisition and uses of literacy are tied to the ideologies surrounding the expected gender roles in the community. Thus during the course of my research project, the questions changed from who reads/writes what in which language to

1   how women live and use literacies
2   why and how their access to secular literacy[3] is controlled by men
3   why these women aspire to literacy and education in a particular language.

Another issue of a more theoretical nature that became pressing as I pursued my research was the one that pertained to my own identity, my own role as researcher. (For a fuller account of the advantages and pitfalls of being an indigenous ethnographer in such communities see Clifford and Marcus 1986; Zubair 1999a.)

The issue of power dynamics between the researcher and the researched is crucial in social science research. Foucaultians and feminists have argued that social science is not a neutral inquiry into human behaviour and institutions. It is a way of exercising power and control over the less privileged and relatively powerless people. Foucault (1980) observes that in modern Western societies power is employed and exercised through a 'net-like organisation'. Power, then, is not monolithic – it does not emanate from a single source; there are various manifestations and dimensions of power, for example class, race, ethnicity, gender, generation, sub-culture, etc. (Warren 1988; Fairclough 1989).

Methodologically, Spivak (1988) has problematised the necessity of speaking for people who have no voices, thus empowering the research subjects. I have used participant observation, case studies and focus groups in an attempt to achieve these objectives, thus empowering the subjects (to some extent) by giving them a voice. I have endeavoured, but with a real sense of the difficulty of the project, to give a voice of their own to these women, these *silent birds* (in their own words) who have not been heard before. The problem of finding a voice for themselves was the main issue identified by some of my subjects. I have tried to achieve this partly through using ethnographic methods.

The data consist of six focus group recordings, forty-five interviews, field notes, literacy documents and participant observation in literacy events.

Power and discourse

Recent contributions to social theory have explored the role of language in the exercise, maintenance and change of power. Language, then, has come to be seen as the major locus of ideology, and so of major significance with respect to power. Foucault's work (1980) has ascribed a central role to discourse in the development of specifically modern forms of power (adapted from Fairclough 1989). It has been argued by social linguists that language, assumptions and meanings, values and attitudes constitute discourse and that the concept of discourse allows us to speak of the importance of language as a way of framing reality and shaping how we see ourselves and the world (Foucault 1980; Horsman 1987; Kress 1989; Gee 1990). Papen (this volume) argues that Foucault's concept of discourse refers not only to language, but to the processes of social interaction through which meaning is constructed, recognised, contested, negotiated and reconstructed. Literacy practices, she argues, are part of these processes. Similarly, Gee (1990) has argued that to appreciate language in its social context we need to focus not on language, but rather on Discourse which he writes with a capital 'D': meanings reside in social practices and discourses rather than in formal properties of language. Discourse is taken as a pattern of using language and the notion of discourse is incorporated in the notion of literacy practices. Literacy practices invoke other practices and larger social patterns as they are rich in individual and social meanings: the larger institutional practices may be subverted or questioned.

191

Within the theoretical framework outlined above, this chapter investigates the gendered uses and perceptions of various literacies in a Seraiki-speaking rural community. The people here have access to three literacies: Arabic, Urdu and English. I describe and explore women's access to and uses of multiple literacies to show how these relate to their social and communal roles. I first describe some gendered literacy practices, resulting from the ideologies perpetuated by the dominant groups.

The descriptions of literacy practices and literacy events are presented to show the diversity of literacy practices and to analyse how the gendering of literacy practices is inextricably intertwined with the power dynamics and 'sexual politics' (Millet 1977). The way women's access to 'secular literacy' is curtailed and controlled by the men in the community shows how literacy can become a major site for power politics and resistance between the powerful and relatively powerless segments in similar other communities around the world. While doing so, I reproduce excerpts and texts from women's writing and speech: by talking and writing about their roles they throw light on the significance and meanings of literacy in their day-to-day lives as well as the possible uses of various literacies. Some of their linguistic choices and emergent themes are analysed to illustrate:

1   how women use literacy to make sense of their lives
2   how power and identities are discursively contested and negotiated
3   how integral literacy is to the smooth running of their social and communal lives as opposed to the appalling literacy rates shown by UNESCO and other aid agencies.

The gendering of literacy

The main use of literacy in women's lives in the community is that of the oral recitation of the Quran, which increases during the month of *Ramadan*. Most people in the village read the Quran either daily or occasionally.

Older women in their forties, fifties and sixties perform their ritual prayers regularly five times daily. They also recite the Quran daily. Some recite it and then read the translation in Urdu. These religious rituals are performed daily at the same set times by these women. The reading of the Quran takes place after early morning prayers in the mornings. This has a deep religious and spiritual significance, i.e., that these women's first and foremost perception of their own identity is that of Muslims. Thus they engage in this religious literacy event every morning. All these religious literacy events are carried out in Arabic and Urdu, the only languages that these older women can read. It is important to note another pattern in the literacy practices of the older women, that they only read the Quran and the local newspapers, sometimes at night, before going to bed. During the day, they engage in household activities of cooking, cleaning, etc. Because they primarily see their social role as housewives and mothers, they only read the paper at bedtime, as a leisure activity because they do not find time to

Table 10.1 Women's uses of literacies

Age	Language	Reading	Writing	Other
50–70	Arabic	Quran prayers		teaching
	Urdu	newspaper television calendars		teaching
30–49	Arabic	Quran prayers		teaching
	Urdu	newspapers magazines calendars cards/letters television	letters diaries record keeping signing legal documents	
15–29	Arabic	Quran prayers		teaching
	Urdu/English	newspapers magazines novels medicine labels cards/letters calendars television	letters diaries record keeping messages notes exam papers sign legal papers/cheques poetry short story	teaching studying

read it during the day. It is interesting as well as pertinent to note that for men the reading of a paper is not a leisure activity but an important prime-time activity, as all read it in the morning hours to learn about the most recent political developments and the latest news.

Most women (particularly from the old and middle groups) daily read the Quran in the early hours of dawn after the *fajjar* prayers. The purpose of recitation of the Quran is not to understand the meanings, but to perform a pious religious ritual. The ritual prayers are also offered in Arabic five times a day. Men go to the village mosque five times a day to offer ritual prayers called *namaz*, and women offer these prayers at home. Although much of what they read in the *Quran* and *namaz* is not understood by the people, the ritualistic readings have a symbolic significance and mean a lot to the village people. The act of reading is symbolic of the assertion and confirmation of their religious identity and beliefs. Women also read other religious material, for example booklets in Urdu, to gain guidance and information about the code and performance of various rituals like *namaz*, *roza*, *zakat* and *haj*, which form the basics of Islamic faith. Table 10.1 shows a detailed list of women's uses of literacies, across age groups.

A common feature – that serves as a contrast to younger women's literacy repertoire – in the literacy histories of the older women is that since most of them have not been to schools, some have learnt to read only, whereas some could write earlier but have lost the skill owing to the lack of practice or the lack of need to write. These women also engage in literacy events which involve negotiation of literacy skills and abilities; for instance some of these women, while confined to their homes, during their leisure time teach poor village children to read Arabic and Urdu.

Women's access to literacy acquisition, in this community, was traditionally limited to Arabic literacy. Therefore, a vast majority of the older women can either only read the Quran in Arabic, or read some Urdu, e.g., newspaper headlines, names on cards, television announcements, etc. However, the middle and younger group of women who can read and write Urdu and English engage themselves in a wide variety of literacy practices ranging from reading of bills and medicine labels to reading of fiction and creative writing. The gendering of literacy practices also manifests itself in women typically reading the electricity bills and writing records of household accounts, whereas the payment of bills and shopping for the house is done by the men in the family. Men and women occupy and function in different domains: women's world is primarily the private domain of home whereas men occupy and function in the public domains. This is also reflected in their *literacy practices* (see above, also Introduction to this book). Men mostly use their literacy skills to accomplish practical goals of daily life, for example payment of bills, reading agriculture manuals, instructions on medicines and pesticides, business news about cotton trade and brokerage, etc.

Men read Urdu newspapers daily outside their homes, in shops or other workplaces. Reading the papers is important for them to keep abreast of the political developments in the country and local politics. They also discuss political news with other men in the workplace or the small teashops where men can watch television and read the local paper free of charge.

Whereas men are particularly interested in political news, younger and middle-aged women are more interested in romantic fiction and women's magazines. Women, unlike men, have to choose times and spaces for reading and writing between heavily gendered home activities. Some women reported reading the newspaper at bedtime as they do not get free time to read it during the day. Discussing literacy time and family time for working-class mothers in England, Mace (1998) uses the word *play* while elaborating on the meanings of literacy in mothers' lives. She argues that certain kinds of literacy behaviour simply looked like *play* in conflict with the work of mothering.

Writing about the practices of reading women's magazines, Hermes (1995) observes that everyday practices, far from being meaningless, are highly significant in that they can be a form of resistance to the mainstream cultural practices. I interpret the young women's reading of romantic fiction and writing of personal diaries in two ways: first as self-expression because women are denied a public voice, and second as a denial of and resistance to the dominant male

194

culture. As for Radway's readers (1987), reading of romances was a declaration of independence: a kind of minor rebellion against the position accorded by the dominant patriarchal discourse, that of the caring housewife and mother.

Diary-writing and diary-keeping is a very prominent literacy use in the community. It exists across genders but there are differences in terms of its use, frequency and maintenance. Reading woman's magazines and writing personal diaries emerge as two very distinct literacy practices that the young women engage themselves in very regularly. It was found to be common and very popular among younger, especially unmarried women. These women daily write diaries. These diaries consist of pages of personal feelings, intimate thoughts, self-reflection. Some women in their mid-thirties wrote diaries before their marriages, but said that they had stopped writing them after marriage but had kept their old diaries as memoirs.

Mace (1998) has argued that literacy engages our imaginations, intellects, emotions and memories, and is a matter of enormous mystery. These literacy practices are tied in to the availability of time and space in their lives, and simultaneously they serve as a means of temporal excursions from the mundane. Following is an excerpt from the diary of a young woman:

> After dinner I took my radio and went upstairs on the terrace. I liked a drama which was on air. It was about an educated daughter-in-law who is a doctor. She wants to work but her husband and mother-in-law do not approve. They want her to remain domesticated. She feels suffo-cated. At last, she leaves her husband and takes up work. She earns her own living, has her own house and car. I thought strange thoughts after listening to this play, whether she made a right decision or not. I kept thinking until I dozed off.

This extract provides evidence of the younger women's use of writing skills as an expression of the self and the conflicting ideologies regarding women's space and role in the community. The young woman's preoccupation with the issues of female education and employment, self-realisation through work rather than marriage, challenging and renegotiating the existing stereotypes regarding personal and social identity, is well illustrated through this quotation from her personal diary. As these younger women become exposed to the Western and local media, they begin to examine their own lives in relation to the new images of women portrayed there. They are gradually learning how to create and take up new opportunities and move into what had always been viewed as 'male jobs' or 'male spaces'. This is reflected in their literacy practices as well as in their public discourse. The problems and issues relating to the traditional roles and the conflict of resolving the personal aspirations with the expectations of their families and the larger community are often the focal points of their writings. The pages of their personal diaries contain a mixture of personal and sociological insights – the quotations, short stories, poems, personal observations, all point to the fact that these women are not merely functionally literate but are able to understand and interpret the world from their own standpoint. They demonstrate the capability, as in the example quoted above from a personal diary, of critically analysing social expectations of women's roles. The problems and issues relating to the traditional roles and the conflict of resolving the personal aspirations with the expectations of their families and the larger community are often the focal points of their writings. The tussle between the contested and conflicting ideologies is also found in their interactions in focus groups (see section on power and discourse).

Men's perceptions of and engagements with literacy are of an entirely different kind. Those men in the village who also keep and write diaries use them for different purposes, e.g., record keeping, memos, and for writing future plans and appointments. One man had written and kept a diary for the past ten years. Whereas men use diary-writing as a way of organising their records, a timetable, women use this literacy event for their emotional catharsis. The main difference, then, between men's and women's uses of literacies is role-related: men use literacy skills to fulfil their role of dealing with the public world in a non-emotive and utilitarian context as opposed to women who use their literacy skills not only to fulfil the domestic role but also for self-fulfilment and expression of their deepest emotions and feelings.

The politics of literacy in discourse

Street (1998) has pointed out that an anthropologist analyses the use of tropes and metaphors in everyday conversation just as a literary critic analyses figures of speech in a literary text. Following from Street (1998) and others (Foucault 1980; Horsman 1987; Barton and Hamilton 1998), I will look at examples from the data to illustrate how identity and power are challenged, contested and negotiated in these discourses.

I found my data replete with juxtapositions of threatening and non-threatening, powerful and powerless forms of literacy. Women belonging to older and middle-age groups frequently used metaphors such as *caged birds* and *silent birds*, to describe their peculiar predicament regarding their lives and literacies; these metaphors not only refer to the act of speech, but also express a desire to find a voice, an individual identity through literacy. I have argued that speech stands for literacy and the ability to articulate ourselves and thus achieve self-realisation. Silence being the antonym of speech stands for illiteracy or lack of literate abilities to enable people to participate and function fully in society (for a fuller account, see Zubair 1999a).

Example 1

M = Moderator is myself, S, R & O = Older women, A = Women in thirties, Z & N = Younger women, F = Male participant in early forties. For a key to the symbols used, see the Appendix.

038 R   [yes absolutely there was *izzat* – if someone came outside we
039 O   [very respectable people
040 R   couldn't tell whether it was a human being or an animal we
041 R   remained indoors like silent birds – *now* there's freedom children
042 R   are also being educated and we also have some awareness but
043 R   for us those times were okay =
044 O   = it was good =
045 R   = it was absolutely fine
046 O   (unclear)
047 R   those times were absolutely fine those elders did right now
048 R   there's freedom – children have an easy life now even for us its
049 R   easier
050 M   umm would you tell me something about it? (signalling towards younger
        participants)
051 A   what do we know? [what shall we (unclear)
052 Z   [I think that there shouldn't be so many =
053 A   = restrictions =
054 Z   = restrictions should not be there because . . . (starts speaking Urdu)
055 Z   one can't sit at home (M: umm) that's our view because the new
056 Z   generation (laughs) would say that one can't sit at home there
057 Z   should be some freedom – at least to move about to meet friends
058 Z   to go out with friends to parks to see movies – there should be a
059 Z   little bit of freedom – too much of it (restrictions) is not good
060 Z   (M: umm) I think if there is too much pressure on a girl she
061 Z   won't be able to do what's right for her (M: umm) that's all
062 Z   (laughs)

Example 2

164 M   why didn't you?
165 F   it's okay if women are literate they become very free Islam is
166 F   about strictly observing *purdah purdah* is obligatory a woman
167 F   must cover herself if she goes out head must be covered it is
168 F   Islamic [Islam
169 S   [(laughs) see
170 F   these are the Islamic rules =
171 S   = (jokingly) he is our Islamic =
172 F   = Islam says teach up to this learn to read that you are familiar
173 F   with the religion but people forget religion and pay attention to
174 F   worldly education more they have [no respect for elders
175 N   [yeah this is also this is
176 N   written meaning that our prophet said that even if you have to
177 N   go to China to get educated you should go this means some

178 N   freedom was given =
179 F   = China that
180 N   this is all made up by them to suppress to kill that 'you are'nt
181 N   going out you aren't learning literacy' when Islam allows one
182 N   to go out to become literate then these these restrictions are
183 N   imposed by man

During the focus groups and personal interviews, the men, whether old or young invariably used the pronouns *we* and *them*, as in, *if we educate women, they become free*, and in *they'll hit us on our heads with their shoes*. Example 2 from focus group illustrates the power politics where F (a man) and N (a young woman) argue about female rights to literacy and education in the light of Islamic teachings.

In example 2, when questioned about not sending his daughter to school, F's response is spontaneous: *it's okay – if women are literate they become very free*. *They* here refers to the women, the other group as opposed to the self. Seeing women as *they* has implications: he regards them as the other group struggling for power and dominance through literacy. *We* and *they* are then two polarities, two groups in competition, and the *we* group is more powerful than *they* and, whether knowingly or unknowingly, does not want to give up its control and power over the other group. Wales (1996) has observed that in semiotic and semantic terms, generalised *we* and *they* are in binary opposition to each other, i.e., positive versus negative, functioning as value-laden antonyms. In social and ideological senses rather than a literal sense, *we* can mean 'more than one': it can mean a collective identity like a Greek chorus.

Further analysis of the lexis and figures of speech in these samples brings out the antithetical juxtapositions of concepts and attitudes, for example antonyms like restrictions and freedom, old and new, then and now, suppression and respectable, etc. These collocations are emblematic of the various strands of thought exemplified by the gender groups in the talk. Thus the use of these antonyms reflects conflicting ideologies. Each word is value laden: language is a site of contest and power struggle between different groups in the community. Russian linguists Bakhtin and Voloshinov emphasise the social nature of language that it is always pulled in opposite directions. Language appears here as the site or space in which dialogic relationships are realised; it manifests itself in discourse, the word oriented towards another (Dentith 1995). These antonyms, i.e., *restriction and freedom, then and now, old and new, suppression and rebellion*, show the participant's preoccupation with these concepts and emphasise the fact that the people in the community are caught between these opposing ideologies, and the notion of women's literacy is inextricably intertwined with these sharp contrasts.

While recounting their literacy histories, women describe themselves as *caged* and *silent birds*. Lakoff (1995) observes that silence is analogous to invisibility. She quotes the example of fundamentalist Muslim societies (similar to the one under study), where women must be veiled in public, which she considers a symbolic public invisibility because even in veil women are perceptible objects on streets.

She goes on to argue that interpretative control, i.e., making of meaning of the private and public discourses, is controlled by men even in Western societies. Interpretative control is hard to recognise because it is done silently by those having cultural hegemony. Similarly, Kramsch (1998) has pointed out that only the powerful decide whose values and beliefs will be deemed worth adopting by the group, and whose voices will be heard. Thus the use of metaphors like *silent birds* and *caged bird* reflects an enforced silence. Kaplan (1990: 312) observes:

> A very high proportion of women's poems are about the right to speak and write . . . that larger subject, the exploration and definition of gender difference in culture, it becomes a distinct issue when women speak or write, and men protest, not only or primarily at what they say, but at the act itself.

Freire (1972) observes that learning to read and write ought to be an opportunity to know what *speaking the word* really means, i.e., a human act implying reflection and action. He goes on to suggest that in the culture of silence the masses are *mute*, they are prohibited from creatively taking part in the transformations of their society and therefore prohibited from being. Thus, the use of such strong and powerful images might be interpreted as a protest at being silenced by the dominant groups. Here these metaphors are emblematic of their collective literacy voice. These birds are not wilfully silent – their voices have been silenced. The consistent use of the passive voice in expressing themselves and narrating their literacy histories strengthens the point that these women were not active agents in decision making about their own lives but rather passive recipients of others' decisions. A tension between the unequal and arbitrary use of power and the threat of certain types of literacy was apparent in their linguistic choices (Zubair 1999b). Quranic literacy is a non-threatening form of literacy, therefore acceptable to the dominant segments of the community. The threatening forms of literacy are not acceptable to the dominant group in the community, hence gatekeeping around Urdu and English literacies. The concept of secular literacy was invariably constructed in these villagers' discourse as an empowering phenomenon (Zubair 1999a). Literacy carries with it a promise and yet fear and threat. It holds a promise as it offers economic and financial gains as well as independence, therefore it is aspired to by younger women, who invest their dreams in literacy. It is also a threat and fear because it empowers the individual, because it implies change in the old system and adapting to new identities and roles. Hence, the younger women's resistance to men's control over secular literacies and aspiration to self-enhancement through literacy and a newer identity.

The power dynamics of literacy were also manifested in some communal and social literacy events that I observed in the community. For example the reading and writing of letters is a very significant family as well as communal literacy event in that it not only helps to maintain relationships, but the participants are often caught up in the power dynamics of literacy in these literacy events. As not all members of a family can read and write letters, family letters are read aloud to the whole family. The whole family usually sit together and the literate person in the family reads the letter even though it may be personal; even if the husband writes to his wife, the letter is sometimes read aloud to the whole family. Thus the person who can read and write has power over those who may not wish their letters to be read communally. Satto, a young woman, said she felt powerless and exposed when she had to take her husband's letter to other women to read out to her. These examples show the communal and power aspects attached to these specific literacy events. Those who can read and write have a certain edge and power over those who are dependent on them for the reading and writing of personal letters. This also results in feelings of disempowerment and dependence among those who do not possess these literacy skills.

Conclusion

The ethnographic approach used in this research project to study multi-literacies captured the conflicting ideologies and perceptions of literacies in the village community. Whereas women's preoccupation with literacy envisages reflection literacy (Hasan 1996) as their target, men feel functional literacy[4] can suffice. Hence, the uses and conceptions of literacy are caught up in a web of power dynamics of family relationships and genders. Within the community there are conflicts and tensions between various groups *vis-à-vis* genders, families, generations and individuals, e.g., between husband and wife, father and daughter, sister and brother.

The conflicting ideologies and perceptions of literacy in my data show that female literacy and education are highly contested notions in this community, and that literacy is a major site for power struggle and resistance. The conceptualisation of literacy is not uniform among the community members: the community is divided in terms of their literacy aspirations and goals. From men's perspective functional literacy is the desirable goal whereas women expect much more from literacy than learning the alphabet. Women, especially the younger generation, aspire to wider education rather than literacy as a set of skills. Younger women's desire for literacy and education complements their acquisition of English literacy and access to the Western media. The younger women negotiate this change through their talk and behaviour whereas younger men are content with their existing roles. Because they are dissatisfied with the prescribed roles, younger women act as agents of change whereas men being content with the existing roles exhibit a fear of change. Hence they fear the consequences of secular literacy and control women's access to wider education.

Women's lives and their encounters with various literacies within the parameters of time and space show that women's access to and uses of multiple literacies are tied in to their social and family roles of mothers and housewives. Owing to the constraints on women's time and space, their access to secular literacy is curtailed. Nevertheless, diary-writing and reading women's magazines in leisure time have special significance in women's lives, as they choose times and spaces between gendered domestic activities to indulge in these little pleasures. Quotations and extracts from the diaries suggest that these literacy practices are not merely temporal excursions, but they have a greater underlying significance for women who are denied a public voice. Thus they endeavour to find a voice for themselves through creative writing. This is their way of establishing their own identity. These non-utilitarian functions of literacy fulfil their innermost needs of self-expression and self-fulfilment, the desire to find a voice and to be recognised as human individuals as opposed to the prescribed social roles of mothers, daughters and wives.

The difference between men's and women's perceptions of literacy is crucial. For men, women's secular literacy proves a threat to their subjugated position. For women, literacy is a means of self-improvement and self-empowerment. Hence, the younger women have a more advanced approach to literacy than older women and men (both young and old). They are more willing to embrace social change, and a new identity which goes hand in hand with the acquisition of secular literacy, because they have more to gain from this than men. They are less committed than the men to the traditionally male-dominated system of agriculture. Since secular literacy is conceptualised as an empowering phenomenon in this community, men fear women's acquisition of secular literacies and women desire literacy for self-empowerment, and self-enhancement. This conflict of interests is central to the way literacy is used and conceptualised by men and women in this community.

Women's clamour for (secular) literacy in this particular context seems ironical considering the fact that no adult literacy programme was on offer in these two villages. Whereas this remains the responsibility of the state and calls for a concerted effort in creating a social environment conducive to female literacy and education, the governments of Pakistan have not done enough to facilitate women's access to literacy. These women's engagements with and their specific needs for literacy (programmes) need to be taken into account by the local NGOs, UNESCO and other international agencies while designing and implementing literacy programmes for these communities.

Appendix

Transcription conventions: key to symbols used

[simultaneous or overlapping utterance
=   contiguous utterances
( )   1. unclear utterances
        2. description of non-verbal activity, e.g., laughs
–   short pause
. . .   long pause

?	functional question
' '	in narrative passages involving reported speech inverted commas are used to establish the provenance of an utterance
Italics	emphasis

Glossary

namaz	ritual prayer
fajjar	pre-dawn
roza	fast
haj	pilgrimage to Mecca
izzat	male pride or ego
kammi	landless
purdah	screen; segregation of sexes at puberty
Ramadan	Muslims' holy month of fasting
mullah	priest
zakat	alms
zamindar	landowner

Notes

1 Some parts of this chapter have appeared in Zubair 1999b.
2 The community is predominantly agrarian. The socio-political structure of the community is based on a feudal system, with two classes of people, the *zamindar* and the *kammis*. These two classes are mutually interdependent for the smooth and effective functioning of the communal and social life.
3 Secular literacy is a term I coined during my research in this community. The village people frequently referred to Arabic literacy as religious or Islamic, whereas other literacies (English, Urdu) were considered literacy for worldly gains, e.g., literacy for employment, etc. Therefore, deriving from villagers' own perceptions, I use the term secular literacy for Urdu and English literacies as opposed to religious literacy in Arabic.
4 The term functional literacy is used to describe basic literacy and numeracy skills to accomplish everyday tasks. The village people did not use this term but they referred to literacy as a limited set of skills, e.g., to be able to read/write letters or to read bills, etc. The men invariably considered these basic skills as desirable, as opposed to education; Rockhill (1993) has observed that when skills become education it is a threat to male power.

References

Alam, A. (1993) 'When Formal Education Does Not Work, Try Non-Formal Methods', in Pakistan newspaper *Frontier Post*, 1 March 1993.

Ang, I. (1985) *Watching Dallas*, London and New York: Routledge.

Barton, D. (1994) *Literacy: An Introduction to the Ecology of Written Language*, Oxford: Blackwell.

Barton, D. and Hamilton, M. (1998) *Local Literacies: Reading and Writing in One Community*, London: Routledge.

Barton, D. and Padmore, S. (1991) 'Writing in the Community', in D. Graddol, J. Maybin and B. Stierer (eds), *Researching Language and Literacy in Social Context*, Clevedon, Adelaide and Philadelphia: Multilingual Matters.

Baynham, M. (1995) *Literacy Practices: Investigating Literacy Practices in Social Contexts*, London: Longman.

Besnier, N. (1995) *Literacy, Emotion, and Authority*, Cambridge: Cambridge University Press.

Cameron, D., Frazer, J., et al. (1992) *Researching Language: Issues of Power and Method*, London: Routledge.

Clifford, J. and Marcus, G. (1986) *Writing Culture: The Poetics and Politics of Ethnography*, Berkeley: University of California Press.

Dentith, S. (1995) *Bakhtinian Thought: An Introductory Reader*, London and New York: Routledge.

Fairclough, N. (1989) *Language and Power*, London and New York: Longman.

Foucault, M. (1980) *Power/Knowledge: Selected Interviews and Other Writings in 1972–77*, ed. C. Gordon, Brighton: Harvester.

Freire, P. (1972) *Cultural Action for Freedom*, Harmondsworth: Penguin.

Gee, J. (1990) *Social Linguistics and Literacies: Ideologies in Discourses*, London, New York and Philadelphia: The Falmer Press.

Hartley, T. (1994) 'Generations of Literacy among Women in a Bilingual Community', in M. Hamilton, D. Barton and R. Ivanič (eds), *Worlds of Literacy*, Clevedon and Adelaide: Multilingual Matters.

Hasan, R. (1996) 'Literacy, Everyday Talk and Society', in R. Hasan and G. Williams (eds), *Literacy in Society*, London and New York: Longman.

Heath, S.B. (1983) *Ways with Words: Language, Life and Work in Communities and Classrooms*, Cambridge: Cambridge University Press.

Hermes, J. (1995) *Reading Women's Magazines*, Cambridge: Polity Press.

Horsman, J. (1987) *Something in My Mind besides the Everyday: Women and Literacy*, Toronto: Women's Press.

Kaplan, C. (1990) 'Language and Gender', in D. Walder (ed.), *Literature in the Modern World: Critical Essays and Documents*, New York and Oxford: Oxford University Press.

Kramsch, C. (1998) *Language and Culture*, Oxford: Oxford University Press.

Kress, G. (1989) *Linguistic Processes in Socio-Cultural Practices*, Oxford: Oxford University Press.

Lakoff, R. (1995) 'Women and Silence', in K. Hall and M. Bucholtz (eds), *Gender Articulated: Language and Socially Constructed Self*, New York: Routledge.

Mace, J. (1998) *Playing with Time: Mothers and the Meaning of Literacy*, London: UCL Press.

Millet, K. (1977) *Sexual Politics*, London: Virago.

Population Census Organisation (1981) *Census Report of Punjab*, Islamabad: Statistics Division, Government of Pakistan.

Prinsloo, M. and Breier, M. (eds) (1996) *The Social Uses of Literacy: Theory and Practice in Contemporary South Africa*, Amsterdam and Johannesburg: John Benjamins and Sached Books.

Radway, J.A. (1987) *Reading the Romance*, London and New York: Verso.

Rockhill, K. (1993) 'Gender Language and the Politics of Literacy', in B.V. Street (ed.), *Cross-Cultural Approaches to Literacy*, Cambridge: Cambridge University Press.

Saxena, M. (1994) 'Literacies among Punjabis in Southall', in M. Hamilton, D. Barton and R. Ivanič (eds), *Worlds of Literacy*, Clevedon, Philadelphia and Adelaide: Multilingual Matters.

Spivak, G.C. (1988) 'Can the Subaltern Speak', in C. Nelson and L. Grossberg (eds), *Marxism and the Interpretation of Culture*, Urbana: University of Illinois Press, pp. 271–313.

Street, B. (1984) *Literacy in Theory and Practice*, Cambridge: Cambridge University Press.

—— (1995) *Social Literacies: Critical Approaches to Literacy in Development, Ethnography and Education*, New York and London: Longman.

—— (1998) 'New Literacies in Theory and Practice: What Are the Implications for Language in Education?', King's College London: Inaugural Professorial Lecture, 19 October 1998.

UNICEF, UNESCO, UNDP (1991) 'World Declaration on Education for All: Meeting Basic Learning Needs', documents from World Conference on Education for all, March 1990, Jomtein, Thailand.

Wales, K. (1996) *Personal Pronouns in Present-Day English*, Cambridge: Cambridge University Press.

Warren, C.A.B. (1988) *Gender Issues in Field Research*, Newbury Park, London and New Delhi: Sage.

Zubair, S. (1999a) 'Women's Literacies in a Rural Pakistani Community: An Ethnographic Study', unpublished PhD thesis, Cardiff University.

—— (1999b) 'Women's Literacy in a Rural Pakistani Community', in T. O'Brein (ed.) *Language and Literacies*, papers from BAAL 1998 Conference held in Manchester, Clevedon Avon, Adelaide: Multilingual Matters, pp. 114–25.

AFTERWORD

Problematising literacy and development

Alan Rogers

This volume of essays sets out to examine, through a series of case studies, how the New Literacy Studies can contribute to a more effective analysis of the relationship between literacy and development. Perhaps the most important result of this collection of papers is to highlight the fact that the easy platitudes of so many development programmes are in fact highly problematic. It may be helpful to look at this in more detail.

Literacy and development: the traditional picture

The traditional picture of the relationship between literacy and development is that there is a *direct* relationship between the two.

Development is seen as the unquestioned improvement in certain key indicators such as health and housing – especially economic indicators. Papen quotes a typical statement: 'The benefits of women becoming literate are well documented, not only in terms of their own emancipation, but also in terms of education, health and economic progress of the whole family and nation' (Papen, this volume, p. 46). This is based on a 'needs' approach to the so-called underdeveloped populations. In a recent World Bank paper, entitled 'Including the 900+ Millions' (thereby implying that the more than 90 million persons whom the rest of the world have designated as being 'illiterate' are somehow 'excluded' from the significant world society), a direct relationship between learning literacy skills and improvements in seven indicators of development (listed as confidence/ autonomy and empowerment; children's effective participation in schooling; family hygiene, nutrition and health; family size; increasing livelihoods; participation in community and political life; and better understanding of radio information) is seen as unquestionable, even when it accepts that the precise way in which the relationship works is not always clear.

Deficits

Two key approaches can be identified to the literacy-leads-to-development equation. The first sees the barriers to development (the causes of underdevelopment) as deficits in the target populations – for example, the lack of skills and of knowledge, or the reluctance of the poor to embrace new attitudes, new technologies and new working practices. The answer to such deficits is inputs – especially education and training directed at the target group. And literacy is seen to be the starting point for this process of education and training – literacy leading to new knowledge.

The equation is a causal one – literacy leads to new knowledge leads to developmental changes.

Thus, for example, as the Nepal case study here shows, traditional aid agencies look to literacy to increase knowledge about health directly. The goal of literacy learning programmes then is 'further learning' (i.e., more education and training). In terms of adult learning theory, we are dealing here with the personal transformation paradigm (Mezirow and other writers) – education and training lead to personal transformation which in turn leads to development.

The relationship between learning literacy skills and the development indicators is then seen as a direct one. Although we hear less today of the earlier statement that a 40 per cent level of 'literacy' (skills) is required for any society's economic growth rate to 'take off', development depends on a prior acquisition of literacy skills on a wide basis. Therefore, as Maddox says, illiteracy is regularly evoked as *the* barrier to economic and social progress (Maddox, this volume, p. 137). Literacy is 'your key for a better future', as the Namibia government tells its people (interestingly, in English) (Papen, this volume, p. 44). Without literacy skills, these 900 million so-called illiterates can never engage in any development programmes; they cannot even understand radio (World Bank paper 2000) or watch television (Stites, this volume, p. 180).

Social transformation

The second approach sees the barriers to development as lying in the systems which surround the 'illiterate'. Instead of the poor alone changing, the whole of society needs transformation to overcome the in-built oppression which the dominant groups assert over the subaltern. The process of development then is not inputs but social action. And once again education and training are required to help the target groups to understand their true lifeworld, to determine their desired course of action, and to implement it against the opposition they face. Again literacy is the starting point for this process of comprehending, deciding and acting (Freire 1972) – learning to 'read the word' is a prerequisite for 'reading the world'. Literacy leads to liberation and a new social order.

Both approaches are based on a 'literacy comes first' ideology. The concept is sequential, linear. At first, illiterate individuals or social groups are thought to engage in no literacy activities at all. Literacy learning programmes thus start a completely new process; and this leads directly to many forms of new literacy activities for further learning and development.

The New Literacy Studies as seen in these chapters have problematised all three parts of this traditional sequence. 'Literacy' itself is now seen as problematic. 'Development' too can no longer be seen as unproblematic. And the 'links' between the two also need much closer examination, especially in the light of the new thinking on literacy and development.

Problematising literacy: whose literacy?

Literacy is now being examined in new ways. It is seen as an integral part of communicative practices. As one of the chapters says, 'Literacy, in this perspective, is not conceived as a single set of competencies, but as different *practices* embedded in political relations, ideological practices and symbolic meaning structures' (Papen, this volume). 'Literacy is not just a set of uniform technical skills to be imparted to those lacking them – the "autonomous" model – but rather . . . there are multiple literacies in communities, and . . . literacy practices are socially embedded' (Street, this volume, p. 2). 'Literacy is a social construction, not a neutral technology: it varies from one culture or sub-group to another, and its uses are embedded in relations of power and struggles over resources' (Herbert and Robinson, this volume, p. 121, citing Street 1984).

According to this view, 'illiteracy' and 'literacy' are social constructs which vary from context to context; not every country defines 'literacy' in the same way. 'In many developing contexts today, the arrival of a literacy [learning] programme and the associated national publicity about the problems of lacking literacy [skills], themselves serve to construct "illiteracy" amongst people for whom the term previously had no salience' (Street, this volume, p. 2). Literacy then is seen to have a social and cultural meaning which differs from place to place. What is more, all societies are changing. In place of a static definition of literacy which applies to all persons for all time (the skill of decoding words from texts), we are faced with a changing scenario in which people are both subjects of change and objects of change. This is as true of the Peruvian Arakmbut as of rural Chinese, of the nomadic Rabaris as of the children in Eritrea, of Pakistan families as of religious groups in northern Ghana. Literacy (and development also) is continually being redefined in a changing dialectic, just as dominant and subaltern cultures are continually redefining their relationships.

In the new approaches to literacy, it is now recognised that 'the "literate" and "illiterate", as subjects of literacy, have relations. They share the same moving social spaces. Within social space, they are constructed as each other by themselves and vice versa' (Chopra, this volume, p. 86). It is a relationship of power: the 'literate' have excluded the 'illiterate' from their society and will only include them on condition that the 'illiterate' acquire the same skills of the same literacy as the so-called 'literate' possess – attitudes which many of the non-literate members of society have internalised, so that they see themselves as deficient and excluded.

But as these chapters show so clearly, literacy is a core activity for both literate and non-literate persons. Literate and non-literate alike have literacy tasks they wish and indeed often feel that they need to engage in; and they adopt many different strategies to engage in such communicative practices. As these chapters show, non-literate persons are not inexperienced in literacy; they engage in literacy activities frequently and often effectively.

Multiple literacies

Ethnographic studies of literacy have thus revealed that instead of one universal literacy (a set of skills), there are different forms of literacy, different literacies. This is a common theme of almost every one of these chapters. Herbert and Robinson show this clearly from their study of literacy and language uses in northern Ghana. Religious, commercial, economic literacies can be identified as well as the so-called 'school-based' literacy of the adult literacy learning programme. Some of these are closely related to language: for instance, in Muslim societies religious literacies are usually (but not always) in Arabic, while the school-based literacies will be in more standardised languages such as Urdu and English (Zubair, this volume, p. 193). In Pakistan, secular literacies can be clearly distinguished from religious literacies.

As the case studies reveal, some of these other literacies are very different from the more formal literacy. Thus in Bangladesh, the different types of economic literacy identified by Maddox 'involve a vocabulary and form that are quite different from those of the literacy primer (which is largely based on discursive texts and development messages, and [which] maintains a separation of literacy and numeracy)' (Maddox, this volume, p. 139). In Namibia, 'there is often little room for the recognition of non-dominant literacy practices which may have been acquired outside schools and are valued within communities and social groups' (Papen, this volume).

Dominant and non-dominant literacies

Nor do all these literacies live together in harmony; they are often deeply in contestation with one another, as Brian Street points out (Street, this volume, p. 8). Some forms of literacy are highly privileged; others are demeaned. Some are more dominant than others. The dominant literacy tends to marginalise the local literacies. But, as Maddox shows, the local literacies used in Bangladesh for economic activities in the home and in the community, are not marginal, they are central to the life of rural men and women:

Bangla literacy, for economic purposes, plays an integral role in the economic life of the peasantry in Bangladesh. Its use is widespread and

central to economic and cultural institutions and the practice of daily
life, rather than being peripheral or marginal. Although the oral culture
and face-to-face relationships are highly valued, literacy plays a part in
nearly all forms of economic activity, and those people who are not able
to do so directly must make use of mediators [and other strategies].

(Maddox, this volume, pp. 140–1)

Different uses of literacy

What is more, the case studies show that literacy (whether in the dominant form
or in one of the local forms) is used by different groups and individuals for
different purposes. Such uses may be related to language issues. Herbert and
Robinson show not only that the dominant literacy can be used for economic
purposes (different from the kind of economic literacies Maddox found in Bangladesh), but also that one person may use different languages when using literacy
for different communicative purposes. In this case, the usages of literacy determined the language used, not the other way round.

The different uses of literacy mean that it is not simply a case of dominant
(central) literacies against local literacies: rather, local communities have different literacies and uses of literacy within them. 'The conceptualisation of literacy
is not uniform among the community members: the community is divided in
terms of their literacy aspirations and goals' (Zubair, this volume, p. 200).

And this means that literacy activities are bound up with the power structures
of any society. It is often argued that learning the formal school-based literacy of
the dominant group will lead to empowerment, while more indigenous forms of
literacy (where they are recognised to exist) will not. This may be true for some
people: in the Pakistan case study, the younger women sought to master the
secular (dominant) literacy as a means to their own independence, while some of
the men sought to restrict their access to this secular literacy for exactly the same
reason. But in other situations, as Aikman's study among others shows, formal
literacy does not always lead to empowerment (see also Gibson in Prinsloo and
Breier 1996); real power often lies elsewhere. Aikman's communities were operating 'in a context where there was little enforcement of the written law, and
however authoritative and forceful it [the written law] sounded on paper, in
practice it could be ignored . . . when the death threats come, they are never
written down'.

While it is true that the dominant literacy will normally be the most powerful,
some of the case studies suggest that any one of the multiple literacies can
become a tool of power (social or personal) when used by different persons or
groups. Indeed, any form of literacy itself can be used to oppress some people.

The uses of literacy in a homogeneous community like this are caught
up in a web of power dynamics of family relationships and gender.
Within the community there are conflicts and tensions between various

groups *vis-à-vis* genders, families, generations and individuals, e.g., between husband and wife, father and daughter, sister and brother. The conflicting ideologies and perceptions of literacy in my data show that female literacy and education are highly contested notions in this community, and that literacy is a major site for power struggle and resistance.

(Zubair, this volume, p. 200)

Gender distinctions form one key here, but the distribution is not only a gender-based one: the younger women (the daughters) were found in this case study using both dominant and religious literacies in different ways and to achieve quite different purposes from the older women in the family (their mothers and grandmothers). In such a context, any weapon (including literacy) will be used to further the goals of the participants in these struggles.

The relationship between dominant and local literacies

One interesting issue raised is that the different literacies and different uses of literacy occupy different spaces and spheres and form part of the communicative practices of different social groups. This can be seen in Herbert and Robinson's study of literacy and languages in northern Ghana. Stites in his study of literacy among one section of rural China also shows that such literacies and literacy usages are part of the different forms of relationship in these communities. 'The unschooled adults I met in Dahu [China] were only "illiterate" when they ventured out of the relatively private spaces of the household and village' (Stites, this volume). As Shirin Zubair shows, literacy is both personal and local in the sense that it can be defined differently by any one individual according to the space which she occupies at the time. Part of the 'attack' on 'illiteracy' launched by formal literacy learning programmes (both government and NGO) is aimed at increasing the number and sizes of those spheres in which formal (dominant) literacy activities take place, and at the same time at reducing the number and sizes of those areas of life where literacy practices are less formal or different, or where they are not felt to be necessary to a full life. The creation of village libraries with approved texts in many countries is an example of this attempt to create new spaces for dominant literacy in local communities (Rogers et al. 1999).

What we appear to have then is a set of contacts between different literacy communities. In particular, in several of these studies, we have the contact between government literacies and local community literacies. We note in Namibia the slogan 'literacy *for* the people' (my italics); i.e., not the *people's* literacy, but the *government's* literacy which they are trying to persuade the people (by rallies, festivals, certificates, etc.) to accept. The dominant literacy through development programmes attempts to assert its superiority over (and even to deny the existence of) other forms of literacy.

210

And many of the people have internalised these dominant attitudes. A young woman in China said that she could never learn to use an electric rice cooker or washing machine, because she was illiterate (Stites, this volume). 'This dominant ideology is largely shared by the rural poor themselves', says Maddox of Bangladesh. The Rabaris see themselves as illiterate, and therefore as being ignorant, helpless, cut off from communication, and constantly being cheated: 'if a woman is educated, she can take care of her household better, she can teach her children how to talk, make them understand properly, and if she teaches the child, the child won't be cheated anywhere else' (Dyer, this volume). Such hegemonic ideas have been fed to them by the dominant literate group. The spread of formal schooling in many countries has helped to spread negative ideas of non-literate persons and led to the demeaning of non-school literacies. The people are asked to become the passive recipients of other people's literacies (Chopra, this volume).

It is important, however, that when we see the resistance which some people put up to this dominant form of literacy, we should not read it simply as a defence against intrusion, a defence of a traditional way of life. Our case studies show that most people are willing to change when they feel that it is in their interest to do so. The Arakmbut adopted enough of dominant literacy to achieve their own ends; similarly, the Rabaris were willing to adopt some dominant forms of literacy so as to achieve their own development goals. In northern Ghana, some Ghanaians use dominant languages and literacies when they want to express power. The resistance to dominant literacies which has been detected elsewhere because of people's earlier experiences of school is not obvious from these case studies.

What then can we see from these studies? I want to suggest that what we are witnessing here – and throughout the developing societies today – is a confrontation of different literacy communities. Different literacy cultures, if you like, with varying literacies and with varying degrees of what may be called 'literacy penetration', meet. What we need to assess is the impact of this meeting on *both* literacy communities. So far we have tended to look only at the impact on the subaltern literacy communities; what is the effect on dominant literacy communities of their continual contact with other forms of literacy? Here is a field of research which still awaits its explorers.

Problematising development: whose development?

The problematising of literacy is of course well known, and has been reinforced in this collection of essays. But 'development' too has recently become problematised in much the same way, particularly with reference to the work on development as discourse (Crush 1995; Escobar 1995).

> Development discourse is embedded in the ethnographic and destructive colonial (and post-colonial) discourses designed to perpetuate colonial

hierarchies rather than to change them. It has defined Third World peoples as 'other', embodying all the negative characteristics (primitive, backward and so forth) supposedly no longer found in 'modern' Westernised societies. This representation has provided the rationale for development experts' belief in modernization and the superiority of the values and institutions of the North.

(Parpart 1995: 253)

Most development workers however still see 'development' as unproblematic. Current orthodoxies stress the relief of poverty, and identify clear indicators of such relief. It is true that, over the last fifty years or so, there have been changing paradigms of development, but this is only part of the search for *more effective* strategies by which to achieve the clear and universally accepted goals of development. The emphasis on participatory approaches to development such as PAR and PRA, for example, is caused by concern that existing strategies are less than effective, and better ways need to be found to achieve the current goals of development. In addition, the rapid changes within the world (globalisation, the new technologies, etc.) call for some changes within the theory and practice of development.

The traditional approaches to development, then, are being increasingly challenged. Development today is seen by some people as a social construct, created by dominant ideologies within a particular context. Escobar talks of:

mainstream development literature, in which there exists a veritable underdeveloped subjectivity endowed with features such as powerlessness, passivity, poverty and ignorance . . . as if waiting for the (white) Western hand to help subjects along, and not infrequently hungry, illiterate, needy and oppressed by its own stubbornness, lack of initiative and traditions. This image also homogenises Third World cultures in an ahistorical fashion . . . that [this description] exists . . . is more a sign of power over the Third World than a truth about it.

(Escobar 1995: 8–9)

Thus, in much the same way as the definition of 'illiteracy' serves to exclude large numbers of society's members, so the term 'underdeveloped' serves to exclude two-thirds of the world from the seats of power; 'development schemes are contributing to their social, economic and political marginalisation' (Dyer, this volume).

Multiple developments

The fact that 'development' is a social construct means that (like literacy), instead of there being one development, there are many different 'developments'. Several of the chapters here demonstrate this very clearly. In the Peruvian Amazon, the development agendas of the state, the churches, the NGOs, the colonising commercial interests and local grassroots organisations are all very different – but they are all designated 'development'. And (like literacies), these various developments are often in contest one with another. For example, the state at times supports and at times opposes the development programmes of corporate organisations. To adapt a proverb, what is one person's development is another person's poison. Aikman's chapter is the most revealing in this respect; but in Namibia, as elsewhere, the state's development agenda is not necessarily the same as that of the groups which it seeks to influence – 'economic development, societal modernisation, nation-building and racial/ethnic reconciliation' (Papen, this volume), issues which overlap with but are not the same (in content or in priority) as the poverty, poor housing, ill health, lack of economic opportunity and lack of access to information which Uta Papen identifies (it is not clear on what basis) as the 'real' issues for the majority of the Namibian population (Papen, this volume). In particular, the state there lays emphasis on 'the rights and responsibilities [of the population] as Namibian citizens' (it is interesting that this aim is directed especially at the 'illiterate' populations). Development for the President means 'to develop a better sense of what it means to be a reconciled, united nation and what we can accomplish when we set out with a will to deal with the inherited inequalities and backlogs which are an obstacle to our development' (Papen, this volume, p. 48). The purpose of the state's development programme (as with its literacy programme) is 'investment in human capital and political socialisation rather than promoting liberation and transformation' (a different development agenda which many NGOs espouse) (Papen, this volume, p. 48). Equally in China, development work (including literacy learning) was an 'effort [by government] to diffuse central ideology and control into peripheral regions, and in so doing to reduce [what government sees as] the marginality of these communities'. Stites (this volume) speaks of the Chinese state's goals for 'social, political and economic development . . . extending the reach of the party/ state' (Stites, this volume). And the strategies created for this form of (state) development, too, often reflect the state's concerns: when popular theatre is introduced in Namibia, 'its main purpose is to help the regions campaign for the [government's] literacy campaign', not to help the people to express their own concerns (Papen, this volume).

Whose development?

The problematic then of development is (like that of literacy), 'Whose development?' There is no one 'development', universal and neutral. There are many developments, all ideologically constructed. Some are privileged and dominant; others are demeaned. Any development worker will be aligning herself with one development agenda against others.

People's self-development

The current fashion for promoting people's self-development (Sachs 1993; Burkey 1994; Rahman 1994) is equally not unproblematic. The development promoted by the state and major NGOs (especially the international NGOs, many of which are really inter-governmental bodies) can be seen (and is seen by some local populations) as an outside intrusion, something to be resisted 'because of its associations with political-economic state-oriented growth models or as the justification for the neo-colonial extraction of resources from indigenous terri-tories' (Aikman, this volume). For the Rabaris, the external 'disastrous devel-opment . . . marks their moral downfall' (Dyer, this volume). Such external development, it is urged, needs to be replaced with a locally created agenda which will be implemented by the people themselves (with any assistance they can get).

But even this has its problems. For, again, we need to ask, which form of development is 'the people's self-development'? Whose voice is heard? Who speaks 'for' the people? Whose among the 'people' are the dominant discourses and whose among the subalterns? There are hints that, among the Rabaris, there were several different self-development agendas. To adapt what Brian Street says in his Introduction with reference to China, what does 'development' mean for those 'rural women [who] have limited access to . . . outside . . . envir-onments and thus have few opportunities to apply and develop the . . . skills and knowledge conveyed in the [development] curriculum'? (Street, this volume, p. 214). Theirs will be a different development from that of many men in the same communities.

And equally, who takes the lead in formulating the people's development goals? What role do external aid agencies (however radical these may be) play in helping local peoples to articulate their self-development agendas? Many of the indigenous people's movements include many non-indigenous activists.

Responses to development encounters

What becomes clear then is that 'development' (including self-development) is complicated. There are many different 'developments', not just one unques-tioned and universally valid development. Some are dominant, others are sub-altern. And the responses which different groups of people make when their own development project[1] encounters the dominant models of development will vary. Three major kinds of responses have been identified in these chapters.

Development as defence

One response is to reject the advances of the dominant development paradigm, and put up a defence of the existing. For example, Aikman shows that in some contexts, defence against the greed and robbery of colonisers, the preservation of a community and of a way of life which some members of the community feel has worked reasonably well for many years, can be seen as a form of self-development. Papen speaks of development for some Namibians as being 'their daily struggle for a decent life' rather than the adoption of a new way of life (Papen, this volume).

Alternative developments

Equally, while rejecting the external development programme, some groups create their own 'alternative development' agenda. As Aikman and others have suggested, this is not likely to be capitalist and the free market but communal in character. Many of these alternative projects are 'outside the culturally based idea of "development" and its Western framework of progress and degeneration'; rather, they are based on 'the ability of indigenous peoples to become self-supporting . . . not [through] privatisation of rural indigenous economies but collective or community developments which are determined by the recipients who become the subjects of development'. The Rabaris saw their own self-development, not so much as defence of their traditional way of life but as the adoption of a new ('improved') way of living (Dyer, this volume) which although it had many elements of the official (dominant) development agenda, nevertheless was their own creation. Indeed, some groups may see their own agendas not as being 'development' (since development for them had negative connotations), but as 'alternatives to development' (Aikman, this volume).

In pursuing such an agenda, many such grassroots groups are willing to pick up and use some of the tools of modern (state/international/capitalist) development programmes, including literacy, as both the Arakmbut (Aikman, this volume) and Rabaris show (Dyer, this volume), and they will use these in their own way, just as the Eritrean teachers created their own form of 'student-centred communicative methodology' which they 'incorporated into already-existing methods, "indigenized" so to speak' in a way which was more effective than the straight transfer of technique would have been (Wright this volume). I note in an innovative 'legal literacy' project in India how the literate and non-literate field workers took hold of the legal texts and used them in their own way, often quite contrary to the ways in which they had been trained by the formally educated legal experts (Monga 2000). I also note what Brian Street says about the way in which some elements in the New Work Order have taken up the terminology of participatory development and turned it to its own purposes (Street, this volume, p. 4).

Pragmatic development

A third approach which these studies identify is for the local participants to pick out from the official dominant development programme those items which it feels will be 'really useful' to them, while rejecting the whole package with its power implications. This was particularly true of the Rabaris; and among the Arakmbut, 'if new technologies or alopathic medicines from the national society make life easier or cure diseases brought from the outside like tuberculosis, they will be welcomed' (Aikman, this volume). Such attitudes reveal that many groups are not opposed to all change but they may be opposed to dominant perceptions of change. They will be selective in their approach to external development plans.

It is this which reveals most clearly what is really going on. We have here, as with literacy learning programmes, the interaction of different development discourse communities – a dominant development and more local developments. And this interaction is embroiled in power relationships. It is from time to time contested – even though many of the participant groups internalise the value systems of the dominant programmes. The tools which the dominant groups use for their hegemony include both literacy and development.

Problematising the link between literacy and development

If we try to reconceptualise both literacy learning programmes and development programmes as the interaction between two or more (unequal) discourse communities, the question of the link between literacy and development is completely changed. Instead of literacy (i.e., the dominant literacy) being seen as the 'motor for the emergence of the "modern man" [and woman] and the development of attitudes and dispositions of flexibility, adaptability, empathy, willingness to accept change, proneness to adopt innovations' (Papen, this volume), rather it can be visualised as the attempted imposition on groups which the dominant section of society has declared to be marginalised, of one set of criteria for acceptance into the so-called 'modern community', with all that that implies.

Causal?

As Anna Robinson-Pant shows, there always were problems with the traditional picture of a direct, straightforward causal link between literacy ('conceptualised and valued as knowledge rather than as skill in reading and writing *per se*', as in China: Stites, this volume) and enhanced development indicators (Robinson-Pant, this volume, p. 152). Apart from the fact that the statistical basis for such judgements has been shown several times to be unsatisfactory, it has never been clear why one *starts* with literacy and proceeds to (for example) health. Why should one not start with health which leads to literacy? We can rewrite the quotation which Anna Robinson-Pant cites in her chapter as follows: 'In the southern Indian state of Kerala, where the infant mortality rate is the lowest in the entire developing world and the fertility rate is the lowest in India, literacy is [almost] universal.' In other words, it may be that healthy women learn the

216

dominant literacy skills more effectively, rather than that dominant-literate women enhance the health practices of themselves and their families.

A common factor?

Again, however, the relationship may not be causal at all, whichever way it goes. Perhaps we should be talking about the 'associations' which literacy has with other activities rather than relationships. For there may be a common 'third factor'. For example, participation in a group activity may be more effective in promoting both health and (the dominant) literacy skills than either factor alone. Robinson-Pant found in her study in Nepal that 'as a social structure, the [literacy-cum-health education] class did not create new bonds between the women but strengthened existing bonds and existing divisions'. The work of Doronilla and Bernardo in the Philippines suggests that the participation of non-literate persons in the activities of literate communities may be more effective than simply attending literacy classes (Doronilla 1996; Bernardo 1998). And other factors clearly affect the progress made in different contexts. For example, one of the studies suggests that in some contexts participants who are mobile may learn more effectively than those who are less mobile: 'women's existing mobility determined how they used the knowledge and skills from classes rather than the reverse, and this [mobility] varied greatly between the two districts studied' (Robinson-Pant, this volume).

This approach would suggest that literacy is not *the* channel to new knowledge, any more (as both current anti-smoking and family planning campaigns reveal) than knowledge is *the* channel to changing behaviour – facts which the contemporary AIDS campaigns need to learn. 'Changing attitudes or behaviour is not simply a matter of providing knowledge or literacy skills' (Robinson-Pant, this volume).

Practical implications of these studies

Researchers such as the writers of these chapters are then increasingly uncertain what the links between literacy and other developmental indicators are, or how 'development' (whichever development is taken) can be promoted by literacy. But in so far as this book is aimed at practitioners in literacy and development programmes, it is designed not to promote a new orthodoxy or methodology, but to help practitioners to look at their own situation in a new way. 'The ethnographic approach represented here is, then, more concerned with attempting to understand what actually happens than with trying to prove the success of a particular intervention or [to] "sell" a particular methodology for teaching or management' (Street, this volume, p. 1).

But at times this leaves a sense of unfinished business. Time and again, I was tempted to ask at the end of a chapter, 'So what?' Robinson-Pant suggested that her research produced 'more problems than benefits for developers'. Indeed, she goes so far as to suggest that the role of researcher and developer are anti-pathetic: 'The developer's task . . . is usually seen primarily as initiating change in people's behaviour (a catalyst) – an aim which is disputed or ideologically unacceptable to many ethnographers who wish to remain observers of change that is happening irrespective of their actions' (Robinson-Pant, this volume). Researchers, she suggests, *cannot* offer advice or advocacy.

Perhaps one cause of this is that most of these researchers try to stand outside of the situation they are examining. 'Research . . . I believe, has a task to do in making visible the complexity of local everyday community literacy practices and challenging dominant stereotypes and myopia' (Street, this volume). In that sense, most of these researchers attempt to adopt an outsider stance towards the situation they are analysing, even when challenging the dominant literacy community. They may see themselves as critics, but they are still observers rather than actors.

Such an approach may be thought to be particularly important if literacy and development programmes and projects can be seen in terms of an interaction between two unequal lifeworlds – an interaction which at times takes the form of a contest. Ethnographic researchers, it may be argued, should be able (as Anna Robinson-Pant tries) to see both sides equally. 'Instead of privileging the particular literacy practices familiar in their own culture, researchers now suspend judgement as to what constitutes literacy among the people they are working with until they are able to understand what [literacy] means to the people themselves and which social contexts reading and writing derive their meaning from' (Street, this volume, p. 9).

But literacy agencies cannot 'suspend judgement'. The question for all literacy learning practitioners is, 'whose side are you on?' If there are dominant and subaltern literacies and different ways in which the dominant literacy is used, which literacies and which uses of literacy are we encouraging? If literacy is tied into the power structures of society, where do we stand? Where do we come from and where are we going?

Researchers such as the writers in this book, however, also come from a particular (development and literacy) community; they operate within an (often chosen) discourse community. And their own ideologies influence the way they look at the literacy contests. Because they are particularly conscious of the power dimension to literacy and development, ethnographic literacy researchers in particular continually find themselves taking sides.

This may be the reason why these chapters are unequal in their balance when addressing this issue of the interfacing of dominant and subaltern forms of literacy and development. The reaction of the subaltern groups to what is seen as the imposition of dominant literacies on other literacy communities is well and sympathetically studied here. But (as we noticed above) the reactions of this interfacing on the *dominant* agencies is not yet well documented. How do they react? How do they change as the contest proceeds? What were the experiences of the Catholic church and state educational agencies in the Peruvian Amazon, or the various aid agencies, government and NGO, working among the nomads in north-west India, the Christian missionaries in northern Ghana or the state officials in China? How did *they* react to the interface of cultures? Did they learn anything from the contacts they made? And why is this dimension lacking from these studies (apart from Anna Robinson-Pant's contribution, which however does not examine the contest between dominant and local literacies or between dominant and local health practices, but rather seeks to understand the conflict she experienced between one set of aid agencies operating within one discourse community and researchers operating within another)?

The issue then is whether it is possible (and desirable) to have any measure of detachment, or whether the researcher is bound within her discourse community. Or again how far the researchers can (and should) take sides and develop a sense of solidarity with one or more of the groups they are researching. I am minded of the words of Richard Rorty:

> Solidarity is not discovered by reflection but created. It is created by increasing our sensitivity to the particular details of the pain and humiliation of other, unfamiliar sorts of people. Such increased sensitivity makes it more difficult to marginalise people different from ourselves by thinking, 'They do not feel it as *we* would', or 'there must always be suffering, so why not let *them* suffer?'
>
> This process of coming to see other people as 'one of us' rather than as 'them' is a matter of detailed description of what unfamiliar people are like and of redescription of what we ourselves are like.
>
> (Rorty 1989: xvi)

Although most of these researches are not strictly neutral: the sympathies of the researchers are in most cases with the subaltern groups, there are few signs (except with Anna Robinson-Pant) of that process of 'redescription of what we ourselves are like'. And the problem with solidarity is that the identification of one group as 'one of us' may inevitably lead to identifying other (often opposed) groups as 'them'.

And this despite the fact that almost all the contributors here come from within the dominant (educated) cultures. I find it strange that most of the practitioners and discussants of ethnographical literacy research, in this collection of essays and in others (e.g., Barton et al. 2000), come from the educational systems of the West. It is hard to find persons rooted within other cultures taking up such studies and employing the same discourses; and as Robinson-Pant shows, it is hard even to engage in dialogue with persons from a different development and literacy discourse community on these matters. Aikman seems to have been able to identify very closely with the lifeworld of her chosen group; but I suspect that she finds it harder to work with those representing the dominant culture; and I also suspect that in the process she has underestimated the influence of dominant ideologies and tools in the process of the Arakmbut creating their own programme of self-development alternatives. Her young village leaders have all been formally educated in state or Catholic schools (Aikman 1995, 1999, etc.).

The missing practical implications

And this identification with the subaltern may also be the reason why there are few words of support for any literacy teaching agency, and relatively few indications of how any form of literacy (subaltern, alternative or dominant) can be effectively promoted. The main practical conclusion drawn seems to be that 'a crude imposition of [Western or urban literacy practices] that marginalises and denies local experience is likely to alienate even those who were initially motivated' (Street, this volume, p. 14). The study of the daily literacy practices of one population in rural China shows how far apart are the state literacy learning programmes from the 'real' literacies of many rural people in the area studied. Equally, in Pakistan, 'these women's engagements with and desire for literacy ... need to be taken into account by the local NGOs, UNESCO and other international agencies when designing and implementing literacy programmes for these communities' (Zubair, this volume).

What conclusions then may adult literacy programmers draw from these studies? Does this book point to any strategies planners may devise to help them to fulfil the wishes of those 'many local people [who (as Street admits)] in the long run do want to change their literacy practices and take on board some of those associated with Western or urban society' (Street, this volume)? I have suggested elsewhere one or two strategies which draw upon local literacy practices in devising literacy learning programmes for adults (Rogers 1999, 2000).

There are hints here and there throughout the book. To adapt part of what Wright is saying of Eritrea, it may be suggested that

> what participant groups in Eritrea and other impoverished parts of the world need is not a radical restructuring of their entire [literacy and socio-economic] systems from the outside, based on what *ought* to exist according to Western standards. Instead of seeing traditional methods as a *problem* to be eradicated, these need to be reconsidered by those within and without the system as *resources* . . . State-of-someone-else's-art [literacy or development] methodology does not serve any purpose, if it is so inapt and inadequately supplied that the practitioners are ultimately disempowered by the very thing that they were led to believe would liberate them.
>
> (Wright, this volume, p. 76)

This is particularly true of literacy. As long as the dominant literacy community neglects or despises traditional local literacies, the imposition of new forms of literacy (state approved and school based) is likely to be at best ineffective, at worst openly rejected. There is some evidence that people drop out of adult literacy classes, not because of lack of motivation but because they are 'pushed out' by what is expected of them from the new paradigms of literacy or development (Robinson-Pant 1997). Instead of one-way literacy instruction, there could be two-way learning between the dominant and subaltern literacy communities. And if this is to take place, then we need to understand exactly what, in any given locality and with any given group, their existing literacy practices are, so that such new learning programmes can relate directly to the existing real-life literacy practices of the participants rather than the new and generalised literacy practices of the dominant group.

This surely is where this group of essays comes into its own. They show us that literacies, like development agendas, are multiple and that the uses of literacy (including the dominant literacy) are multiple. They seem to suggest that we need to 'start where the people are', with what they already do, and help them to transform their own lives in their own ways for their own purposes, rather than to impose our literacy for our own purposes on them, in the process ignoring or despising their existing patterns of literacy and development practices.

At the heart of this issue lies the attitude of the dominant community – that illiterate persons are 'them', 'other than us', the 'excluded' who need to be 'included' into 'us'. These chapters show that the basic assumptions that non-literate persons do not engage in literacy activities and that illiterate persons cannot engage in development activities are false. Non-literate persons are already engaging in literacy activities on their own, using their own strategies: and if they feel that these strategies are adequate, they will never be motivated to change to a new form of literacy. Non-literate persons are already engaging in their own development projects, and they can fulfil these without necessarily developing the dominant form of literacy. Building new programmes of literacy and development enhancement on the basis of what the people are already doing and on what they want to do is likely to be more effective than assuming nothing exists and starting from scratch.

Note

1 I use the term 'project' here in the sense in which philosophy studies use it: the key project which the whole activity seeks to achieve.

References

Aikman, S. (1995) 'Language, Literacy and Bilingual Education: An Amazon People's Strategies for Cultural Maintenance', *International Journal of Educational Development* 15: 411–22.

—— (1999) *Intercultural Education, Literacy and Development*, Amsterdam: John Benjamins.

Barton, D., Hamilton, M. and Ivanič, R. (eds) (2000) *Situated Literacies: Reading and Writing in Context*, London, Routledge.

Bernardo, A.R. (1998) *Literacy and the Mind*, Hamburg: UNESCO Institute of Education.

Burkey, S. (1994) *People First*, London: Zed Books.

Crush, J. (ed.) (1995) *The Power of Development*, London: Routledge.

Doronilla, M.L. (1996) *Landscapes with Literacy*, Hamburg: UNESCO Institute of Education.

Escobar, A. (1995) *Encountering Development: The Making and Unmaking of the Third World*, Princeton, NJ: Princeton University Press.

Freire, P. (1972) *Pedagogy of the Oppressed*, London: Sheed & Ward.

Mezirow, J. (1991) *Transformative Dimensions in Adult Learning*, San Francisco: Jossey Bass.

Monga, N. (2000) *Knowing Her Rights*, Beyond Literacy Series, Mumbai: ASPBAE.

Parpart, J.L. (1995) 'Post-modernism, Gender and Development', in J. Crush (ed.), *Power of Development*, London: Routledge.

Prinsloo, M. and Breier, M. (1996) *Social Uses of Literacy: Theory and Practice in Contemporary South Africa*, Amsterdam and Johannesburg: John Benjamins and SACHED Books.

Rahman, Md Anisur (1994) *People's Self-Development*, London: Zed Books.

Robinson-Pant, A. (1997) 'Some Aspects of Post-Literacy in Nepal', paper prepared for research project into post-literacy, available from Education for Development, Reading.

Rogers, A. (1999) 'Improving the Quality of Adult Literacy Programmes in Developing Societies: The "Real Literacies" Approach', *International Journal of Educational Development* 19: 219–34.

—— (2000) 'Literacy Comes Second: Working with Groups in Developing Societies', *Development in Practice* 10(2): 236–40, Oxford: Oxfam.

Rogers, A., Maddox, B., Millican, J., Newell Jones, K., Papen, U. and Robinson-Pant, A. (1999) *Re-defining Post-literacy in a Changing World*, London: DFID Research Report 29.

Rorty, R. (1989) *Contingency, Irony and Solidarity*, Cambridge: Cambridge University Press.

Sachs, W. (1993) *Development Dictionary*, London: Zed Books.

Street, B. (1984) *Literacy in Theory and Practice*, Cambridge: Cambridge University Press.

World Bank (2000) 'Including the 900+ Millions', Draft Sector Paper 2000 (I owe this reference to John Oxenham).

INDEX

Italic numbers denote pages with illustrations.

Non-Governmental Organisations
(NGOs) 124–5, 126, 137, 139, 140,
188, 210, 213, 214
Nujoma, S. 45, 48

OECD (Organisation for Economic
Cooperation and Development) 11
Osmani, S.R. 139
Oxenham, J. 47

Pakistan 100–1; ethnographic data
190–1; low literacy in 188
Pankhurst, R. 63
Parpart, J.L. 212
Pashuara, H. 29
personal literacies 131–2
Peru 65, 72; as modernising state 109–10;
political/economic situation 104–5,
see also Harakmbut
Plan Karene, economic sustainability
component 113; funding for 112;
and importance of oral/literate
practices 116, 117; and legal literacy
event 114–15; as part of indigenous
movement/self-development goal 113,
114–16; support for 117; territorial
component 112–13; and training in
small-animal husbandry 115–16
Population Census Organisation 188
Pottier, J. 105, 107
power, in discourse 191–2; female 201;
of literacy 199–200; manifestations of
191
Pozzi-Escot, I. 106
Prinsloo, M. and Breier, M. 1, 5, 10, 122,
189, 209

Quran, education in 63, 127–8; as
non-threatening literacy 199; reading
of 192–4

Rabarin, D. 30
Rabaris 3, 22–3, 211, 214, 215, 216;
and cheating 31–2; described 28–9;
education for 37–8; and female
researchers 33–5; and Indian
development strategies 28, 30;
information concerning 29; migrations
of 29–30; and notions of literacy 27,
28, 30–1, 32, 35–7; and peripatetic
teaching 32–5; status of 30, 31
Radway, J.A. 195

Rao, A. and Rao, D. 150
Rashid, S. 138
Rassool, N. 42
religious literacies 127–9
Robinson, C.D.W. 122, 123
Robinson-Pant, A.P. 2, 7, 8, 56, 100, 153,
221
Rockhill, K. 41, 160, 189
Rogers, A. 5, 56, 153, 220; et al. 55, 56,
155
Rorty, R. 219
Rummenholler, K. 109

Sachs, W. 214
Sainath, P. 137
Salzman, P. 28
Sarasola, S. 109
Saxena, M. 189
School for Life (NGO) 126
school literacy 122
Scribner, S. and Cole, M. 150
Shanin, 150
Shore, C. and Wright, S. 44
Shue, V. 173
SIL (Christian-based NGO) 125
Skaria, A. 150
Smith, C. 154
Social Welfare and Community
Development Department (Ghana)
126
Spivak, G.C. 88, 89, 137, 191
Stites, R. 171, 173; and Semali, L. 171
Street, B. 2, 6, 7, 8, 9, 12, 27, 46, 79,
100, 107, 110, 121, 122, 123, 140,
153, 186, 189, 196, 208, 214–15,
217–18
Stromquist, N.P. 153
subaltern literacies 137, 220
Swift, J. et al. 27

Tabouret-Keller, A. et al. 133
Taylorism 3
team working 3–4
Tegborg, M. 49, 53
Territorial Consolidation and Sustainable
Development (Harakmbut, Madre de
Dios), *see* Plan Karene
Timm, R.W. 140
Toivo ya Toivo, A. 45, 46, 48, 49
Total Quality Management (TQM) 3–4
tourism 4–5, 58
Triebel, A. 121